I Won't Grow Up!

I Won't Grow Up!

The Comic Man-Child in Film from 1901 to the Present

Anthony Balducci

McFarland & Company, Inc., Publishers
Jefferson, North Carolina

ALSO BY ANTHONY BALDUCCI

The Funny Parts: A History of Film Comedy Routines and Gags (McFarland, 2012)

Lloyd Hamilton: Poor Boy Comedian of Silent Cinema (McFarland, 2009)

All photographs are from the author's collection unless indicated otherwise.

Frontispiece: The childlike playfulness of *In the Navy* (1940) is conveyed in this image of Bud Abbott and Lou Costello getting dropped off in town by a friendly truck driver.

LIBRARY OF CONGRESS CATALOGUING-IN-PUBLICATION DATA

Names: Balducci, Anthony, 1958– author.
Title: I won't grow up! : the comic man-child in film from 1901 to the present / Anthony Balducci.
Description: Jefferson, N.C. : McFarland & Company, Inc., Publishers, 2016. | Includes bibliographical references and index.
Identifiers: LCCN 2015044245 | ISBN 9781476662084 (softcover : acid free paper) ∞
Subjects: LCSH: Emotional maturity in motion pictures. | Men in motion pictures. | Boys in motion pictures.
Classification: LCC PN1995.9.E45 B36 2016 | DDC 791.43/653—dc23
LC record available at http://lccn.loc.gov/2015044245

BRITISH LIBRARY CATALOGUING DATA ARE AVAILABLE

**ISBN (print) 978-1-4766-6208-4
ISBN (ebook) 978-1-4766-2221-7**

© 2016 Anthony Balducci. All rights reserved

No part of this book may be reproduced or transmitted in any form or by any means, electronic or mechanical, including photocopying or recording, or by any information storage and retrieval system, without permission in writing from the publisher.

Front cover image of *left to right* Ed Helms, Zach Galifianakis, and Bradley Cooper from *The Hangover*, 2009 (Warner Bros./Photofest)

Printed in the United States of America

*McFarland & Company, Inc., Publishers
Box 611, Jefferson, North Carolina 28640
www.mcfarlandpub.com*

To my Uncle Sonny,
who prides himself on being
an 81-year-old Peter Pan

Table of Contents

Introduction 1

1. The Crib Years 5
2. Act Your Age 17
3. "I'm a Baaaad Boy!" 39
4. Masculinity and the German Occupation of France 56
5. A Major Minor 68
6. Further Post-War Immaturity 85
7. Forever Young 105
8. Young Again 120
9. "I know you are but what am I?" 132
10. Problem Child 146
11. Jack and Jill 168
12. Girls 175

Epilogue 190
Chapter Notes 195
Bibliography 202
Index 203

Introduction

[T]o be able to laugh at yourself is maturity.—William Arthur Ward, *Fountains of Faith*

In 2014, Seth Rogen turned up as a guest on Kurt Andersen's *Studio 360* podcast to promote his latest feature comedy, *Neighbors*. Before Rogen was introduced, Andersen attempted to put the actor's success into perspective, noting, "In the last decade or so, the man-boy has pretty much become the comic archetype in American movies."[1] He spoke of Rogen finding a prominent place in this popular trend as "the intelligent but clueless bro who can't quite get a grip on the adult world."[2] This brief introduction adequately summed up Rogen's success. For years, the man-boy or man-child has dominated comedy films, creating controversy with every crude sex joke, offensive barb and gross scatological gag. While diehard fans are laughing, others are complaining. It isn't new for the highbrow film critic to disparage a comedian for resorting to childish antics, but now the general public is coming forth in increasing numbers to express their weariness with the overabundance of juvenile humor. They complain in social media and, even more importantly, they refuse to buy tickets to the latest coarse gagfest. The truth is that the Hollywood comedy does not make as much money as it once did.

It could be argued that it is the job of the fool to act callow and that comedy is, by design, childish. But film comedy has not always been this way. Comedy has changed and, more significantly, the definition of maturity has changed. Childish has come to mean uninhibited and vulgar rather than naïve and inept. Today, a comedian is considered childish if he draws humor from jokes about penises, women's breasts, and bodily functions. Bob Fischbach of the *World-Herald* complained about Adam Sandler's *Grown Ups 2* (2013), "Of course the humor is juvenile.... It took all of 30 seconds into the movie to get to the first urine joke. It would not be the last. Sandler managed to last 15 minutes before the first fat joke, calling a kid 'a beanbag with arms and legs.' The first poop joke came ten minutes later, the first joke about women with big breasts soon after, and the inevitable projectile vomiting and gay jokes followed as expected. Repeatedly."[3] Other Sandler films have hit a nerve with critics. In a review of *That's My Boy* (2006), *Variety*'s Justin Chang complained of "multiple gags involving erections, ejaculation, incontinence, public urination and vomiting."[4] How this immoderate trend came to dominate film comedy is worth examination.

Physician Lewis Thomas believed that it is through maturity that the "real show of humanity emerges on stage."⁵ What is emerging on the grand stage on which these comedians perform? Marlon Wayans engages in a breast-feeding routine in *Little Man* (2006). Jim Carrey squats and defecates on a neighbor's lawn in *Me, Myself and Irene* (2000). Rob Schneider tongue-kisses a 76-year-old woman in *Grown Ups* (2010). This is a dubious form of amusement and self-expression.

A child is expected to negotiate the path to maturity. Adults are required to help children by providing guidance and presenting a good example. Every adult who encounters a child has an obligation to serve as a mentor. How does a comedian fit into this vital social process?

Standards of maturity have changed from decade to decade. Lou Costello was known for his childish ways in the 1940s. Seth Rogen is known for his childish ways today. But these comedians are hardly interchangeable.

Costello played a childish stooge, a character he carefully developed while working for years in burlesque, film and radio. He succeeded because he fully committed to this comic persona, whom he assured was believably childish in every conceivable way. He had a childish innocence, childish fears, a childish ungainliness, a childish high-pitched voice.

Rogen has built a career playing an easygoing, pot-smoking goof. He is not clumsy or confused. He could easily understand that the first baseman on Bud Abbott's team is named Who. He is not innocent or sexless. He is willfully childish, embracing his immaturity as if it were a badge of honor. *New York Times* critic A.O. Scott wrote, "The desire of the modern comic protagonist ... is to wallow in his own immaturity, plumbing its depths and reveling in its pleasures."⁶ This arrogant clown insists on the right to be selfish, foolish and reckless. Rogen's screen persona is, by the actor's own description, "a lazy, self-involved manchild."⁷ This same description could not be applied to Costello. Costello was eager to please others and, if he ever failed in his endeavors, it was never because he hadn't

Lou Costello expressed a childlike innocence and naiveté that made him endearing to wartime audiences. This publicity photo of the comedian was distributed to promote *Who Done It?* (1942).

work hard. Unlike Costello's lovable but helpless boob, Rogen's doobie-puffing slacker is in control of his actions. This is simply the person that he chooses to be.

Rogen is a reflection of a particular type of man in contemporary society. In his recent book *Guyland*, sociologist Michael Kimmel wrote: "Guyland is ... a bunch of places where guys gather to be guys with each other, unhassled by the demands of parents, girlfriends, job, kids, and the other nuisances of adult life. In this topsy-turvy, Peter Pan mindset, young men shirk the responsibilities of adulthood and remain fixated on the trappings of boyhood."[8]

A large gap exists between the fumbling, well-meaning idiot and the irresponsible, self-gratifying lout. Costello derived humor from the mistakes, failings and weaknesses that we, as human beings, expose at various times in our lives. Unlike Rogen, he was neither self-indulgent nor narcissistic. Costello represents who we are. Rogen represents who we, at our core, wish we could be—playful, free-floating, free of responsibility.

This book will trace the evolution of cinema's comic man-child from André Deed, who debuted on screen in 1901, to Seth Rogen and his contemporary man-child peers. As we examine changing cultural attitudes about maturity, we'll determine what it means to be an adult, what it means to be a child and how today those two things are more confused than ever.

There will be snacks along the way if anyone gets hungry and I have brought along games to make the ride fun. But I swear, if I hear anyone making a fuss while I am trying to drive, I will turn this car around and take everyone home.

A sign of maturity is gratitude. I thank you for reading my book.

1

The Crib Years

Maturity is the desired outcome of a person's emotional, social and moral development. Maturity has distinct markers in those qualities that we, as a society, uphold as virtues. Prominent among those virtues are strength, courage, pride, industry, resolution, self-reliance, discipline, and honor. A person is expected to attain a level of excellence to function favorably in the world. Otherwise, it is believed, they will spend their lives as ne'er-do-wells.

Consider the alternative. A world without virtue is a world without adults. When our political leaders fail to show virtue, we wonder if our country is being run by children. When the people around us refuse to follow rules or show consideration for others, we worry that the world is populated by nothing but rascals and hellions.

Contrary to popular opinion, stupidity is not a vital element of comedy. Far more important to comedy is immaturity, which compels the comic hero to struggle awkwardly with emotion, desire and ego.

Robert Moore and Douglas Gillette identified four types of mature men in *King, Warrior, Magician, Lover: Rediscovering the Archetypes of the Mature Masculine*. The King represents wisdom, leadership and selflessness. The Warrior represents vigor and aggression. The Magician represents mastery and transformation. The Lover represents sensitivity and connectedness. But Moore and Gillette should have added a fifth archetype: the Jester. The Jester is present to mock the other four types if they ever stray onto the wrong path. The archetypes can easily go awry. The King can become a tyrant, the Warrior can become a sadist, the Magician can become a trickster, and the Lover can become a weepy mama's boy. We can see Charlie Chaplin firmly committed to the Jester's task of mocking the Tyrant in *The Great Dictator* (1940). Chaplin makes it clear in his portrayal of dictator Adenoid Hynkel that this sort of ruthless man is maldeveloped. When Hynkel dances with a large, inflatable globe, it becomes obvious that he is a child who regards the Earth as his own personal toy. Hynkel engages in a pointless game of one-upmanship with Benzino Napaloni (Jack Oakie), dictator of Bacteria. When the two dictators sit in barber chairs, each tries to pump their seat higher than the other until Hynkel's chair reaches its limit and collapses. This tense meeting between dictators ends in a food fight, which hardly shows either man as a mature individual.

Not much maturity is seen in comedy films today. Steve Rose's article for *The Guardian*, "Why are there so many movies about guys who won't grow up?" shines a

Charlie Chaplin plays a dictator who craves power like a baby craves milk in *The Great Dictator* (1940) (courtesy www.doctormacro.com).

disapproving light on the subject. "There they'd have found the solution to the plight of American masculinity: don't grow up. Just stretch out that period between adolescence and parenthood to the extent it becomes a prolonged state of infantile bliss. Teenage hedonism on a grown-up salary; being old enough to smoke weed but still having your mum do your laundry; not having to share your Star Wars figures with anyone. This is the new American dream."[1] Rose singled out *Jeff, Who Lives at Home* (2011) for discussion. "Jeff, played by Jason Segel, is the latest in a long line of movie men-children with no great urge to fly the nest, and why should he, when his mum feeds him, puts him up, lets him smoke weed in her basement and no doubt does his laundry?"[2]

Men and women are expected to grow up at some point. But a person can struggle to let go of their carefree youth and accept adult responsibility. As Rose suggests, we start out in infantile bliss and eventually graduate to teenage hedonism. This period of life is so enjoyable that a rational person cannot leave it behind willingly. It is just too appealing to imagine yourself indulging in perpetual freedom and delight.

The late bloomer has become common in our culture, but a long delay in a person's maturity can disrupt the transition. A person who lingers too long in an extended youth is likely to establish habits that they can never break. The greatest risk is that what should be a transient life stage will end up as a permanent lifestyle. It's different today in that less social pressure is exerted on the individual who wants to remain in a permanent state of immaturity.

We cannot have this discussion without considering J.M. Barrie's 1904 stage play, *Peter Pan, or The Boy Who Wouldn't Grow Up*. The play's hero, Peter Pan, enjoys perpetual childhood on the island of Neverland. He is a boastful and careless boy. At the end of the play, a narrator explains that this fearlessly cocky young adventurer would never be capable of leading an adult life. He says simply, "He could never quite get the hang of it." In today's world, an increasing number of people are unable to get the hang of adult life and manage to avoid it by building their own personal Neverlands.

Most modern filmmakers do not abide by traditional notions of maturity and they are not inclined to condemn boyish antics. Their man-child comedies, which celebrate juvenile behavior, have more than likely contributed to this social trend. What has gone wrong?

Film director Judd Apatow said, "All comedy is about bad behavior and immaturity. Go watch any comedy from the past 75 years—go watch Harpo Marx try to grab some girl's boobs. The only thing that's funny in comedy is bad behavior. A normal, polite person is a bore. A person saying the worst things ever is the person whom you find hysterical."[3] Is Apatow correct?

Comedy stars will never be held up as models of maturity. Comedy and maturity are at odds for several reasons; the first and foremost is that maturity produces order while comedy produces disorder. Maturity is represented by calm, steady behavior, but behavior that is calm and steady does not usually get laughs. There are exceptions, of course. A rare comedian (Jack Benny comes to mind) could get big laughs without making a fuss. The restrained type of comedian need not perform a pratfall when he can get a laugh with just a look. But it isn't easy. Benny could afford to be subdued because he had spent years letting his audience get to know his idiosyncrasies.

Much greater scrutiny is needed to expose the deep-seated flaws and anxieties of the mature person. The child inside us may be suppressed, but he will never leave us. This is the reason that an adult can sometimes feel like a child playing the part of an adult. Maturity is about getting it together and holding it together, but those childhood anxieties can be a driving force that threatens to make us burst apart at the seams. This is the real problem. Maturity is about a person suppressing their fears and controlling their desires. A comedian has to be much more open than that. He must express his fears and confess his desires to have the slightest hope of amusing a crowd.

The challenge of making an outwardly mature individual laughable can be daunting. Why should a comedian bother frustrating himself with a type of role that is not immediately funny? These roles could turn out to be, as Apatow says, boring. It is much easier and safer for a comedian to serve strictly as a counterpoint to the responsible adult. Therefore, many comedians fully commit to acting immature. They display an unrepentant childishness, approaching slapstick and other forms of humor as a form of subversion.

The parent who wants to properly shape their child will often tell the child, "Don't act silly!" This is a direct call for a person to act mature. But it is the job of the comedian

Harpo Marx uses an old seduction move in *A Night in Casablanca* (1946).

to act silly. Comedy films are typically designed to dispute established notions of maturity.

The problem with Apatow's bad behavior proposition is that Apatow sees comedy as representing only vice, never virtue. This is a narrow modern-day perspective. Comedy provides insight into our humanity, which is a much richer source of material than Apatow imagines it to be. Life's challenges, difficulties and pains are not always imposed on us through our own bad behavior. Trouble can find a person whether that person is flawed or not. Often, comic complications arise out of forgivable miscalculations, reasonable misunderstandings, unforeseeable twists, and unfortunate circumstances that are beyond the protagonist's control. We love many of the classic comedians for the good behavior that they display in the worst situations.

The constructs of masculinity amass whatever qualities are perceived as virtues between men. Those qualities that define masculinity have long been intertwined with the qualities that define maturity. The mature man is a masculine man. How does this apply to comedy films? What are the virtues of the comedy hero? The term "comedy hero" may be a contradiction of terms. Comedy characters are not built as heroes. They can be skinny and fragile. They can be fat and clumsy. They can be weak, perverted, or mad. Heroes are inspirational. But comedy, which allows us to laugh at our flaws, is by design more comforting than inspirational. The antics depicted in these films are often an avoidance of maturity. This could understandably raise doubt if a comedy film has the ability to illustrate virtuous behavior.

Apatow has made it clear in interviews that he is a king among the doubters. Simply stated, he doesn't believe that virtue or maturity has a place in comedy. He said in a 2007 interview, "Nothing is funny that is mature. Isn't it all just doing things wrong and screwing up and learning lessons?"[4] But a film that genuinely emphasizes the learning lessons part is, in the end, a film about maturity.

Commedia dell'arte's Arlecchino expressed a childlike simplicity. Something as sophisticated as morality was simply beyond his grasp. It created good comedy to set a childlike figure like Arlecchino against rule-bound authority figures. The minstrel show comedians were invariably childlike. They were spontaneous, carefree, unambitious, and unfocused. Life to them was endless play. Later, vaudeville comedians could expect big laughs when they played bratty children in schoolroom sketches.

A long line of childish men have existed in films. The slapstick comedy that dominated early films promoted childishly impulsive behavior. Self-control, which we learn as we get older, is the most vital component of maturity. Without it, a man's id will inevitably take control and the man will run rampant. Men running rampant was a trademark of early comedy films, which often climaxed in manic chase scenes. The chase comedies presented slapstick at its fastest, most inhibited and most destructive. The first film star to emerge out of this madcap genre was André Deed, who ran around like a bratty child on a sugar high. When Deed turned to the camera with a foolish grin stretched lavishly across his face, he wanted to communicate to the viewer that he was not a restrained or serious-minded adult. His objective, clearly, was to do something foolish to make the viewer laugh. He was fun and free-spirited. He expressed impish glee, engaging in destruction and risky behavior for the pure thrill of it.

The eternal child is unbounded and undisciplined. He covets freedom, chafes at boundaries, and finds restrictions of any kind intolerable. In his stubborn determination to remain childish, he refuses to assume appropriate adult social roles and responsibilities. A physical comedian can be as free and playful as the eternal child.

In many of his films, Deed played a bratty child dressed in a boy's sailor suit. This was the case in the 1910 comedy *Foolshead Has Been Presented with a Football* (originally released in Italy under the title *Cretinetti e il pallone*). The plot is simple. Deed manages by carelessly tossing about a football to smash valuables in his family's home and cause similar destruction in his neighborhood. In *Cretinetti in the cinema* (1911), Deed slips into a projectionist booth at a movie theater and fiddles with the controls of the projector. It isn't long before he upsets the theater's patrons by causing the film to run in reverse. It is inevitable that Deed, as most naughty boys, will be punished for his misdeeds. Film historian David Robinson described Deed walking with "his bottom thrust out in a constant—and rarely disappointed—anticipation of a kick or a spanking."[5]

Deed appeared in several films as a hapless adolescent who is forced by his parents into various jobs. Deed's father gets him a job as a pastry cook in the 1907 Pathé Frères comedy *Jim's Apprenticeship* (released originally in France under the title *Les Apprentissages de Boireau*). Film historian Richard Abel wrote, "[A]fter being given an apron and hat, [Deed] promptly grabs a cream tart, sits down at a table to devour it with relish, and (angry at being interrupted) tosses another one in a female customer's face."[6] Like a baby, he eventually tires of working and takes a nap on a soft bed of dough. Deed gets a job as an apprentice to an architect in the 1908 comedy *Jim Gets a New Job* (released originally in France under the title *L'Apprenti architecte*). Abel wrote, "Both parents this time use their influence to get him this job, and he is much more deferential in the architect's office (continually bowing to his new boss) and even timid—the man's rough handshake sends him leaping into his mother's arms."[7] While gathering up blueprints, the awkward apprentice gets punched about by several draftsmen and ends up knocking over tables and cabinets.

Ernesto Vaser followed Deed's example in his "Fricot" series for Ambrosio. A good example is the 1913 comedy *Fricot and the fire extinguisher* (released originally in Italy under the title *Fricot e l'estintore*) which focuses on Vaser as he merrily skips through town blasting an inexhaustible fire extinguisher at everyone in sight.

A man-child is the title character of the 1910 Pathé Frères comedy *A Shy Youth* (released originally in France under the title *Les Timidités de Rigadin*). Charles Prince plays the shy suitor of a bold young society woman (Mistinguett). Prince is seated on a tiny stool while the woman, according to Abel, "tower[s] over him with her formidable crested headpiece."[8] The woman loosens up Prince by getting him to drink wine. Soon Prince is stomping around audaciously. When the woman's father arrives home and sees the way that Prince is behaving, he delivers a hard kick to his backside. Prince flees the home and, once outside, he sits on a step and sobs like a child.

A culture of immaturity was prevalent in the Keystone comedies, which were produced from 1912 to 1917. We are supposed to emerge from our childhood as restrained and productive adults. But this is not the behavior that is on display in a Keystone comedy. A mature individual lives by a strict moral code. This means that, unlike the Keystone characters, the person does not sneak out of work to get liquored up at a bar or dally at the beach with a neighbor's spouse. These characters suffer from poor judgment, poor insight, and poor impulse control. They are willing to pursue their own desires at all cost. Walter Kerr, a *New York Times* theater critic, examined the Keystone comedies at length in his well-regarded tome *Silent Clowns*, writing, "[I]t is primeval play, play in the treetops before *mores* were heard of, play without cause or consequence or social feeling. It is erupted volcanically, as though from the bowels of the earth; long-buried impulses in man simply shot to the surface at incredible speed to splatter wantonly over the landscape."[9] Noted theologian Karl Rahner wrote, "How often I have found that we grow to maturity not by doing what we like, but by doing what we should. How true it is that not every 'should' is a compulsion, and not every 'like' is a high morality and true freedom."[10]

Comedy often comes from a character making bad decisions or failing to control his deep desires. Our deep desires emanate from that unorganized part of our personality structure known as the id. The Keystone characters are living embodiments of the id, acting wildly and impulsively to serve pleasure-driven urges. They know what they want and they go after it with vigor. Often, their wildness can turn to violence. An immature person is unable to view the world from another's point of view. They cannot understand the pain or hardship that their selfish acts inflict on another person. Because of their indifference to other people's feelings, they will not hesitate to act cruelly towards others.

The problems that arise among the Keystone players are quickly and decisively resolved with brute force. It could be argued that the strength and directness of their actions are masculine. Without a doubt, manly character can be demonstrated in rugged play. Alan Bilton, the author of *Silent Film Comedy and American Culture*, referred to this as "masculine exuberance."[11] But so much of what happens in a Keystone comedy is random and unproductive. These characters lack discipline and purpose, which makes them fall far short of maturity or masculinity standards. Psychologist David F. Bjorklund of Florida Atlantic University believes that, in our immature forms, we are "inefficient structures."[12] It is important for people to be productive members of society and this can only occur if people are responsible and competent.

The Keystone comedies were never about accepted standards of conduct or taste. No one in these madcap adventures look or act in a conventional way. It was a specialty of the studio to present a grotesque reversal of expected order. For instance, oversized harridans were matched with husbands who were frail and submissive. Models of masculinity were nowhere to be found in the studio's special mix.

At the time, the Keystone comedies were phenomenally popular with the American public. They may have been successful because they took an adult back to their childhood. It can bring an adult pleasure and relief to watch a comedian defying the rules. Geoff King, a lecturer in film studies at London's Brunel University, wrote that a "key pleasure"[13] of comedy films comes from the filmmaker giving viewers "the space to enjoy the spectacle of childish regression."[14]

Of course, man rarely takes great strides forward without first enduring the occasional stumble. Order progresses from disorder, which makes disorder essential to maturity. Novelist Tom Robbins wrote, "Humanity has advanced, when it has advanced, not because it has been sober, responsible, and cautious, but because it has been playful, rebellious, and immature."[15] Orderly principles of film comedy were to emerge from the playful, rebellious and immature nature of the Keystone farces.

Early films relied on Georges Méliès' stop-trick camera effect to present all sorts of magical transformations. One such transformation was an age regression that occurred in a 1914 Pathé Frères comedy called *Uncle's Finish*. An 80-year-old man is able to recapture his youth by drinking water from a special spring. He becomes a hale young man, but the transformation has made him aggressive and insatiably hungry. He eats everything in sight. He becomes even younger and his hunger grows. This makes sense as children are, without question, fixated on consumption. This is the reason that the childish André Deed ravenously stuffed the creamy tart into his mouth. The man now continues to regress and, before long, he turns into a monkey. The film is saying that children are, in fact, one step above monkeys. *Uncle's Finish* serves to support Kerr's analysis of the Keystone comedies. Kerr was no doubt alluding to monkeys when he talked about the early ancestors of man playing in treetops.

A person must grow up internally at the same time that they grow up externally. Abraham Lincoln wrote, "You have to do your own growing no matter how tall your grandfather was." The alternative is that a person will end up as a small child in a big body. This is something that, though troubling in real life, is the sort of amusing contrast that is welcome in a comedy film. Often, this disparity is visually represented by a comedian wearing clothing too small for his body. This brings us to Roscoe Arbuckle. Arbuckle, a fat man with the round, plump face of a baby, looked like an overgrown child in his tight-fitting clothing. Comedian Chris Farley referred to this as "fat guy in a little coat" comedy. Arbuckle furthered his boyish image with his irrepressible playfulness. His boyish inclinations were never more evident than the times in *The Waiter's Ball* (1916) and *The Cook* (1918) that he interspersed cooking chores with an exuberant juggling of kitchen utensils. He came across as an oversized boy on other occasions, certainly when he played hide-and-seek on a farm (*The Hayseed*, 1919), or when he stuck out his tongue to express his anger at his wife (*Fatty's Chance Acquaintance*, 1915), or when he sat on a beach with a child's bucket and shovel (*Coney Island*, 1917), or when he bawled after seeing a cream pie hurled against a windshield that he had just finished cleaning (*The Garage*, 1920). But he lacked the vulnerability of a child. A large and powerful man with a rambunctious nature, especially one who will not hesitate to pummel a rival with a broom, is a formidable presence. He is not vulnerable.

Bilton believed that Arbuckle depicted on screen "a baby's appetite blown up to gargantuan proportions."[16] Arbuckle's appetite centered around three great passions: women, alcohol and food. The first two passions hardly made him childlike. Arbuckle ogles and leers at pretty young women, which suggests very adult inclinations. A child is sexless, but Arbuckle is not. Arbuckle is, at best, a hormonal adolescent. But Arbuckle's passion for food puts him squarely in the realm of a child. He has accepted eternal youth at the expense of an insatiable appetite (which is the premise of every vampire film). Bilton wrote, "[H]is wife in *Chance Acquaintances* won't give him money for an ice cream so he is forced to try and steal her purse like a naughty schoolboy."[17] Bilton recognized the dichotomy, writing, "[I]n many of his films, [Arbuckle's] persona seems to shift uncertainly between adult and monstrously inflated infant."[18] Bilton offered a fair summary of Arbuckle's nature in the following passage:

> [W]hether he's been caught by his wife chasing some young thing, or simply swiping a freshly baked pie from the kitchen counter, Roscoe looks straight to the camera and fixes

the audience with his trademark, beseeching grin, the epitome of the naughty child asking for forgiveness. Arbuckle deploys this shot in virtually every one of his movies, and while it is very different from Chaplin's appeal for pathos, it operates on a similar level: Fatty, the kid who can't help it, whose appetites are greater than his restraint, but whose innocence disarms any thought of punishment or responsibility. Was this, then, the key to Arbuckle's huge popularity? Forgiveness for all our childish failings, all of our insatiable appetites.[19]

Another Keystone comedian, Mack Swain, sometimes played an overgrown mama's boy. Take, for example, *His Bitter Pill* (1916), which featured Swain as a kind-hearted small town sheriff known as Big Jim. Big Jim is too shy to express his affection for the beautiful Nell. He is so nervous sitting close to Nell that he finds himself at a loss for words. He merely smiles at her while tensely squeezing his hat. As his nervousness increases, he raises the hat to his face and desperately gnaws the edges. Jim is devastated when Diamond Dan, a city slicker, persuades Nell to marry him. Film historian James L. Neibaur wrote, "One of the funniest [scenes] has Big Jim taking solace from his doting mother.... Once mom leaves the room, Jim collapses onto the couch and starts crying while flailing his arms and kicking his legs. The tantrum stops abruptly upon mother's return."[20] The mother, who can tell that her son has been crying, lifts the hem of her apron to wipe away his tears.

Lloyd Hamilton was the original full-fledged man-child of Hollywood cinema. He came along before Harry Langdon, before Curly Howard, before Lou Costello. Hamilton, sweet-natured and well-mannered, had a little boy's charm. He mostly expressed his immaturity in his social awkwardness. His mother's mollycoddling, though well-intentioned, had made him shy with peers and ungainly around women. His films derive tension and incongruity from their boy-in-a-man's-world misadventures. Unlike Arbuckle,

A boy and his dog: Roscoe Arbuckle and his dog Luke.

Hamilton expressed a childlike vulnerability. The actor was adept at expressing the deep apprehension that is felt by a defenseless child. Whenever he did something wrong, the comedian looked as if he was in great fear of a vigorous spanking. He would sometimes produce a pouted lip as he set out to flee and hide from the victim of his latest misdeed.

Hamilton, whose hair was neatly combed and whose clothes were clean and ironed, resembled a boy whose mother had sent him out to play. A child, though in the process of learning to control their impulses and follow rules, is not permitted to roam the earth as a wild and chaotic beast. A child must live under the supervision of parents, whose job is to exert strict and loving control of their developing youngster. A good parent assures that a child's life is simple, precise and structured. The influence of good parents is distinctly reflected in Hamilton, who is careful, courteous and obedient.

Charley Chase specialized in playing weak-willed mama's boys in his early films, including *The Fraidy Cat* (1924), *Hard Knocks* (1924), *Jeffries Jr.* (1924), *Fighting Fluid* (1925) and *Bad Boy* (1925). The plots typically centered on a meek young man who has to learn to toughen up.

In *The Fraidy Cat*, Chase breaks out in tears when a bully (Earl Mohan) rips the lapels of his jacket and splits the tail of the jacket up the middle. When the bully persists in his efforts, Chase scurries into his home and hides behind his doting white-haired mother, who thrashes the bully with a broom. It is later, when he wrongly believes that he is dying from an incurable disease, that Chase is finally able to muster courage. He defiantly thrusts out his chest and declares that he is "going to die like a man." This is a false transformation as it isn't insight or love or danger that brings out bravery in him. It is an equally false transformation that Chase undergoes in *Fighting Fluid*, in which he finally demonstrates manly aggression after he mistakenly gets drunk. This is similar to a comedy trope in which a cowardly man becomes brave under hypnosis. This was a more cynical take on a plot commonly used by Harold Lloyd, a subject that we will discuss in the next chapter.

A more probable plot can be found in Chase's *Hard Knocks*. Chase is a mild-mannered office clerk who must learn assertiveness before he can demand a raise from his boss and propose marriage to the boss's daughter (Beth Darlington). In the climax, Chase comes upon a shady co-worker (Eddie Baker) attempting to break into the company safe. Without a thought, Chase attacks Baker and saves the company's cash. Now a hero, he has the confidence to press forward with his career objectives and his romantic aspirations.

The best film in this category is *Bad Boy*. This time, Chase plays a pampered socialite who looks forward to working at his father's steel mill and marrying his girlfriend (Martha Sleeper). The problem is, both his father and his girlfriend are disgusted with his wimpy ways. Not surprisingly, he does poorly on his first day working in the foundry. Considerable humor is derived from the sensitive, thin-limbed comedian trying his best to fit in with his burly, pugnacious co-workers. It is a hopeless situation for Chase, who lacks the minimal muscle required to lift steel bars. That evening, Chase is persuaded by his mother to dance as a wood nymph at her lawn party. His fey prancing fails to convince either his father or his girlfriend that he is capable of toughening up.

In the end, Chase rallies sufficient wit and courage to safely escort his girlfriend out of a rough dance hall.

Female comedy stars also depicted characters who struggled with maturity. Louise Fazenda was expert at playing wide-eyed, clueless farm girls. Fay Tincher performed in many films as unruly tomboys. Gale Henry never came across as fully developed with her gangly limbs and gawky gestures. Mary Desjardins, Associate Professor of Film and Media Studies at Dartmouth College, was able to identify childlike qualities in the heroines portrayed by Colleen Moore. These characters, which were described by Desjardins as "dreamy" and "socially incompetent,"[21] are straining with all of their might to move into adulthood.

Harry Langdon made his film debut in 1924. Langdon's Little Elf character is by no means a fully formed adult. It is a question if he is, in fact, a human being. This person could not have possibly survived in the real world. Impossibly childish clowns reside in an absurd alternate reality. Langdon was a dreamlike character whose misadventures occurred in a world much more forgiving than our own. His nickname is accurate because he is no less a fantasy figure than a tiny, pointy-eared elf that inhabits a

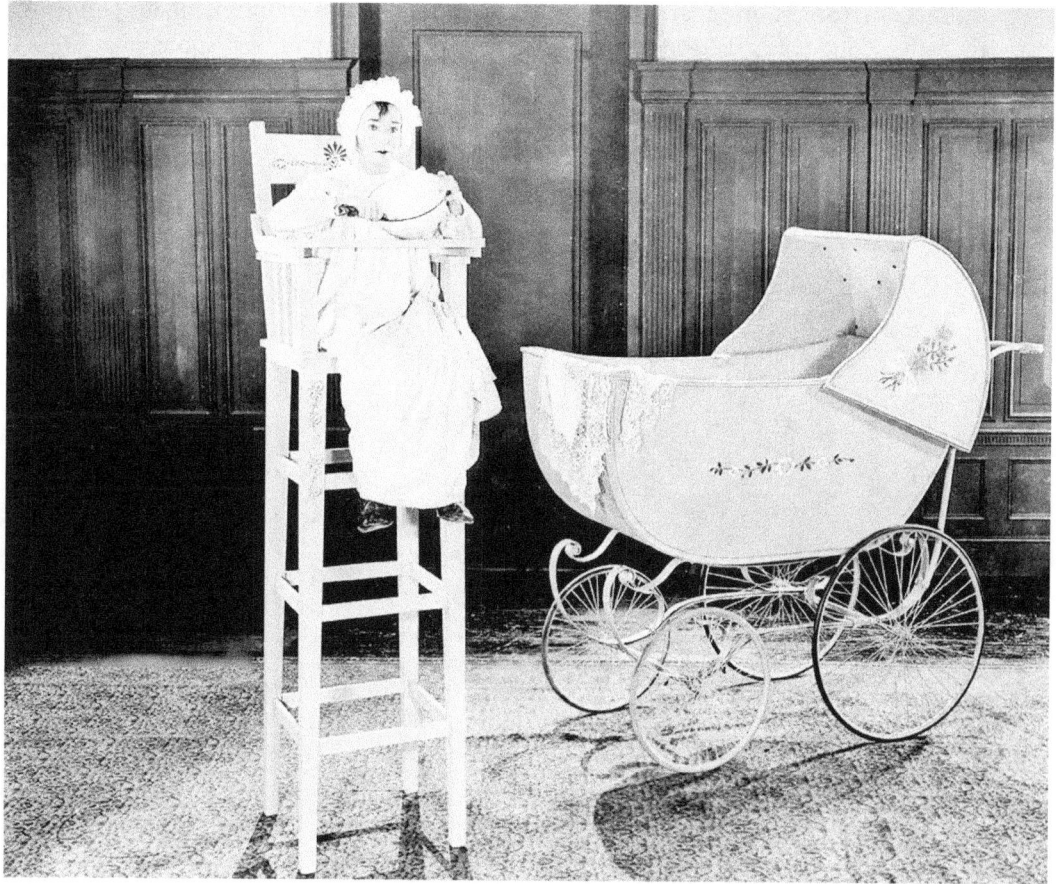

Harry Langdon plays his own infant son in *Tramp, Tramp, Tramp* (1926) (courtesy Tim Greer).

tree. Characters of this sort can also be found in *Pee-wee's Big Adventure* (1985), Will Ferrell's *Elf* (2003) and *Mr. Bean's Holiday* (2007).

The comedian who portrays this sort of character must, himself, strain glaringly to maintain the character's impossible youthfulness. Rowan Atkinson, who played Mr. Bean from 1990 to 2012, then refused to continue in the role. He said, "[I] think someone in their 50s being childlike becomes a little sad. You've got to be careful." In 2013, Will Ferrell swore that he would never star in an *Elf 2*: "I just think it would look slightly pathetic if I tried to squeeze back in the elf tights: Buddy the middle-aged elf." Only Paul Reubens, the 61-year-old actor who plays Pee-wee Herman, has been unwilling to retire his old character. He told *Entertainment Weekly* in 2006, "Am I nervous about being Pee-wee again? Not really. Not since I found out about digital retouching!"[22]

Langdon is best remembered for his childlike mannerisms. His every hesitant gesture speaks of inexperience and uncertainty. Kalton Lahue and Sam Gill, authors of *Clown Princes and Court Jesters*, described Langdon having the "stiff gait of an infant learning to walk."[23] Like a child in early development, he constantly looks to more mature figures as role models. He observes their behavior and does his best to imitate it. Kerr wrote, "[Harry] is endlessly rehearsing the act of growing up."[24]

Langdon came along at an interesting time. While he was emphasizing his childish ways, other comedians believed that it was time to grow up and be responsible.

2

Act Your Age

In the 1920s, film comedy entered a new age: The major comedy stars graduated from short films to feature films. A comedian could not simply play the fool if he wanted to sustain a well-structured, feature-length story. His actions could no longer be random or futile. Now a full-fledged protagonist, he had to take logical steps to get from one part of the story to the next. He had to be substantial and clear-headed to come upon his motivation, undergo personal development, and make timely decisions to overcome obstacles and achieve goals. In other words, he had to act like an adult.

The feature-length comedy required a protagonist with a greater purpose than visiting a skating rink (Harold Lloyd's 1919 short *Don't Shove*) or wiring a house for electricity (Buster Keaton's 1922 short *The Electric House*). This meant that the protagonist needed to have foresight and ambition. It serves society well when a person shifts from pleasure to purpose, but it isn't enough if a person's pursuits are shallow and short-term. A dog that runs to fetch a stick has purpose and direction, but its efforts will never amount to anything significant or interesting.

Men must have an elaborate moral code for which they are willing to fight. For men, maturity has been inexorably intertwined with this masculinity code. Douglas Fairbanks emphasized this point in his 1913 Broadway comedy hit, "The New Henrietta." The play put forth the clear message that a growing boy must become a robust and righteous fighter before he can be considered a man. The plot developments of the play functioned together to, according to David Bordwell, "turn [a sissy] into a red-blooded man."[1] This formula carried on to Fairbanks' early comedy films, including *The Lamb* (1915), *Reggie Mixes In* (1916), *His Picture in the Papers* (1916), *Wild and Woolly* (1917) and *The Mollycoddle* (1920). In *The Mollycoddle*, Fairbanks plays a pampered young rich man. He has descended from a long line of stalwart Western frontiersmen, but growing up in the cultural centers of Europe has made him soft. Fortunately, the tenacious spirit of his ancestors comes alive in him when he comes up against a murderous diamond smuggler (Wallace Beery).

This type of story, which Bordwell called the "lamb-to-lion plot,"[2] later became an influence on the work of Harold Lloyd and Buster Keaton. The formula was already fully evident in the plot of Lloyd's 1921 feature *A Sailor-Made Man* (1921). An idle playboy (Lloyd) falls in love with a pretty society girl (Mildred Davis), but the couple cannot marry unless the playboy can prove his manly worth to the girl's businessman father. He chooses to prove himself by joining the navy.

The young men that Lloyd portrays are not willing to linger in their youth. It is assumed that, when the time is right, these characters will embark with vigor on their rite of passage. By the end of the story, they will in all likelihood have overcome their awkwardness with women, proven their ability to hold a job, and stood up to the threat of a rival. In Lloyd's first official feature, *Grandma's Boy* (1922), his protagonist, a country boy known simply as Grandma's Boy, is cowed by a bully. It is considered immature to be a craven weakling. To bring to the fore the character's immaturity, Lloyd followed Arbuckle's example of wearing an outfit too small for his body. The sleeves of his coat barely extend beyond his elbows, the pants legs only reach as far as his ankles, and the coat is too tight for him to button it properly around his stomach. Lloyd's grandmother gets the young man to overcome his fears by convincing him that an umbrella handle

Harold Lloyd lacks the courage to eject a surly tramp (Dick Sutherland) from his grandmother's property in *Grandma's Boy* (1922). Providing Harold with back-up is his grandmother (Anna Townsend) and a neighborhood boy (Jackie Morgan).

is a magic amulet that once transformed his grandfather into a war hero. By the end of the story, he has clobbered the bully, captured a dangerous tramp, and become engaged to the girl that he loves.

Fairy tales often promoted maturity. "Jack and the Beanstalk" involves an immature boy who must quickly attain maturity to prevent himself and his mother from starving to death. The conflicts in a coming-of-age story are tests. A problem is presented to a young person, who must find a mature response.

In a comedy, a character's bungling is usually the result of drunkenness, stupidity or immaturity. The immature bungler is the most sympathetic of the group because he has the chance to learn and succeed. A viewer can forgive Lloyd his mistakes as they know that he is still learning and he will get better as a result of his experiences. He is a hero in the making, possessing the potential for growth and the hope for a prosperous future.

Many comedy films begin with a pretty young woman turning a young man's head. The libido rushes a young man headlong into adulthood. Lloyd often started out a story falling in love. In *Bumping into Broadway* (1919), Lloyd feels sympathy for a struggling young actress (Bebe Daniels) who is about to be evicted from their boardinghouse. He gives her the little money that he has to pay her overdue rent. Unfortunately, his own rent is overdue and he now has put himself in jeopardy of being tossed into the street by the landlady's burly bouncer. But Lloyd is so smitten by the actress that he hardly cares. At one point, he is delighted to accept a flower from the actress. With a dreamy look in his eyes, he sits down on a curb to savor the flower's fragrance and caress its soft petals.

In *Girl Shy* (1924), Lloyd's interest in the fairer sex inspires him to write a book entitled "The Secret of Making Love." The joke is that, by all indication, this young man has only made love in his imagination. At the time, film critics often described Lloyd as "boyish." (Lloyd himself added to this "quiet, normal ... clean, sympathetic, not impossible to romance.") This was a reasonable description as Lloyd appeared on screen as a naïve young man whose mind was filled with romantic illusions. A person with a youthful spirit and romantic illusions is liable to defer commitments, obligations and growing up, but it is different with Lloyd. Lloyd's youthful spirit and romantic illusions are the forces that drive him steadily towards adult ambitions and adult commitments. Lloyd does not want to escape into his fantasies. He wants to make his fantasies come true.

Lloyd's go-getter persona, known as the "Glasses Character," is in no way characterized by immobility and failure. He achieves maturity by developing a sense of self, finding intimacy, and achieving productivity. Bilton wrote about comedy characters who were weak and indecisive. He specifically referred to them as "mooncalves and milksops."[3] This doesn't at all describe Lloyd, who understands that he must measure up as a true man before a woman will be willing to marry him. Famed developmental psychologist Erik Erikson believed that marriage and parenthood provide an important framework for human development. Lloyd accepted this idea, which he applied to his film stories. His character's simple and distinct goal is to marry and have children.

David D. Gilmore, the author of *Manhood in the Making*, found that almost every society has an idea of a "real man" that shares three common imperatives: A male must

Harold Lloyd is a dreamy romantic in *Girl Shy* (1924). Little does he know that the girl of his dreams (Jobyna Ralston) is standing above him on the bridge (courtesy www.doctormacro. com).

protect, procreate, and provide. These are, in fact, the imperatives of a husband and father. We talked about Lloyd clobbering a bully, which proved his ability to protect. We will discuss Lloyd's ability to procreate in a later chapter. That leaves Lloyd's ability to provide.

A man cannot provide for his family unless he is capable of productivity and social integration. Productivity, which begins with finding a purpose and assuming commitments, leads a man to undertake challenges and risks. Equal amounts of discipline, nerve and intelligence are required to fulfill these undertakings. Lloyd had those qualities, which is particularly evident in *Safety Last* (1923). The film begins with country boy Harold bidding his mother and fiancée farewell at a train station. He intends to become a big success in the city so that he and his fiancée can marry. But attaining success isn't as easy as Harold expected. He finds himself continually harried working as a sales clerk at a department store. Because he wants more than this, he commits himself to working hard and looking forward to the first opportunity to earn a promotion. His chance comes when the department store manager offers a thousand dollars to an employee who can come up with a successful promotion for the store. Harold proposes

Harold Lloyd was quick to assume the role of protector in his relationships with women. Lloyd is protecting Mildred Davis from Noah Young in this scene from *I Do* (1921) (courtesy www.doctormacro.com).

that they attract crowds by having a "mystery man" climb up the exterior of the building. When the man scheduled to climb the building gets into trouble with a police officer, Harold, determined that the promotion be a success, sets aside doubt and trepidation to climb the building himself. He nearly falls several times during his climb, but he keeps going and he manages to reach the rooftop in the end. Never at any point in the film does Harold run out of spirit, ideas, or resolve. He employs initiative and industry for a fixed purpose and he manages in the process to become a man.

Lloyd's stories shared elements with Horatio Alger's classic novels. Lloyd and Alger were both master storytellers who liked to show a poor boy achieve success. Russel Crouse, who edited a collection of Alger's work, essentially described the heroes of Alger's stories as honest, cheerful, ambitious and manly. Lloyd's earnest and indomitable characters certainly fit within this mold.

The metaphor of *Safety Last* was obvious. This man willing to climb a tall building to achieve success was, in every sense, a social climber. But Lloyd does not meet everyone's standards of maturity in his rise to the top. It could be argued that nothing about his climb up the side of a tall building is sober, responsible or cautious. Should we cheer this fellow or not? Lloyd certainly works hard to elicit our cheers and he takes necessary risks to achieve an important objective.

Lloyd was also good at social integration, which requires conformity. Unlike other comedy characters, Lloyd's characters did not reject conformity. He wanted to be liked and fit in with others. In *Speedy* (1928), Lloyd sees an advertisement for "The Well-

Harold Lloyd's go-getter character was wonderfully enshrined in *Safety Last!* (1923). In this scene, Lloyd works hard as a department store clerk in the hope that he can earn enough money to marry his hometown sweetheart (courtesy www.doctormacro.com).

Dressed Man." He looks at the illustration of a smartly attired man in the ad and he immediately adjusts his pocket handkerchief and straightens his tie to make himself look more like this man. An awkward youth who doesn't know proper etiquette and dress can live his life as a lonely misfit. Lloyd is willing to relinquish his individuality to be accepted.

In sharp contrast to Lloyd, Groucho Marx defies social rules in his resistance of integration. It is no wonder that Groucho's most famous line is "I don't want to belong to any club that will accept people like me as a member." Maturity involves a person aligning themselves with accepted standards. Groucho, an iconoclast, could never do that. He behaves like a bratty boy in the way that he is surly to authority figures, shows off for girls, and makes rash decisions. Unlike the stylish Lloyd, he immediately stands out in a crowd with his dusty swallowtail coat. The Marx Brothers, as a whole, were defiantly childish in their war against authority and convention. Harpo stood out for his boyish mischief. Frequent co-star Margaret Dumont said of the Brothers, "They're just like a bunch of school boys.... Everything they do is in the spirit of fun...."[4]

So much of what happens in a Lloyd film is a test of virtue, self-worth and masculinity. This is even the case in *Speedy* (1928) when Lloyd breathes as hard as he can into a "Test your Lungs" machine at an amusement park. In *Girl Shy*, Lloyd plays a tailor's shy apprentice, who aspires to be a writer. He expects to have the confidence to propose marriage to a young socialite, Mary Buckingham (Jobyna Ralston), once he sells his first book. Disappointed when his manuscript is rejected, Harold sadly gives up his pursuit of Mary. Then the publisher changes his mind and sends him a $3000 advance. Harold learns that Mary is about to unknowingly marry a bigamist. He relies on various modes of transportation, including an automobile, a motorcycle, a horse and a trolley car, in an urgent race across town to stop the marriage. This takes courage, confidence, vigor, determination and resourcefulness, which are traditional qualities of a mature and masculine man. Confidence is the most important quality in Lloyd's character. Lloyd may experience self-doubt from momentary setbacks, but he is always successful in the end and he comes away from his experiences with great self-confidence.

In *The Kid Brother* (1927), Lloyd appears to be an undersized weakling compared to his father and two brothers, all three of whom are tall, broad-shouldered and muscular. Keaton already exploited this type of contrast in *My Wife's Relations* (1922), *Our Hospitality* (1923) and *Battling Butler* (1926). The difference with Keaton, though, was that he was dwarfed in size by the father and brothers of a girlfriend. It makes Lloyd feel painfully inadequate to have grown up as the runt in his own family.

Harold's steely dad, Sheriff Jim Hickory, is entrusted with a fund collected for the construction of a county dam. He holds the cash in safekeeping in a strongbox at his home. A medicine show huckster learns about the fund and enlists the aid of the show's strongman to steal it. The men sneak into the sheriff's home, break open the strongbox, and leave with the money. Sam Hooper (Frank Lanning), a nemesis of the Hickory clan, is quick to accuse the sheriff of stealing the money and convinces other townsfolk to throw the sheriff in jail. Determined to clear his father's name and get him released from jail, Harold devotes himself to capturing the true thieves and returning the money.

Harold finds that it is much easier to locate the thieves than it is to subdue them.

The Marx Brothers are engaged in their usual mayhem in *The Cocoanuts* (1929). (courtesy www.doctormacro.com.)

He needs to be resourceful to defeat these rough folk. He learns that the strongman, who is unable to swim, is afraid of water. He uses that knowledge to his advantage by lifting the strongman onto a dolly and dumping him into a river. The strongman flails around in panic and eventually becomes exhausted. Harold now has little trouble taking his weakened adversary into custody. By using courage, wit and perseverance, Harold has been able to capture the thieves, restore his family's honor, and prove his worth to his father. The fact that he acted with foresight and planning did more than anything else to establish his maturity. The next year, elements of *The Kid Brother* turned up in Keaton's *Steamboat Bill, Jr.* (1928), in which Keaton appeared to be an undersized weakling compared to his brawny father and he proved his worth by securing his father's release from jail.

Hot Water (1924), a foray into domestic comedy, gave Lloyd an opportunity to explore the intimacy of marriage, which is the next stage of human development. It would have made sense for Lloyd to illustrate the significance of marriage considering that marriage was the primary goal of his previous film characters in *Safety Last* and *Girl Shy*. But the film is trite and pointless compared to the comedian's other silent features. Lloyd had no real interest in exploring marriage. The drab, put-upon husband was not a role that suited his vigorous style of comedy. His determined and exuberant character must remain, like Peter Pan, a cocky young adventurer.

In looking back on his childhood, Lloyd associated himself with another boy in popular literature. "I was," Lloyd said, "a good example of Tom Sawyer."[5] It followed then that Lloyd should develop his Glasses Character in the mold of the iconic Saywer, who was known to be enterprising, lively and adventurous. It seemed even more important to the comedian to distinguish his comic persona from Tom's lawless and rebellious best friend, Huck Finn. Huck hated civilized life. Twain wrote, "[W]hithersoever he turned, the bars and shackles of civilization shut him in and bound him hand and foot."[6] American literary scholar Henry Nash Smith wrote that Finn rejected conformity in his fidelity to "the uncoerced self."[7] He led a carefree life free from societal rules. That was not Lloyd.

Tom started out as a mischievous boy who wanted to emulate bad boy Huck, but he managed by the end of Twain's novel to give up the freedoms of childhood and accept adult order. He urged Huck to embrace respectability and responsibility, but this was beyond his friend's capability. I wrote earlier about Lloyd recognizing the importance of dress. Forget about Huck ever becoming an impeccable, well-dressed citizen. He hated clothes; collars were too tight and shoes were too binding. He told Tom, "I got to wear them blamed clothes that just smothers me, Tom; they don't seem to any air git through 'em, somehow; and they're so rotten nice that I can't set down, nor lay down, nor roll around anywhere's...."

Lloyd's continued reliance on "coming of age" stories became a problem for him as he got older. He was still acting as if he was on the threshold of manhood in *Movie Crazy* (1932) even though he was close to 40 years old at the time. Now he did look like an immature goof, which no doubt contributed to his decline at the box office.

A true man is not passive. He competes, explores, and takes risks. This what it takes to be successful and stand out, which is important. It is through his achievements that a man gains power and privilege, which serves to improve his chances to procreate. In *The Freshman* (1925), Lloyd proves himself in a championship college football game, which elevates his status. In *The Sin of Harold Diddlebock* (1947), satirist Preston Sturges subverts our assumption that Lloyd's success in the game has securely elevated his status and set him on the path to great success. Diddlebock, a college football hero, ends up stuck in a dull, low-paying bookkeeping job for 23 years. He has never been able to achieve financial security, which means that he has been unable to become a husband and father. It takes him getting terribly drunk one night to get him to abandon social rules. Without his inhibitions, he buys himself a garish outfit, which includes a ten-gallon hat and a checkered sports jacket. This is no longer the hopeful young man who was so attentive to the "Well-Dressed Man" advertisement. But it is by breaking the rules and abandoning conformity that Diddlebock finally manages to achieve success and get the girl.

Keaton sought outright absurdity when he played a bratty child in his early short comedies *Oh Doctor!* (1917) and *The Play House* (1921). It was incongruous to see the resourceful and hard-edged Keaton act childishly.

Keaton essentially adopted Lloyd's coming-of-age template for his feature films. Steven D. Greydanus of *Decent Film Guide* wrote, "Lloyd's Glasses Character persona is always a mild-mannered underdog hero, too bashful to speak to the pretty girl and too slight to take on the brawny bullies. For awhile he gets by on cleverness and trickery, until finally some crisis or event rouses him to genuine valor and heroism, and he finds an unexpected and hidden strength he didn't know he had."[8] His underdog-turned-hero stories, which are essentially a boy-turned-man stories, are not at all different than the type of stories that Keaton employed in his features.

Little was underdeveloped about Keaton. The characters that he portrayed were

Harold Lloyd sees a clear path ahead for himself and his girlfriend (Jobyna Ralston) in *The Freshman* (1925) (courtesy www.doctormacro.com).

2. Act Your Age

fully formed adults: physically fit, motivated, focused, and resourceful. Let's examine the plot of *Our Hospitality* (1923), in which Keaton portrayed young Willie McKay. When McKay turns twenty-one, the estate of his late father is transferred into his name and he is summoned to claim the estate as part of his inheritance. This transaction marks Keaton's arrival into adulthood, at which time he is expected to assume the same responsibilities his father once had. This is the time for Keaton to demonstrate virtue and meet the challenges of adulthood. Keaton never gives us a doubt that he will beat his rivals, win the girl, and prove his virility. While Chaplin gains our sympathy and Lloyd gains our support, Keaton is able with his breathtakingly clever and heroic exploits to gain our admiration. It's not that we are eager to know *if* he will succeed, it's that we are eager to know *how* he will succeed. Keaton may be short in stature, but he is a manly figure nonetheless. He is strong, able, and defined by action. He stands as a virtuous protagonist whenever he takes vigorous and direct action to solve problems.

One Keaton character that seemed at the outset to be less than manly was Rollo Treadway, the wealthy young heir he portrays in *The Navigator* (1924). Rollo is introduced by a wide shot that also offers an expansive view of his lavish bedroom. He is

Buster Keaton found great humor in portraying an idle rich brat in *The Navigator* (1924) (courtesy www.doctormacro.com).

sitting in a silk robe at the edge of a large bed and leisurely sipping a cup of tea, which a valet has delivered to him on a serving cart. The valet stands attentively beside Rollo awaiting his next command. The valet provides this rich scion with whatever he needs before he even knows that he needs it. This can have the effect of stopping a person from engaging in intelligent thought. Rollo is so unthinking that he steps into a sunken bathtub without remembering to remove his robe.[9]

We know everything about Rollo that we need to know from this one scene. He is one of those deplorable idle rich, spoiled and lazy and wholly dependent on the care of his faithful valet. When he looks out his bedroom window, Rollo sees a car with a "Just Married" sign and a bride and groom joined together in a joyful embrace. He looks blankly at a portrait of Betsy O'Brien (Kathryn McGuire) that sits on top of his dresser. He tells his valet, "I think I'll get married." He has the valet arrange a honeymoon cruise to Honolulu while his chauffeur drives him across the street to Betsy's home. In an oft-cited gag, Rollo's limousine makes a simple U-turn to deliver Rollo from the front of his house to the front of Betsy's house. Rollo is so helpless that, after this blink-of-an-eye trip, he needs a footman to help him out of the vehicle.

Rollo enters Betsy's living room and hands her flowers. Then, without prelude, he asks her to marry him. Betsy is startled, confused and insulted by this bold and tactless proposal. She reacts with indignation, flatly rejecting the offer. When he leaves, Betsy feels so hurt and upset by his actions that she sheds a single tear, which rolls down her cheek. The tear makes it clear that she truly cares for Rollo. Rollo figures to go on his honeymoon cruise without a bride. He looks heartbroken as he rips up Betsy's ticket. Rollo would likely be on his way to marry if he expressed this sort of emotion when he proposed. The problem, it seems, is that neither Rollo nor Betsy are willing or able to reveal their true feelings to one another.

Betsy accompanies her father (Frederick Vroom) to retrieve papers that he left on his steamship, the *Navigator*, which a foreign nation has just purchased for their war effort. Betsy waits in the car as her father walks on the pier toward the ship. Saboteurs leap out of the shadows to capture Betsy's father. After hearing her father cry for help, Betsy races aboard the ship to find him. Rollo ends up on the wrong pier and he, too, boards the *Navigator*. The saboteurs set the ship adrift with its two unwitting passengers. One film historian described the couple being "faced with the reverse–*Robinson Crusoe* challenge of setting up housekeeping in the over-technicalized environment of a ship built for thousands—and not a servant in sight" (notes for the University of California's 1981 American Comedy Festival). Shipwrecks create good stories. A number of popular stories, including *Robinson Crusoe* and *Swiss Family Robinson*, involve a shipwreck that strands passengers on a desert island. Rollo's ocean liner is not wrecked by storms or currents. Its hull remains seaworthy for the majority of the film. The twist to the story is that, instead of being stranded on an island, the passengers find themselves stranded on the ship itself.

Crusoe used materials salvaged from the ship, including beams and iron bolts, to build a table and chairs. He carved a canoe out of a tree trunk. He used planks from the shipwreck to build a hut. He made clothing out of animal furs. He tricked out a makeshift boat with sails and an umbrella. He realized that there was nothing he wanted that he couldn't make. At first, Rollo can't even open a can of food, but he soon proves to be a resourceful young man. He salvages parts from the ship to create a spectacularly mechanized kitchen. Like Crusoe, he becomes self-reliant. He also learns to be brave and selfless. When the ship runs aground and the hull is damaged, he summons the courage to put on a diving suit and go to the ocean floor to make repairs. When he finds that Betsy has been captured by cannibals, he rushes to her rescue just as Crusoe once rescued his island companion Friday from cannibals. Rollo must think for himself when his valet is no longer around to serve his needs and, in the end, he rises to many unexpected challenges, which means that the appropriate manly virtues were latent inside of him all along.

Pampered socialites are generally seen as immature. *The Navigator* is more optimistic than J.M. Barrie's 1902 stage play *The Admirable Crichton*, the plot of which was nicely showcased in Lewis Gilbert's 1957 film adaptation. When a family of aristocrats gets shipwrecked on a desert island, only their butler has the skill and resourcefulness to assure the group's survival. But *The Navigator* takes a different tack with Rollo, who is able to do well on a desert island (with cannibals, no less) without his servants. Keaton was playing a variation of Bertie Wooster, a popular literary character that satirist P.G. Wodehouse introduced in 1915. Wooster was meant to symbolize the foolish and dimwitted folk who comprised Britain's idle rich. The character's survival depended on the dutifulness and resourcefulness of his valet Jeeves, who was constantly required to rescue Wooster from awkward situations. Novels and plays had long relied on resourceful valets to help to solve problems for their masters. Other famous valets of literature included Passepartout, Dromio, Figaro, Leporello and Baptistin. But, of all of these characters, Jeeves had the most impact on Hollywood's valets. The Jeeves character hung around in Hollywood for decades. Proof can be found with the kind valet Coleman (Denholm Elliott) who helps Eddie Murphy in *Trading Places* (1983). The one valet who broke the mold was Burt Kwouk's immortal Cato Fong, the valet of police detective Jacques Clouseau (Peter Sellers) in the *Pink Panther* series. Cato was the only valet authorized to launch sneak attacks on his employer, who considered the attacks a necessary part of his self-defense training program.

Keaton plays the Lover archetype in *The Navigator*. Film critic Ed Howard, author of the Only Cinema blog, wrote, "Keaton's attempts to comfort and help his companion reveal a tenderness and compassion not revealed by his characteristic stoic expression and the deadpan way he'd approached romance earlier in the film. This undercurrent reaches its apex with a wonderful shot in which Keaton and McGuire struggle to light some candles while their shadows seem to kiss on the wall behind them, enacting the romance that they never quite consummate in the flesh."[10] To move on to a mature relationship, Rollo has to develop sensitivity and connectedness. These qualities are not regarded as explicit masculine qualities, but they serve a man in his efforts to achieve intimacy and social integration. Although French actor Jean Gabin was a manly figure in his films, he often connected to others on screen with distinct expressions of tenderness. Gabin will be discussed at length in a later chapter.

Crusoe was on the island for twenty-four years before he met Caribbean tribesman Friday. Once he was joined by Friday, he learned how to cooperate with another person and develop a close, binding and mutually beneficial relationship. Rollo forms a similar relationship with Betsy and the couple is close and loving by the end of the film.

In the comedies of this era, the man who won the fair lady was not the man with a sense of entitlement or the man with alpha-dog status. The pretty maiden was quick to reject the aggressive, arrogant and often well-to-do suitor who was willing to improve his situation by lying, cheating and bullying. No matter how charming and lavish these men could be, the women recognized their sleaziness and wanted no part of what they had to offer. Both Lloyd and Keaton emphasized their characters' high moral standing in their early features. Keaton's superior virtue comes through in his rivalry with the womanizer (Ward Crane) in *Sherlock Jr.* (1924). Lloyd's superior virtue comes through in his rivalry with the bigamist (Carlton Griffin) in *Girl Shy*. The women were drawn to Keaton and Lloyd because they made sincere and reliable suitors. Lloyd, for all his pluckiness, was always polite, gentle and affectionate to his girlfriend.

In *Battling Butler* (1926), Keaton plays Alfred Butler, yet another effete, pampered

The Navigator (1924) presents the story of a man and woman learning the importance of cooperation and intimacy. Buster Keaton and Kathryn McGuire, whose pride and selfishness kept them apart before, must now find a way to work together to survive aboard a deserted ocean liner adrift in the Pacific Ocean (courtesy www.doctormacro.com).

playboy. Alfred's leisurely lifestyle has become an annoyance to his industrialist father, who instructs a valet (Snitz Edwards) to take Alfred on a hunting and fishing trip to make a man out of him. When we first meet Alfred, he is sitting on a sofa exerting minimal effort as he smokes a cigarette. Alfred's white-haired old mother sits down beside him to delicately break the news of this unpleasant trip that his father has arranged. Rollo Treadway may have had servants at his beck and call, but at least he lived on his own and didn't have his mother at his side to coddle him. Alfred's valet goes as far as smoothing down a stray hair on Alfred's head and removing the cigarette from Alfred's mouth so that he can flick the ashes into an ashtray. It is a perfect tableau that tells you everything you need to know about this helpless character.

The trip goes on as scheduled. Not surprisingly, Alfred proves to be inept as a hunter. This is never more evident than when he causes his rowboat to sink while making a clumsy effort to shoot an evasive duck.

Later, Alfred is holding his rifle backwards while he takes aim at a chicken. When he finally pulls the trigger, he nearly puts a bullet into a mountain girl strolling through the woods. The girl (Sally O'Neil) fervently reprimands Alfred, but all that he can think about is how pretty she is. When Alfred accidentally fires another shot in her direction, Sally throws rocks at him until he flees inside his tent. Then she smiles. It seems that she really likes this muddled hunter after all. It is inevitable that this couple will fall in love.

The couple wants to marry, but Sally's family does not approve of Alfred. Her brother and father, a pair of big and brawny men, are unimpressed with this runt. The brother says, "That jellyfish couldn't take care of himself—let alone a wife!" The father adds, "We don't want any weaklings in our family." Alfred has the financial means to care for a wife and children and he derives extraordinary power from his wealth, but his girlfriend's family sticks to the primal notions of a protector and provider: a manly woodsman who can build a cabin, battle a bear, and produce strong and healthy children. It isn't only that Alfred is not tall and muscular. A much bigger issue is that he lacks vigor. Basic human drive is useless to this young man when, as described by Keaton biographer Edward McPherson, he has "a manservant at the end of a bell."[11] He informs his valet as succinctly as possible what he wants and then he tells the man, "Arrange it." These are magic words that can make anything he wants come to be. It raises the question if a man as impotent as this can father children.

It just so happens that a boxer who is also named Alfred Butler, otherwise known as Battling Butler, is making headlines for an upcoming championship bout. The valet tells the family that Alfred is Battling Butler. Who has more vigor than a champion boxer? The father and brother now have respect for Alfred and support him marrying Sally. Alfred and Sally wed in a joyful celebration, but Alfred must continue to cover up his lie. Alfred reads in the newspaper that Battling Butler will be training in Silver Hot Springs. He leaves for the training camp so that he can send his wife letters from the location. He passes his time at the camp by engaging in his own training regimen, which is limited to taking jabs at an overly springy boxing dummy. Problems arise when Battling Butler's flirtatious wife becomes friendly with Alfred, which infuriates her jealous husband. When Battling Butler learns that Alfred is pretending to be him, he tells his manager that he wants to teach Alfred a lesson by having him take his place in the upcoming bout with the Alabama Murderer. The Battling Butler's trainers agree to work with Alfred.

Alfred, who was unflappable when his boat sank, should not be expected to look worried as he climbs into the training ring. True to form, he confronts his opponent in his familiar stoic manner. He looks nothing more than attentive and inquisitive as he is instructed on stance and balance. Presumably, he is prepared to cope with whatever comes his way and master the skills necessary to succeed in this combat sport. But, as soon as he pitted against his hard-fisted sparring partner, the reality of the situation hits home. He couldn't look more startled when the sparring partner barrages him with punches. He races around the ring to avoid his violent opponent and, like a child seeking a parent's protection, he leaps into the referee's arms. This is the most vigor that Alfred has displayed since he was introduced to us.

Battling Butler is a brutal and bloodthirsty man. He is the Warrior as sadist. The boxer shows more than ever before that he is a mean-spirited bully when, in the final minutes of the film, he attacks Alfred in his dressing room. Alfred is helpless at first,

Buster Keaton, a pampered and naive young man, fails to anticipate the brutality of the boxing ring in *Battling Butler* (1926) (courtesy www.doctormacro.com).

but then he sees his wife in the doorway. She is staring in horror as the man that she loves is being beaten. Refusing to be humiliated in front of his wife, Alfred suddenly fights back with a startling fury and batters the boxer into a wobbly heap. The scene is most remarkable because, from beginning to end, it does not produce a single gag. We accept that, at that moment, Alfred is making the very serious passage from helpless child to vigorous man. The scene mirrors the climax of Harold Lloyd's *Grandma's Boy*. Harold's beloved grandmother is present to witness Harold thrash a bully who has harassed him throughout the film. The fight, which is vicious from beginning to end, does not include a single lighthearted moment. It, too, ends with the bully limp, ragged and barely conscious. Keaton's earlier passivity signified his unresolved personality. But after taking decisive action against Battling Butler, he's become a fully formed adult.

In *Steamboat Bill, Jr.* (1928), Keaton plays Willie Canfield, Jr., the small, dandified son of a rugged, burly riverboat captain, Captain William "Steamboat Bill" Canfield (Ernest Torrence). At an early age, Willie was sent to Boston to be educated. His father, who hasn't seen Willie for years, is excited to receive a telegram that his son is coming to visit. "Must be a big lad by now," he tells his first mate (Tom Lewis). "I'll bet he's bigger'n me."

Captain Canfield is appalled when he finally gets to meet Willie, who is not the manly offspring that he expected. As the captain suspiciously scrutinizes his son, his attention is instantly drawn to the young man's foppish attire. He sees no sartorial splendor in Willie's striped blazer, checkered bow tie, or French beret. He is even less pleased with the thinly groomed mustache that adorns Willie's upper lip and the ukulele tucked underneath his arm. His patience reaches its limit when he sees Willie calm a crying baby by prancing before the baby's carriage and playing a spirited tune on his ukulele.

The captain commits to remake his son in his own image. To start, he snatches away the ukulele and hides it under his coat. Then, he drags Willie into a barber shop and tells the barber, "Take that barnacle off his lip." Finally, the captain takes Willie to a tailor shop and tells the tailor, "Fix him up with some working clothes for the boat." In the next scene, Willie shows up on the dock in a stylish yachting outfit. His father can't believe his eyes. His first mate offers him a pistol and tells him, "No jury would convict you."

Willie ends up replacing his beret with a black wool boating cap (also known as a fiddler cap), the same type of headpiece that his father wears. In general, his new outfit closely resembles his father's outfit. He has, in this way, become a miniature version of the captain.

Willie may look like a man now, but he still has to learn how to act like a man. The captain orders a deckhand to give Willie lessons in the engine room. Later, when Willie gets into a fight with a crew member of a rival steamboat, the captain teaches his son how to throw a punch. In either case, Willie proves to be a less than apt student. His father is particularly upset when Willie crashes their boat into another boat. His father says, "I'm trying to teach you to run it—not wreck it."

The two men finally have a chance to bond when they share a plug of chewing tobacco. But it isn't long before the warm scene is spoiled. When his father heartily

A father and son conflict is at the center of *Steamboat Bill, Jr.* (1928). Riverboat captain Bill Canfield (Ernest Torrence) is appalled to find that his namesake son, Bill, Jr. (Buster Keaton), has developed into a foppish young man (courtesy www.doctormacro.com).

slaps him on the back, Willie swallows the tobacco and faints. This hardly helps Willie to overcome his father's perception of him as a weakling.

Later, Captain Canfield confiscates Willie's clothes to keep him from a rendezvous with Kitty King (Marion Byron), the daughter of his rival, but Willie steals an outfit belonging to his father and runs off to meet the young woman. In the oversized outfit, he looks like a little boy playing dress up. But, in the end, Willie demonstrates mettle

A steamboat captain (Ernest Torrence) attempts to mold his son (Buster Keaton) into his own image in *Steamboat Bill, Jr.* (1928) (courtesy www.doctormacro.com).

and resourcefulness by surviving a massively destructive cyclone and rescuing several people, including his father, Kitty and Kitty's father.

Contrary to his manly exploits on screen, Keaton expressed a youthfully mischievous spirit in real life and he grew increasingly childlike as time went on. In his later years, the veteran comedian maintained an elaborate model railroad in working order at his ranch in the Woodland Hills. His wife Eleanor said, "The toy train came out of the kitchen on a track that ran the length of the pool alongside the fence, and curved over a trestle to a round table. We used it to deliver soft drinks and hot dogs to guests."[12]

Comedians often remain young at heart. Keaton's rival Harold Lloyd was no different. During his retirement, Lloyd reverted to boyhood. He practiced magic tricks, collected cars, listened to his stereo, played handball, and ran around with his Great Danes. He formed a photography club with a group of other actors. His granddaughter, Suzanne Lloyd Hayes, said, "Most of the time they'd exchange slides and talk about meters and filters and strobe lights and new kinds of film. They were just mad shutterbugs, especially when they had some new gizmo to play with."[13] It takes an eternal child to keep a large permanent Christmas tree in their sitting room, which is also something that Lloyd did during this period.

Were Keaton and Lloyd being completely sincere when they promoted the pursuit of maturity in their films?

In *Tramp, Tramp, Tramp* (1926), Harry Langdon does not have a bearish father, not like Keaton's steamboat captain father in *Steamboat Bill, Jr.,* or Lloyd's sheriff father in *The Kid Brother*. Harry's father is a frail old shoemaker confined to a wheelchair. He tells Harry that he is about lose his business. Harry's only concern is that, if his father goes out of business, he won't have the money to buy Harry a bicycle. The bicycle was later used as a foremost symbol of a character's childishness in *The Errand Boy* (1961), *Pee-wee's Big Adventure* (1985) and *The 40-Year-Old Virgin* (2005). Harry realizes that his father cannot provide for him and this means that he must take steps to become an adult. Taking steps becomes literal when he sets out to win a $25,000 cash prize in a cross-country foot race. Harry succeeds in enduring tornado winds and other hardships on his way to the finish line. He collects the prize money, which he uses to save his father's business. It would have been impossible for Harry to have attained the virility of a steamboat captain father or a sheriff father, but he could manage through his fleet-footed performance in the race to more than match up to his own father's limited physicality. The obstacles and expectations had to be lowered for the Little Elf, who could never develop as fully as Keaton's Willie Canfield or Lloyd's Harold Hickory.

Chaplin's Tramp, a destitute everyman, was usually unwanted wherever he went. The character, vulnerable, alone and victimized, wanders through life like an orphan child. Russian filmmaker Sergei Eisenstein said, "[Chaplin] has preserved the outlook and spontaneous reactions of a child.... Hence his freedom from the ordinary fetters of morals...." Chaplin, who envied children, said, "I feel rather inferior to children. Most of them have assurance, but have not yet been cursed with self-consciousness."[14]

Chaplin started out in the film industry at age 25 with a distinctly youthful appearance. He was, according to film critic Ignatiy Vishnevetsky, "slightly built and smooth-cheeked."[15] At first, the actor took the time to paste on a mustache and paint on artificial wrinkles to make his Tramp character look older. Eventually, though, he saw it best to redesign the Tramp to make him an ageless icon. It was for this reason that he made it part of his makeup regimen to apply white-face to erase the slightest lines in the Tramp's face. The Tramp was to remain youthful for as long as he could.

The scarcer the resources, the more men need to be good at being men. This means that, when the going gets tough, the tough get going. But Chaplin's Tramp, whose resources are scarce, does not resort to aggressive means to keep himself fed. Joan Mellen wrote in her book *Modern Times*, "[Chaplin] remains, always, a fortuitous step away from homelessness and starvation."[16] Chaplin finds various ways to stave off starvation, including stealing food off a lunch wagon (*A Dog's Life*, 1918) or eating his boot (*The Gold Rush*, 1925). Keaton believed that Chaplin's reoccurring thievery created a significant distinction between their on-screen personas. He said, "Charlie's Tramp was a bum with a bum's philosophy. Lovable as he was, he would steal if he got the chance. My little fellow was a working man and honest." Chaplin is not a hunter, a warrior or a laborer. He is a rover and a scavenger.

Chaplin clearly demonstrates his willingness to steal when, in *City Lights* (1931), he conspires to fake a boxing match in order to split the $50 prize money. Unfortunately, his partner finds out that the police are after him and he quickly flees the premises. This leaves Chaplin to go up against a tough, no-nonsense opponent (Hank Mann) in a real fight. Chaplin does not bother to act hostile and menacing when he and the prizefighter meet in the locker room prior to their bout. Instead, Chaplin adopts a friendly and submissive demeanor in the hope that he can charm the big and brawny boxer and get him to show him a modicum of mercy. It does not work. Chaplin lights the boxer's cigarette only to have the man blow smoke into his face.

Chaplin comes across as effeminate in his affable interactions with the boxer. Throughout his film career, the comedian behaved effeminately in a variety of circumstances. He often acted in a dainty and flirtatious way to tease or disarm a bigger and stronger foe, which was something that he did quite well with Eric Cambell in *The Cure* (1917). That was a strategy that was later adopted by Bugs Bunny, who would go as far as planting a big wet kiss on an adversary. In his early days, Chaplin could be sensitive or he could be tough. He could prance about playfully or he could give a large foe a swift kick in the backside. But Chaplin's Tramp character had become softer by the time that Chaplin made *City Lights*. Unlike the stoic Keaton, he expresses an undeniable queasiness about participating in a boxing match.

Responsible fatherhood has long been regarded as a sturdy and robust form of manhood. The father role is one of the most powerful concepts in the history of man. Regardless of the era, nothing has ever inspired more respect than a father caring for his child. The father is, according to cultural analyst Jürgen Martschukat, an "embodiment of responsibility, reliability, and rationality."[17]

This is apparent when the Tramp adopts an abandoned baby boy in *The Kid* (1921). In the next five years, he acts as caregiver to the child. He makes sure that he has a place to sleep and food to eat. He teaches him how to get along in life, educating him on proper manners and showing him how to defend himself against bullies. But his role as a father is challenged. When a doctor discovers that the Tramp is not the child's legal guardian, welfare officers take custody of the boy (Jackie Coogan) and lock him the back of a wagon.

The Tramp demonstrates full-blown virility as he battles to regain the child. He races across rooftops to catch up to the wagon and then jumps into the wagon when it passes beneath him. After he pummels the welfare official, he advances so fiercely on the wagon driver that the man flees in terror. This is not an anomaly in Chaplin's films, which show the Tramp at his most manly when he feels a need to protect those that he loves.

In *The Gold Rush* (1925), Chaplin develops affection for a saloon girl (Georgia Hale) and defends her against a burly patron who has insulted her. This is a brave act for Chaplin, who is not a rough and ready brawler. The patron, Jack Cameron (Malcolm Waite), laughs as he shoves and kicks the Tramp. Chaplin is not sure how to handle the situation. He stumbles while trying to back away from Cameron. But there is no backing away from the villain, who smiles sadistically as he stalks his defenseless prey. Chaplin is unable to hide the fear in his eyes while Cameron edges menacingly closer. Just as

Cameron is about to grab Chaplin, a grandfather clock suddenly falls on Cameron and knocks him unconscious. If fate hadn't intervened, the Tramp may have been beaten into the floorboards of the saloon. Does this show the Tramp to be masculine? It is unmanly to act vulnerable and frightened. Masculine confidence is something that should be unbreakable. But let's take a few other facts into consideration. Throughout the film, the Tramp shows bravery and perseverance as he journeys through icy fields and snowy mountains, contends with intense cold and the lack of food, and shoots an ornery bear. Chaplin may have sought humor in placing the sensitive Tramp in a manly environment, but the Tramp rose to the challenges and came across as manly.

Charlie Chaplin shows his mettle by enduring the harsh elements of the frozen Klondike in *The Gold Rush* (1925) (courtesy www.doctormacro.com).

In *The Strong Man* (1926), Harry Langdon battles a drunken bar patron who has made a rude remark about his sweetheart Mary (Priscilla Bonner). This is similar to the saloon scene in *The Gold Rush*. Unlike Chaplin, though, Harry is brave and forceful in his response. He socks the drunk man in the jaw and breaks a bottle over his head. This may be the most manly that the Little Elf has ever been. The film ends with this newly minted man walking a beat as a police officer. But Harry is still a child in need of motherly support. He takes only a step or two before he stumbles over a rock and falls into the gutter. Mary rushes over to him and helps him to his feet. Before the final fadeout, the pair continues along Harry's beat arm in arm.

3

"I'm a Baaaad Boy!"

A child has yet to conform to social conventions, which allows them to maintain their innate purity as an individual. The Three Stooges, who specialized in childish squabbles, are beloved for their purity and for their ability to break through false social conventions. This is the reason that the Stooges are the most effective when they are put into conflict with upper class snobs.

No comedian known to the moviegoing public conveyed childlike mannerisms more wonderfully than the Stooges' Curly Howard. Only a child would express his frustration by squealing in a laughably high pitch or spinning around on the floor.

Comedy is at its best when it addresses the simple truths of life. Who better to deliver a simple truth than a character with a childlike simplicity? A child's worldview needs to be simple. During childhood, we are required to process a large amount of information. A child's sensory limitations restrict the flow of new information to make the learning process manageable. This creates in the mind of a child a simplified and comprehensible world.

The Stooges lack the capacity for self-management and they possess a poor perception of risk. This is evidence of developmental immaturity, which could provide justification for a diminished responsibility defense in court. So, in fact, the Stooges may be criminally stupid. In *Termites of 1938* (1938), Moe creates a device that he calls the Simplex Rodent Exterminator: When a mouse comes out of his hole, it will step onto a string which will detonate a cannon. This could never have been seen by a reasonable person as a practical invention. As an inventor, Moe displays the type of faulty logic that you would expect from a child. Predictably, the cannon blows a hole in the wall while the mouse escapes unharmed.

Much more often, the Stooges would rather play than work. Curly is not seriously committed to his job as an ice man in *An Ache in Every Stake* (1941). He is distracted by a variety of fun activities as he travels his route. At one point, he takes careful aim before he bowls a block of ice down a walkway to knock down a collection of milk bottles. In *Tassels in the Air* (1938), the Stooges are supposed to be painting an office, but Larry and Curly are playing a game, moving paint cans around like game pieces on a checkered tile floor.

The Stooges are the world's worst workmen. They will wantonly destroy a home and then Moe, delusional as he is, will present the homeowners with a bill for their services. This is the comedians at the peak of their absurdity.

Let us compare the Three Stooges to Laurel and Hardy. Producer Hal Roach said, "Basically the Stan and Ollie characters were childlike, innocent. The best visual comedians imitate children really."[1] Laurel and Hardy may be irresponsible and destructive but, unlike the Three Stooges, they are not reckless or delusional. Ollie works hard to be a responsible adult. He is very much concerned with doing a job well and earning respect and gratitude for his services. He wants nothing more than to have others perceive him as a dignified and courteous Southern gentleman. The disparity between his objectives and his accomplishments is a rich source of humor. Ollie's friend Stan is not as complicated. He is, for all his lovable quirks, funny devices, distinctive mannerisms and elfish tricks, essentially a childlike simpleton.

Brats (1930) is unique in that it presents Laurel and Hardy as parents, but the further twist is that Laurel and Hardy's pre-school children are portrayed by the comedians themselves. The mothers have gone out for the evening, which leaves the dads in charge. The film opens with the fathers playing checkers while the children play with blocks. Stan Jr. and Ollie Jr. are very much like their fathers except that they prefer to

A deleted scene from *Three Little Pigskins* (1934). The Three Stooges expressed the clumsiness and confusion of the inner child that resides in us all. The children in the photo are, from left to right, Alex Hirschfield, Billy Wolfstone and Joe Levine.

3. "I'm a Baaaad Boy!" 41

express themselves with action rather than words. After all, childhood is action and instinct rather than intellect and ego. Unlike his father, Ollie Jr., does not care about objectives or relationships. He does not care about preserving his dignity or avoiding "another nice mess." Most of all, he doesn't care about language the way that his father does. The grandiloquent Hardy is sadly incomplete without words. It must be said that,

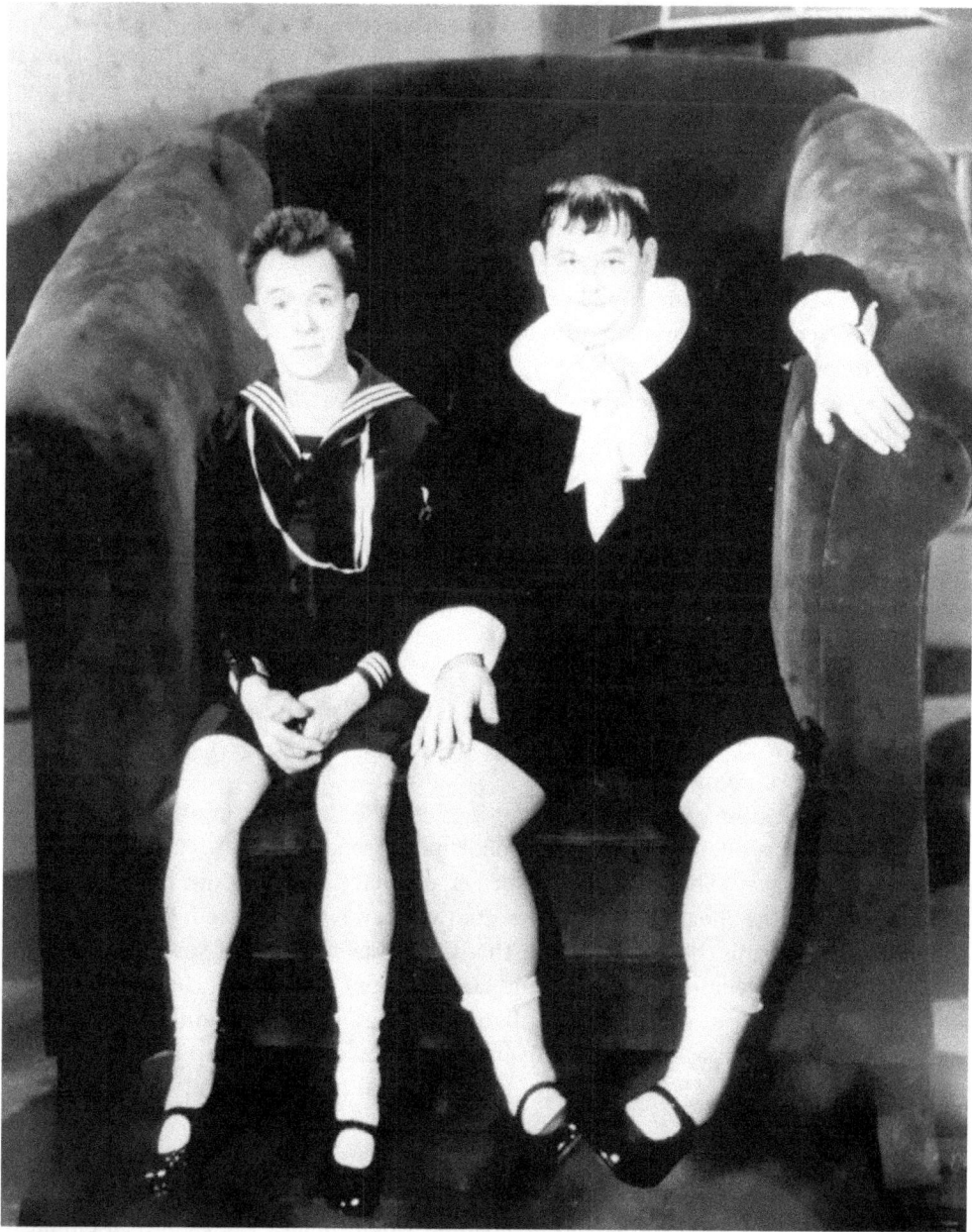

Stan Laurel and Oliver Hardy play rambunctious children in *Brats* (1930) (courtesy www.doctormacro.com).

in his entirety, the young and purely childish Hardy is not nearly as interesting as his elder.

Ollie remains a sadly conflicted character. He struggles to uphold adult principles while being largely propelled by childish impulses. He has the sense and willingness to act like an adult, but he remains stuck at the emotional level of a child. His inability to maintain control, restraint and logic is inevitably the reason for his downfall.

Let us examine a key scene of *Towed in a Hole* (1932), which makes it clear that Ollie easily fluctuates between adult behavior and childish behavior. Stan and Ollie get into an argument as they attempt to repair a boat. In a fit of blind anger, the two men employ buckets and hoses to engage in an all-out water war. The tit-for-tat pattern of this exchange shows that the battle has rules and structure. The nature of the fight—showering each other with water—is childish, but the way the fight is organized is adult. Give children water balloons and watch their giggly, chaotic attacks on one another. Stan and Ollie patiently take turns, behaving methodically in the way that they assault one another. After he dumps a pail of water down the front of Stan's overalls, Ollie is suddenly overcome with shame and realizes that this is not a proper way for men to resolve a dispute.

"Now, wait a minute," he says. "Isn't this silly? Here we are two grown up men acting like a couple of children. Why, we ought to be ashamed of ourselves. Throwing water at one another."

"Well, you started it," Stan insists.

"No, I didn't."

"Yes, you did."

"Well, I didn't."

Stan breaks out in tears. "You certainly did."

Ollie shouts, "*Well, I didn't!*"

Stan gets choked up. "You certainly did," he squeaks out.

"Well, I know that I didn't."

"You did, too!" Stan snaps back.

"Well, if that's the way you feel about it...," says Ollie as he scrambles to retrieve his bucket. Then, suddenly, he stops himself. He feels ashamed again. "Can we stop this quarreling?" he asks. "That's why we never get any place. Let's put our brains together so that we can forge ahead. Remember, united we stand, divided we fall."

Of course, it is in the next moment that Ollie slips on a bar of soap that Stan left lying on the deck. He falls off the boat and lands in a puddle of mud. He finds it impossible to be diplomatic at this point. The battle resumes. Ollie is an adult man trying to get past childish pettiness and vindictiveness to resolve a conflict in a calm and reasonable way, but he finds it impossible to hold it together during the relentless adversity and chaos that he must endure as Stan's partner.

Child development specialists say that, by six years old, a child should be able to express displeasure with language rather than tantrums or physical aggression. It is important for a child to build social behaviors, which includes self-control, empathy and cooperation. Ollie falls far short in this area.

Ollie can also be considered immature because he is easily disappointed and frus-

Stan Laurel and Oliver Hardy lack mature strategies to address problems or resolve conflicts in *Towed in a Hole* (1932) (courtesy www.doctormacro.com).

trated by his failures. Maturity enables a person to maintain their dignity in the midst of frustration. After all, we are expected as adults to calmly persevere when things don't go well.

Stan frequently amuses himself with childish tricks. In *Towed in a Hole*, he blows on his finger and then leans back against a wall to cause his derby to tilt up. This creates a dippy illusion of cause and effect: Stan blew into his finger, which caused air to travel out of his head and lift the hat. This humor very much appeals to young children, who are likely to draw a relationship between two separate events that are otherwise unrelated. This is called transductive reasoning. My research material included an example in which a child heard a dog bark and then a balloon pop. The child came to the conclusion that the dog's bark *caused* the balloon to pop.

Children in the post-operational stage show no signs of metacognition or problem-solving and they have difficulty understanding cause and effect relationships. Let's take a look at the Three Stooges' *A Plumbing We Will Go* (1940). A homeowner needs a plumber to repair a small leak in a basement pipe. Enter the Stooges, who set out to repair the leak, though they have no training or experience. Through various missteps, the Stooges cause a floor to collapse, dig a gaping hole in the front lawn, tear out electrical wiring, split open a heating pipe, and flood the home. It is painfully clear they have no awareness of their own limitations and are inadequate when it comes to crucial problem-solving skills. So much of the Stooges' comedy comes out of their appalling approach to problems. You know it's not going to turn out well when Moe gets out a mallet and tire iron to help Curly get out of a tight sweater (which happens in 1940's *How High Is Up?*). Moe understands the essentials of critical thinking, but he always goes awry in deliberating on a problem, developing a perspective, and coming up with a solution. It is an understatement to say that Moe's reasoning and decision-making skills are poor. Moe is not the thinker's thinker.

Moe is hindered by the fact that he is poorly informed and overconfident. He overestimates his abilities on a broad range of tasks. His faulty strategies can never possibly generate a successful outcome. This, too, is a childlike aspect of his personality. It is normal for a child to lack awareness of his own ignorance. Psychologist Martin E. Seligman proposed that children's overly positive view of their abilities is helpful to their cognitive and social development. He wrote, "Nature has buffered our children not only physically—prepubescent children have the lowest death rate from all causes—but psychologically as well, by endowing them with hope, abundant and irrational."[2] Psychologist David F. Bjorklund wrote, "When children have poor metacognitive skills, they believe that they are capable of more than they really are. This encourages exploration of new territories and reduces fear of failure in young learners."[3] This is fine if the young learner is attempting to ride a bicycle for the first time or is working to solve a math problem for homework. It proves to be disastrous, though, when childish adults like the Stooges are allowed to work with sledgehammers and blowtorches.

Children can act carefree because they have no authority or responsibility. Philosopher Jean Jacques Rousseau wrote, "I would like no more to require a young child be five feet tall than that he have judgment at the age of ten. Indeed, what use would reason be to him at that age? It is the curb of strength, and the child does not need this curb."[4] The Stooges, who are capable of widespread destruction, need to be curbed.

Young children often blame inanimate objects for causing an accident. For instance, a child might believe that the sidewalk was mad and made them fall down. Curly becomes angry with the leaking pipes because he believes the pipes are intentionally working against him. Child development specialists call this animism. Animism is also at work when Harry Langdon confronts a tornado in *Tramp, Tramp, Tramp* (1926). Harry is so angry at the tornado that he throws pebbles at it. When the tornado suddenly dies down, Harry assumes that he succeeded in intimidating this great force of nature. It is also interesting to observe Curly talking to himself as he tries to work his way through a problem, which is the way that a child functions.

The question remains that, if the Three Stooges were so incompetent, how were they able to feed and shelter themselves. In *A Plumbing We Will Go*, the Stooges plan to get themselves a meal by catching a fish from a pet store aquarium tank. We find in *Movie Maniacs* (1936) that the Stooges have set up house in a boxcar loaded with furniture. They live the hobo's life. Living accommodations are acquired largely through underhanded means. Today, we wouldn't accept Jason Segel eating aquarium fish or

3. "I'm a Baaaad Boy!" 45

living in a boxcar. The hobo model is no longer viable. So, how does someone as inept as this survive? He lives in his parents' basement and, when he's hungry, he asks his mother to make him a sandwich. This is one way in which film comedy has become more bound to reality.

Lou Costello always behaves like a boy venturing out into the world for the first time. Much of his comedy comes from his unfamiliarity with the world and the confusion and exasperation that this causes him. In comparison, Bud Abbott often comes across as wise and worldly. In *Hold That Ghost* (1941), Abbott easily recognizes a piece of 18th century furniture called a highboy. He makes reference to the highboy, but Costello is completely oblivious and thinks that Abbott is saying, "Hi, boy!" He waves back at Abbott and says, "Hi, Chuck!" Abbott knows everything and Costello knows nothing. It is a key element of their humor. How Abbott has attained expertise of antique furniture is anyone's guess.

No one would have a problem identifying Costello as childlike. The descriptions of Costello available on the Internet include "childlike buffoon," "roly-poly childlike cutup" and "helpless childlike patsy." Of course, Costello identified himself as a child with his catchphrase "I'm a baaaad boy!" A line that Costello delivers in *In Society* (1944) plainly informs the viewer of his early stage of development. A butler (Arthur Treacher)

Lou Costello won Martha Raye's affections with his boyish charm in *Keep 'Em Flying* (1941). The actor who plays the balloon vendor is unknown.

offers to undress Costello. This appalls Costello, who replies, "The last person that ever undressed me was my mother, and that was a year ago."

The narrative rules of the comedy feature were meticulously established by Charlie Chaplin, Harold Lloyd and Buster Keaton. But those rules were gradually abandoned as the comedy feature became more anarchic in the 1930s. What is the plot of the Marx Brothers' *Duck Soup* (1933) or Abbott and Costello's *Buck Privates* (1941) or W.C. Fields' *The Bank Dick* (1940)? Little time was taken in these loosely structured films for story development or character development.

Chaplin, Keaton and Lloyd's features presented realistically dramatic dilemmas that addressed mature concerns. This provided a serious framework into which the comedian could find the occasional space for a gag or a routine. But let's look at those very different comedians who succeeded Chaplin, Keaton and Lloyd. In the early 1940s, the comedy presented by the Three Stooges or Abbott and Costello was not connected to a narrative. Both teams shifted their attention away from storytelling to focus instead on the gags and routines. Although Abbott and Costello headlined feature films, their characters were rarely responsible for driving the plot forward. Other characters carried the stories, leaving the pair to appear occasionally to interject a comedy routine.

Audiences couldn't help but feel sorry for sweet-natured Lou Costello when he got bullied and battered by bigger and stronger adversaries. In this scene from *Keep 'Em Flying* (1941), Costello is about to take a punch from William Davidson as Bud Abbott looks on.

Buck Privates, a military comedy, could have been a film about a pair of lowly con artists who learn commitment and sacrifice in the service of their country. But, no, this film did not focus on character development or convey a serious message. The characters that Abbott and Costello play in the film have no real story that we can examine. They do not achieve new identities in context to the military institution. In the same way, the Three Stooges have no past or future. They exist only in the here and now and their spectacles of violence have no moral purpose. The Farrelly brothers' Stooges reboot erred in giving the Stooges a back story. They didn't need one.

Abbott and Costello and the Three Stooges were throwbacks to older and purer forms of comedy. But, elsewhere, new writers and directors were trying to make film comedy more sophisticated. Compare Bud and Lou's random boot camp experiences with the carefully structured misadventures that occur in two other comedies of the same period, *Arsenic and Old Lace* (1944) and *Hail the Conquering Hero* (1944).

The protagonist of *Arsenic and Old Lace*, Mortimer Brewster (Cary Grant), is not outwardly childish. The man is a celebrated book author and theater critic. He has had his greatest success writing books in which he gleefully ridicules marriage. Three of the books are mentioned by name in the film—*The Bachelor's Bible*, *Marriage: A Fraud and a Failure* and *Mind Over Matrimony*. Now Mortimer has fallen so madly in love with a minister's daughter, Elaine Harper (Priscilla Lane), that he is willing to burn his books and pledge his lifelong devotion to her. The couple sneaks off to the marriage license bureau and completes all of the necessary paperwork. They are about to leave on their honeymoon when Mortimer discovers a dead body in a window seat of his aunts' home. He learns that his beloved aunts are mad and that they have murdered twelve lonely old bachelors by serving them elderberry wine spiked with arsenic, strychnine and cyanide. This discovery throws Mortimer into a tizzy and he forgets about his honeymoon and, instead, he races around to get rid of a corpse and get his aunts committed to a sanitarium. Complicating matters further is the sudden arrival of Mortimer's criminally insane brother, Jonathan.

It is during this crisis that we learn the real reason that Mortimer opposed marriage so strongly. Mortimer has long been troubled by his family history. It is with difficulty that he finally breaks down and shares his concerns with Elaine. "Look," he says, "I probably should have told you this before, but you see ... well, insanity runs in my family. It practically gallops." It could not have been pleasant growing up surrounded by dark and demented people. The volatile and sadistic Jonathan was undoubtedly a problem. Jonathan glares menacingly at Mortimer as he tells him, "Have you forgotten the things I used to do to you when you were tied to the bedpost? The needles under your fingernails." Mortimer has a second brother, Teddy (John Alexander), who believes he is Theodore Roosevelt. Influenced by Roosevelt's famous charge up San Juan Hill, Teddy likes to draw a sword and yell "Charge!" just before he runs upstairs to his bedroom.

In the final scene of the film, Mortimer's aunts reveal to Mortimer that he was adopted into the Brewster clan. His Aunt Abby explains, "Your mother came to us as a cook. And you were born about three months afterwards. And she was such a sweet woman and such a good cook, we didn't want to lose her. So brother married her. Your real father was a cook, too. He was a chef on a tramp steamer." Mortimer, happy to hear that he is not really a Brewster, lets out several whooping cries. Then he rushes to the window and shouts out the good news to Elaine, who has been waiting for him outside. He says, "I'm not really a Brewster! I'm the son of a sea cook!" The anti-marriage books were a smoke screen for Mortimer, who feared that he was not adequate to become a

Cary Grant maintains doubts about starting a marriage with his newlywed bride (Priscilla Lane) in *Arsenic and Old Lace* (1944) (courtesy www.doctormacro.com).

husband and father. Mortimer cannot move on to his honeymoon and the consummation of his marriage until he frees himself from his childhood anxieties. To become a husband and father, he must shed his shame and doubt and he must find his own true identity. As the film ends, Mortimer is more eager than ever to make love to his bride. He lifts her onto his shoulder and runs off yelling, "Charge!"

The script for *Hail the Conquering Hero* was originally titled *The Little Marine*. The story takes many exquisite twists and turns, which is not surprising considering that it was written by the witty and wily Preston Sturges. As the story begins, Woodrow Truesmith (Eddie Bracken) is drowning his sorrows at a bar. Woodrow meets a group of Marines and he confesses to them that is a fraud and a failure. He explains that he revered his father, who died fearlessly in war, and he meant to follow in his father's footsteps by becoming a Marine. He wanted nothing more than to demonstrate bravery in battle as his father once did. His father, who was killed in the Battle of Belleau Wood, was posthumously awarded the Congressional Medal of Honor, which Woodrow wore as a child. "I grew up with it," he said. "They hung it on me." This boy who grew up wearing his daddy's medals, was, as the original title suggested, a little Marine, but he expected to someday become a big Marine and wear his own medals. Sadly, though,

Cary Grant is reminded of his dark childhood years when his criminally insane brother (Raymond Massey) suddenly returns home in *Arsenic and Old Lace* (1944). Looking on (to the far right) is Peter Lorre (courtesy www.doctormacro.com).

his plans did not work out as he envisioned. He was able to join the Marines and was sent off with fanfare by family, friends and neighbors, but it wasn't long after his fond farewell that a bout of hay fever got him discharged from the military. Worried about disappointing his mother, he informed her in a series of letters that he was fighting overseas.

Woodrow's deception only escalates as a result of his encounter with the Marines. Master Gunnery Sergeant Heppelfinger (William Demarest), who coincidentally served with Woodrow's father in World War I, is determined to help Woodrow out of his predicament. He has Woodrow swap coats with one of the other Marines and then instructs his fellow servicemen to load the coat with their various medals. Woodrow is now able to return home to his mother wearing a military coat festooned with medals. He is again a child playing dress up. A group of citizens is so impressed to be welcoming home a war hero that they put up Woodrow as a candidate for mayor. After further complications, Woodrow summons the courage to finally tell everyone the truth. He expects to receive scorn and rejection for his lies and he promises to leave town rather than cause further trouble or embarrassment. However, Heppelfinger takes the blame for the deception and explains that Woodrow only went along because he was afraid of disappointing his mother. He convinces the townsfolk that Woodrow demonstrated true nerve to confess. The townsfolk decide that Woodrow has just the right qualities to be their mayor and maintain their support of him for the upcoming election.

It is important that Sturges equates moral courage with courage in the line of fire. Being a man is about more than waging war. Woodrow's confession, which showed courage and honesty, marked this youth's passage into manhood.

Hail the Conquering Hero shares key elements with *Battling Butler*. Keaton's Alfred Butler, who poses as a champion boxer (another type of conquering hero), is hailed at a train station by an enthusiastic crowd of small town citizens. A marching band leads Alfred and his fans through town in a lively parade. It is a celebration of manly dominance that Alfred has not truly earned. This is identical to what happens to Woodrow. Woodrow, though, is in a more difficult situation. His mother maintains a shrine for her late husband in a prominent place of her home. We see now why Woodrow felt compelled to be like his father. Woodrow started out with what he saw to be a harmless deception. He had a boot camp buddy send his mother letters from the Pacific just as Alfred had once deceived his wife by sending her letters from the training camp. Then, due to this first lie, he became stuck playing the hero, which was the same thing that happened with Alfred. The biggest difference in these stories is that, unlike Alfred, Woodrow did not need to assert his masculinity with violence. His liberation from his insecurities and doubts did not need to manifest itself in fisticuffs.

The ultimate masculine role is that of protector. It is a key part of the male code. Men, by nature, are meant to protect their families. Governments have routinely exploited the male code, tapping into this powerful resource as a way to persuade men to protect their country. This is why the American flag represents Mom and apple pie. This is the reason that a person's country is referred to by politicians as the motherland. It is clear that this doctrine is used at times in manipulative and unreasonable ways.

It is easy for the Warrior's energies to bring about destruction. It is man's dominance-seeking nature that leads him so often into war. War is what makes societies ambivalent about masculinity. The general belief is that males need to be cautiously socialized to inhibit their bad impulses. We want our men sturdy and vigorous but not destructive.

A man's toughness is put to the test in a war film unless, of course, the war film is a comedy. Charlie Chaplin plays a World War I soldier in *Shoulder Arms* (1918). In the film's climax, Chaplin disguises himself as a tree to sneak behind enemy lines. He manages to defeat German soldiers and capture the Kaiser. Chaplin, who began the film as an awkward and apathetic recruit, has now been transformed into a war hero. But not really. It is revealed in the final moments of the film that Chaplin has been sleeping during training and simply dreamed his heroic exploits. He started the film as an awkward and apathetic recruit and he ended the film as an awkward and apathetic recruit.

Bilton pointed out that Chaplin's *Shoulder Arms* character "oscillates between childish anxiety ... and childish wish-fulfillment."[5] Chaplin often looks like a child in comparison to the larger and stronger men who seek to do him harm. The German soldiers of *Shoulder Arms* look especially big. It elicits our sympathy to see a child facing a great threat. The dream in which Chaplin captures the Kaiser represents the character's wish fulfillment. Bilton wrote, "Charlie is inexplicably, almost magically, a crack shot, faster, smarter, stronger; when he single-handedly returns to the trench with an entire battalion of giant German prisoners in tow, he offers by way of explanation one of the most famous jokes of the war: 'I surrounded them.'"[6]

A war comedy might also present a protagonist as an accidental hero. In *Pack Up Your Troubles* (1932), Laurel and Hardy rout a German military unit when they break through the enemy line trapped inside a runaway tank.

Keaton provided something unique in *Doughboys* (1930): A group of starving German soldiers are happy to surrender to Keaton, who has shown up with food. Keaton is cordial and sympathetic as he takes the soldiers

Charlie Chaplin readies for battle in his foxhole in *Shoulder Arms* (1918) (courtesy www.doctormacro.com).

into custody. The soldiers don't seem broken up that they won't be able to kill or die for the glory of their homeland. This was as anti-war as comedies of the period got until the Marx Brothers' *Duck Soup* (1933).

One of the most critically acclaimed war comedies is Keaton's *The General* (1926). It opens in Marietta, Georgia, on a sunny spring day in 1861. News arrives that the

War gets grim and gritty for Buster Keaton in *Doughboys* (1930) (courtesy www.doctormacro.com).

Northern army has fired upon Fort Sumter, which marks the beginning of the Civil War. Keaton plays a train engineer named Johnny Gray. In comedy films, it is not unusual for a bratty child to play a prank on the hapless comic hero. The child might think it's funny to hurl a rock at the man when he's not looking. But Keaton is not belittled in this fashion. The children in this film adore the train engineer, who they follow around faithfully. We can tell immediately by the behavior of the children that Gray is a well-respected member of his community.

Gray is rejected for military service, but he is not rejected because of flat feet or hay fever. He is rejected because the military believes that he is more valuable to them in his role as a train engineer. Their decision is understandable. Gray is needed to operate his mighty locomotive, the General, which will be needed to deliver supplies to the troops. He is sidelined from battle for the same reason that Lieutenant Doug Roberts (Henry Fonda) would later be sidelined from battle in *Mister Roberts* (1955). Keaton isn't told the reason that he is not allowed to join the Confederate army. He assumes that they are rejecting him due to his short height and small frame. Still, he is confident

Buster Keaton escapes the Northern army in his beloved locomotive, The General, in *The General* (1926) (courtesy www.doctormacro.com).

that he has skills and abilities that would make him valuable as a soldier. He sees himself as so valuable that he doesn't see how the army can do without him. "If you lose this war," he says, "don't blame me." We see through the course of the story that he, in fact, possesses strength, wisdom, valor and determination. These are exceptional qualities that serve him well as a train engineer and eventual unofficial soldier.

The General climaxes with a large-scale battle. The scene is mostly serious, with soldiers being shot and killed as they try to ford a river. But, in the midst of the action, Keaton manages to include a dark gag. As he raises a sword into the air, he loses grip of the sword, which sails through the air and becomes fatally embedded into an enemy sharpshooter.

The logical climax of a war film is a life-threatening battle, but this was something generally absent from a war comedy. An early exception to this rule was provided by the 1912 Cines comedy *On the Firing Line* (originally released in Italy under the title *Medaglie di bidoni*). The film's star, Primo Cuttica, becomes a hero during a critical battle. But the battle scene is devoid of Cuttica's usual comic antics and, in the end, it looks no different than a battle scene in a war drama. A funny battle scene did end the Marx Brothers' war spoof *Duck Soup*. Groucho fires off a machine gun before he learns that he's shooting at his own troops. For the most part, though, the brothers aren't interested in taking up arms. When asked to clean out a machine gun nest, Chico offhandedly says that he'll call in a janitor. It's not as if the brothers are in danger. The incoming gunfire from the enemy has no effect except to send Harpo's tricorne hat twirling around like a pinwheel. Groucho remains playful throughout the battle. At one point, he slides curtain rings to the end of a curtain rod to keep track of the number of soldiers that Harpo and Chico have knocked unconscious with a brick. In the end, the brothers prove to be the most comfortable throwing fruit at their enemies.

In military comedies, the comedians spent more time socializing in the barracks and marching on the parade grounds than they did fighting on the battlefield. Battlefield action was kept to a minimum if it was present at all. Film historian Hal Erickson found this battle ban to be particularly conspicuous in a World War II–era military comedy, *What Next, Corporal Hargrove?* (1945). He wrote in *Military Comedy Films: A Critical Survey and Filmography of Hollywood Releases Since 1918*, "[T]hough we hear the sounds of guns and cannon fire, no one is even slightly wounded; when Hargrove is captured by Germans, then rescued when the Germans themselves are captured, nary a shot is fired."[7] Of course, there were occasional exceptions, especially in later years. The most likable character of *How I Won the War* (1967), Musketeer Gripweed (John Lennon), dies in a field with a bleeding hole in his chest. In *Stripes* (1981), Bill Murray and Harold Ramis drive an urban assault vehicle into Czechoslovakia and take heavy artillery fire from a cannon positioned atop a roof. In *Pack Up Your Troubles* (1932), Laurel and Hardy seek to avoid the bullets and the bombs by hiding out in a tank, but Stan starts the tank by mistake and they inadvertently drive it through the enemy's foxhole. A comedian under fire does not demonstrate the manly qualities of fortitude and stoicism. He yelps, he cringes, and he scurries for cover. This is perhaps a more natural and relatable reaction to the threat of death than marching gallantly into the fray.

The pacifist comedy went by the wayside in *Pineapple Express* (2008). Three pot-smoking layabouts, Dale Denton (Seth Rogen), Saul Silver (James Franco) and Red (Danny McBride), are unexpectedly thrown into a drug war and must find the primal savagery inside of themselves to survive.

Forget about the work ethic and productivity with these weed-mellowed gents. Dale defines the perfect job as, simply, "a job where you don't do shit." Pot-smoking is what's most important to them. It's virtuous. It is transcendental. It's religious. Saul says of his special brand of pot, "It smells like God's vagina."

But they become aggressive to protect their sacred way of life. Their struggle is, in this way, a holy war. War is also about soldiers defending their loved ones. Dale is greatly motivated by his commitment to protect his friend and his girlfriend from a violently crazed gang of drug dealers. The merry trio comes to murder their foes in a bloody, protracted battle scene that ends the film. The entire film leads up to the comical image of fat stoner underdog Dale blasting at the bad guys with an AKM assault rifle. The blood and death exhilarates and liberates the rookie warriors. Hollywood has been making military comedies for more than a hundred years, but we never saw Lou Costello jam a gun under a German tank commander's chin and blow his brains out the top of his head. We never saw Oliver Hardy deliver the crushing weight of a truck over a Japanese sniper's chest. In *Pineapple Express*, the comedians perform these sort of brutal acts, leaving a path of destruction in their wake.

A very odd conversation about death rouses Red to battle:

RED: Man, I'm just into Buddhism, and I'm at peace with the fact that me, as this person, probably gonna not be around. Think about a hermit crab, okay? And it's a shell. It's like, they go from one shell to the next. And that's what I am. I'm just a hermit crab changin' shells.
DALE DENTON: Except if you're a dick your whole life, your next shell will be made of shit, okay? If you're an asshole, you're gonna come back as a cockroach or a worm or a fuckin' anal bead, okay? If you're a man and you act heroic, you'll come back as an eagle. You'll come back as a dragon. You'll come back as Jude Law, okay? Which would you rather be?
RED: Maybe the anal bead, depending on who it belongs to.
DALE DENTON: Belongs to me.
RED: Then the dragon.

The battle turns them into a band of brothers, but they become overly sentimental in the end. Red says, "Seriously, I know this sounds weird, but can we be best friends? Just us, for real?" These three bloodied and bruised men talk about sharing a heart locket that can break into three pieces. Never have comic soldiers been more violent and never have they been more tender.

4

Masculinity and the German Occupation of France

Masculinity is more than muscular aggression. It is comprised of profound qualities that men recognize as virtues and proudly present to one another as a demonstration of their worth. Nothing can facilitate perceptions about masculinity more powerfully than film.

It is by a young man's attainment of masculine qualities that he achieves maturity. The hero's masculinity is an important element in a dramatic story, but masculine qualities do not receive the same amount of attention in comedy films as they do in dramatic films. So, before we further explore masculinity and maturity in comedy films, we should first take a look at the important role that these traits can play in a dramatic film. By looking at the influence that masculine ideals can have on the hero of a serious story, we can better understand the more subtle and indirect influence that the same ideals can have on the hero of a funny story.

In films, the traditional male hero conveys his maleness with strength and directness. He is characterized by self-determination and an immediacy of action. He is disciplined, comradely, and unselfish. However, the blood-soaked battles of war changed how the French conceived of masculinity. Nearly 1.4 million French, both soldiers and civilians, died in the First World War. The Battle of Verdun, a six-month conflict on the Western front, claimed the lives of 315,000 French soldiers. Cities were destroyed. Resources were depleted. The Europeans who took part in this war suffered a great collective trauma afterwards. They could never fully recover from their experiences, becoming what some have called the Lost Generation.

The French became obsessed for years with mourning the dead and erecting memorials in thousands of towns and villages. Films, often the aftershocks of social crisis, would inevitably reflect this mood. In the late thirties, before the Second World War, these dismayed and melancholic people found a new male icon in movie star Jean Gabin, who displayed a wounded and vulnerable masculinity. Gabin did not express his masculinity in a boastful or celebratory way. He was no Douglas Fairbanks showing off his muscular torso and demonstrating his athletic skills.

Gabin became a popular anti-hero playing a gangster in *Pépé le Moko* (1937). He could be dark and brutal, but he could also be tender. This French matinee idol with rugged good looks and somber temperament paved the way for Humphrey Bogart,

Robert Mitchum and John Garfield. Critic John Doyle Wallis wrote, "His appeal lies in his masculinity, his take charge nature, his 'get what I want' attitude, which makes him both attractive and deadly."[1] Renoir said of the actor, "Gabin, with the slightest tremor in his face, could express the most violent feelings."[2]

In *Pépé le Moko*, Gabin and his fellow gangsters form an all-male family. The close bonds between these men are made clear in the way the characters are physically close in the frame and call each other affectionate names like "my little chicken." Pépé plays father to Pierrot, a young member of the group. Ginette Vincendeau wrote, "His stern words or slap in the face to Pierrot are always accompanied by a show of affection."[3] Gabin shows himself to be deeply loyal to the members of his gang. Vincendeau found this warm and close fraternity to be conspicuously absent from the more traditional Hollywood remake, *Algiers* (1938).

Gabin is doomed and trapped in this film as he would be in subsequent vehicles. Thereafter, Gabin played a working class hero: a factory worker, a locomotive engineer, a tugboat captain. *La Bête humaine* (1938) presents Gabin as an alcoholic locomotive engineer who finds himself entangled in a murder plot. He spends the film passing hopelessly through a series of dark alleys and grimy hovels. The French, who were tired of war, had no problem accepting Gabin as a military deserter in *Quai des brumes* (1938). The men in the film's port city setting are generally drunk and despondent. The film was widely criticized for its pessimism, but director Marcel Carné defended his drama by calling it a barometer of the times.

Gabin's vehicles were fatalistic dramas in which the hero, despite his manly vigor, was defeated by forces he could not control. The men who struggle through films like *Pépé le Moko*, *Quai des brumes* and *Le Jour se lève* (1939) do not command their destiny. Gabin often ends up dead, either being murdered or taking his own life. He comes to the latter end in three of his best known films, *Pépé le Moko*, *La Bête humaine* and *Le Jour se lève*. Vincendeau wrote, "[T]he Gabin persona included attributes traditionally considered feminine: gentleness and caring, but also weakness and passivity. Masculinity is traditionally defined by action and power; in the Gabin persona it is characterized by immobility and failure."[4] It intrigued Vincendeau that this "paralyzed and disturbed hero" came to "epitomise the virile French worker."[5]

Director Jean Renoir cast Gabin in his anti-war classic *La Grande Illusion* (1937). Gabin, in the role of Lieutenant Marechal, is an officer in the French air squadron during the First World War. Marechal, a mechanic in civilian life, presents a more rugged figure than his aristocratic commanding officer, Captain Boeldieu. The two men are thrown together when they are captured by a German ace, Captain von Rauffenstein, but they find themselves somewhat separated by their class differences. Marechal cannot relate to a prisoner who devotes his days to translating ancient Greek poetry or another who keeps himself busy drawing pictures. He is certainly not one to follow the example of von Rauffenstein, who lovingly tends to a prized geranium. He is interested in nothing more than taking action to escape. After he is thrown into solitary for disorderly conduct, he becomes so enraged that he bellows like a trapped beast. A German guard hopes to comfort him by giving him a harmonica to play. It proves true in this case that music has charms to soothe the savage breast.

The story gradually focuses on a relationship that develops between Boeldieu and Rauffenstein, who share similar backgrounds. The intimate and tender bonding that occurs between these men has a decidedly feminine quality. Critic Tom Block wrote, "[W]hen they plop down on a window-seat for a chat about the good old days, with Boeldieu curling one leg underneath his body, they have the familiarity of sorority sisters."[6] Later, Boeldieu, who runs from German soldiers in an apparent attempt to escape, is shot by von Rauffenstein. As Boeldieu lies dying in bed, von Rauffenstein nurses his wounds and begs his forgiveness. Boeldieu replies, "I would have done the same thing. French or German ... duty is duty." The men speak to one another in gentle, hushed tones.

Boeldieu's death scene has the potential to cause a redblooded male to snicker if not outright cringe. These sentiments are appropriately conveyed in a British spoof by Rowan Atkinson. In the Atkinson scene, German ace Baron Manfred von Richthoven (Atkinson) enters a prison cell to visit British squadron commander Lord Flashheart (Rik Mayall). The baron brightly announces, "Ah, and the Lord Flashheart. This is indeed an honor. Finally, the two greatest gentleman fliers in the world meet. Two men of honor, who have jousted together in the cloud-strewn glory of the skies, face to face at

Aristocratic officers, Captain de Boeldieu (Pierre Fresnay) and Captain von Rauffenstein (Erich von Stroheim), easily bond though they fight on opposite sides of a bloody war in *La Grande Illusion* (1937).

4. Masculinity and the German Occupation of France

last. How often I have rehearsed this moment of destiny in my dreams. The panoply to encapsulate the unspoken nobility of a comradeship." Flashheart whips out a gun and shoots von Richthoven dead. "What a poof!" exclaims Flashheart. This, according to tradition, is how real men relate to one another in war.

While Boeldieu lies dying, Marechal is escaping back to France. He has been joined on his trek by a fellow prisoner and French officer, Rosenthal. The men develop a close bond, but they rarely share soft, friendly words. A crucial scene features a boisterous argument between the exhausted refugees. Marechal is frustrated that Rosenthal, who has sprained an ankle, is unable to travel quickly. He becomes loud and insulting. Critic Ivana Redwine writes, "Marechal considers abandoning him and starts to walk away. Then Rosenthal starts to sing 'Un Petit Navire,' a silly song about a little ship, and this plays on Marechal's emotions, causing him to come back for the injured Rosenthal."[7] Again, music has soothed the savage breast.

Gabin's career was at its peak at the arrival of World War II. However, the war radically changed the country and its film industry. Military defeat creates national feelings of humiliation and shame. These injuries to national prestige are, largely, injuries to the nation's manhood. The male death rate of the two wars had been high for the French. Some town squares were devoid of men. Luc Capdevila wrote in "The Quest for Masculinity in a Defeated France," "[T]he limitless violence unleashed by the total wars of the industrial era ... gave rise to a number of revisions of the virility myth. As far as gender is concerned, recent conflicts contributed to, and provided a focus for, a crisis of masculinity. Now no sector of society was immune to ... the direct experience of war; the male population as a whole discovered the brutality of combat—discovered that war destroys, mutilates, disfigures and humiliates endless ranks of men."[8]

The defeated young men felt inadequate compared to the mythologized heroes of the previous war, but at the same time they could hardly see manliness in their maimed veteran fathers, many of whom were blind and missing limbs. The Vichy government, the Nazi-controlled regime in power during the German occupation, called upon men to be men again, but these officials offered a poor example. The Vichy government, disarmed and demobilized, had been, according to Capdevila, "subjugated, enslaved—in another word, emasculated."[9] Truly masculine action would be resistance of the occupying German forces. Manly honor would command French men to stand tall and keep up the battle.

The town square was all the more empty for the absence of Gabin. Gabin initially fled his troubled homeland for the sunnier climes of Hollywood, where he went to work for RKO Pictures. This was no doubt a disappointment to some, who had to accept that Gabin was more cultured and privileged than the heroes he played on screen. Vincendeau indicated that the actor, who was so raw and unpretentious on screen, was known to unsettle onlookers when he showed up in public clad in elegant outfits. Soon, though, the actor's manly vices ended his time in Hollywood. Gabin became embroiled in a passionate and troubled affair with actress Marlene Dietrich and he became embroiled in an even more passionate and troubled affair with RKO when the studio refused to cast Dietrich in his latest film. After being fired, Gabin left the lights and glitter of show business and fought as a member of the Free French Forces in North Africa.

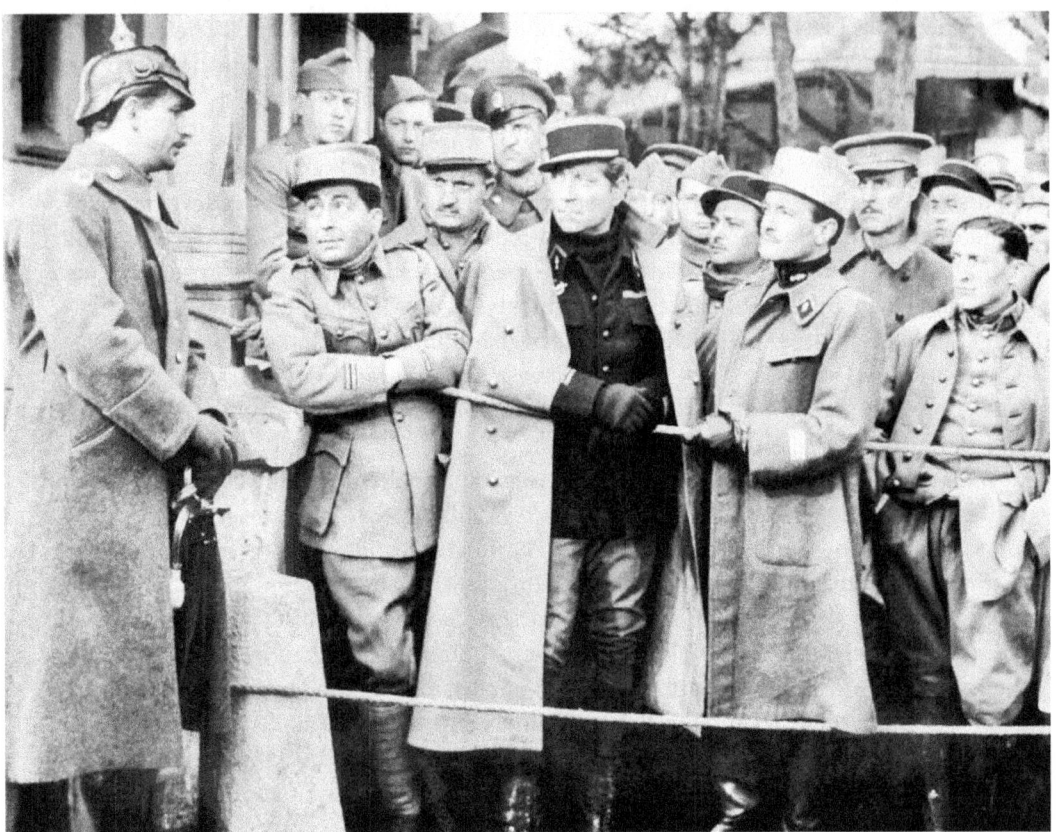

Jean Gabin stands out among his fellow soldiers in *La Grande Illusion* (1937).

Still, Gabin left behind one film before his departure from France. The film, *Remorques*, featured Gabin as yet another working class hero, tugboat captain André Laurent. He is fatherly to crew members, tough or tender depending on the circumstances. When a crew member behaves drunkenly at a party, he has him soak his head under a water pump to sober up. He caringly counsels a crew member who believes his wife has been unfaithful. When the tugboat company threatens to sell the vessel, he need not worry as he is financially secure, but he argues strenuously on behalf of his crew. His crew, who are equally protective of him, frets over their captain when he becomes despondent over his own marital troubles. The captain's dilemma is that, despite his commitment to his wife Yvonne, he has fallen helplessly in love with another woman, Catherine.

Laurent is a man who prefers action to talk. Without giving it a second thought, he punches a man who has tried to cheat him. He reacts angrily when Yvonne tries to get him to talk about his feelings. He accepts, without complaint, that a man is meant to lead a harder life than a woman. He tells his wife that he can't stay ashore with her and knit by the fireplace as this would require him to abandon his duty and deny his very nature.

The moment he announces to Catherine that he is leaving his wife, a crewman visits to tell him that Yvonne has suddenly taken ill and is close to death. Lightning flashes outside the window as if this news has arrived by way of cosmic forces. Laurent rushes to Catherine's bedside in time to see her die before his eyes. Laurent is, as one critic described him, "distraught" and "incredulous."[10] Fate punished him for his infidelity, leaving him to deal with shame, confusion and remorse. The film ends hauntingly with Laurent, in stony silence, steering his tugboat out onto dark and stormy seas to answer a distress call. He must accept his loss and carry on with his work. This is, after all, the nature of a man's life.

The film, in this way, perhaps supported the principles of the Vichy government, which called for men to be faithful to their wives and carry on with their duties. Capdevila wrote, "Restoring masculinity was central to government ideology under Pétain: men must recover their authority as fathers and husbands and cherish their families."[11]

France was, at the time, cut off from the world. Evelyn Ehrlich wrote in her book *Cinema of Paradox*, "What characterizes this cinema is not simply its avoidance of subjects of daily life, but its sense of remove from this life."[12] Many of these films are set in other times or other worlds. Material came not from present reality but from history, fantasy and classic literature. Filmmakers focused their attention on biographies and myths. The filmmakers, as Ehrlich observed, "closed themselves off from the actual world in the fantastic, the supernatural, the magical and spiritual beyond."[13] The fantasy genre was dominated by *Les Visiteurs du soir* (1942), *L'Éternel Retour* (1943), and *La Fiancée des ténèbres* (1945). Other lesser films fell into this category. *Le Baron Fantôme* (1943) concerns the mystery of a mad old nobleman who has disappeared inside a decaying castle. *La Main du Diable* (1943) centers on a poor artist who sells his soul to the Devil. These were not films about strong, able heroes.

These films have, according to Ehrlich, a "formal perfection"[14]: The decors are too perfect, the dialogue too literary, and the photography too artistic. "It is as if the films of this period were played out under glass," wrote Ehrlich, "the characters suffocating in an airless environment, observed from a detached, scientific distance. These films subordinate text, characterization, and other narrative elements to composition of the images, generally composition of a highly stylized kind.... [Filmmakers refused] to show the world through the eyes of its characters or to draw the spectator into the drama."[15] This caution came, in part, out of a fear of censorship and reprisal. This point is made in *Laissez-passer* (2002) when a scriptwriter working in wartime France talks about a period film being "a good medium for putting ideas across." He explains that a person in a period costume does not pose a threat as someone in a modern suit and tie.

Perhaps, too, the filmmakers sought to protect audiences from the shame and horror of the immediate world, which was being plagued by male aggression, and felt compelled, at the same time, to reject the fascists' destructive obsession with virility. *L'Éternel Retour* takes place in a non-specific time and place. It is an alternate reality, a fantasy place in which the director recreates the mythical romance of Tristan and Yseult. Because the hero is too immature to recognize and act on his sexual longings, it remains a story of unrequited love.

The male characters of *L'Éternel Retour* invariably suffer from immaturity, impairment, or impotence. When Uncle Amédée is introduced, he stands droopy and deflated as he is admonished by his braying wife, Gertrude. It is only when he lifts a rifle he has removed from his gun collection that he gets a gleam in his eye and sticks out his chest. The gun, shown at an angle that emphasizes the length of the barrel, stands out in the frame as if an erect appendage emerging from the uncle's body. This has significance coming at a time when French men were disarmed and feeling a lack of virility. It is another gun from this collection that will later lend lethal power to the uncle's malformed and underdeveloped son, Achille (Piéral).

The most acclaimed film of the period is *Les Enfants du paradis* (1945), which is set among the Parisian theater scene of the 1820s and 1830s. It is notable that the film's characters were modeled on actual historical figures. The central character is a beautiful courtesan named Garance (Arletty). Garance has four eager suitors—the mime Baptiste Debureau (Jean-Louis Barrault), the actor Frédérick Lemaître (Pierre Brasseur), the thief Pierre François Lacenaire (Marcel Herrand), and the aristocrat Édouard de Montray (Louis Salou)—but the free-spirited Garance remains unattainable.

The men in the nostalgic *Les Enfants du paradis* are childish and foppish. Lemaître, the actor, lacks manly discipline. He is wild and impulsive in his pursuit of pleasure. He spends money without concern for paying his creditors. He romances women without concern for their husbands. When challenged about his bad acts, he responds with a gleeful smirk, as a schoolboy caught putting a tack on his teacher's chair. Baptiste, a boyish and lovelorn mime, is filled, according to critic Girish Shambu, "with dreamlike passions and fragile sensitivity."[16]

Baptiste defends himself in a barroom fight with a graceful balletic kick. This is not the bare-knuckle punch in the teeth moviegoers expect from a drunken brawl. Baptiste is certainly different than Gabin's character, Jean, in *Le Quai des brumes*. In a *Le Quai des brumes* review, Jake Euker extolled Gabin for executing his duties as leading man "with square-jawed efficiency."[17] Efficient, he is. At one point, Gabin gets into a struggle with a man who threatens his lady love Nelly and uses a large rock to beat the man to death. Nothing graceful about that.

Baptiste also reacts differently than Gabin when it comes to the woman he loves. Baptiste is invited into bed by Garance, but he refuses as he doesn't believe Garance has the love for him that he has for her. That's not how Gabin reacts in a similar situation. After a night of unbridled passion with Nelly, Gabin is ready to go at it again. He grabs Nelly, the two embrace, and they fall together onto the bed. Unlike Baptiste, he is not tentative or emotionally needy. He knows what he wants and he knows what to do to get it.

Lemaître and Baptiste were not, as Gabin, taciturn. They gushed forth with fanciful, long-winded speeches, doing a considerable amount of talking for a movie that is principally the story of a mime. They also dressed stylishly, which separated them from Gabin's working class heroes. The working man is not obsessed with pretty clothing and he never demands to have the feel of silk threads against his flesh.

Most of all, a man expresses aggression with directness, plainness, and purpose. Aggressive impulses are expressed in more deviant ways in *Les Enfants du paradis*. The sadistic count, Edouard, regularly engages in duels so that he can casually murder men for no more than a vaguely perceived insult and then pretend the murder was an act of civility and honor. He exposes his hypocrisy when he later criticizes Shakespeare's plays for their "debased violence" and "lack of decorum."

Lacenaire, egotistical, sneaky and cruel, is comparable to the twisted child who pulls the wings off of flies. Near the end of the film, he murders the count without a clear motive. He certainly doesn't have a "Nelly" who is in immediate danger. Shambu wrote that this frustrated playwright "ends up mounting a real-life assassination with the loving detail of a theatrical production."[18] Shambu added, "After the meticulous murder of the Count, the murderer waits calmly after the 'performance' for the arrival of the police."[19] His actions are, in fact, calm, meticulous and, most of all, affected. It is a high art performance he enacts in view of his henchman, Arvil, who has been brought along for no clear reason other than to observe the murder. It was established earlier in the story that Arvil was squeamish and so now, when he predictably reacts with horror, Lacenaire could not be more pleased. The exchange between these characters has a sexual tinge. Lacenaire acted to titillate Arvil with his brutality and Arvil, with his excited reaction, managed in turn to titillate Lacenaire.

The real-life Lacenaire was indeed a murky and twisted individual. He was driven to crime by a desire to emulate Vidocq, a celebrated French bandit. His main goal, according to his autobiography, was to become "the scourge of society."[20] He reveled in standing in court and confessing to his crimes in great detail. This poet and assassin was an unstable bundle of contradictions. He was cynical and romantic, courteous and petulant, charming and vicious. He was, in his own mind, socialite and sociopathic.

Another popular historical drama of the day was *Le Destin fabuleux de Désirée Clary* (1942). The film, based on a novel by Annemarie Selinkos, is a true-life love story of Napoléon Bonaparte and Désirée Clary. It would, in contemporary terms, be categorized as chick-lit. The film shows a tender, loving side of the great conqueror. Jean-Louis Barrault, the wistful and sensitive mime Baptiste of *Les Enfants du paradis,* makes a skinny, fragile Napoleon. A 1954 Hollywood remake featured Marlon Brando, then the preeminent American male icon, as a more masculine Napoleon. Brando, in his then-recent portrayal of Stanley Kowalski, had forever impressed himself on the American consciousness as brutish and sexual. It was a long stretch from the Barrault Napoleon to the Brando Napoleon.

Le Corbeau (1943), which introduces the subjects of suicide, abortion and murder, is a film about death. The film's title translates into English as *The Raven,* the lustrous dark bird which is the perennial symbol of death. Dr. Rémy Germain, played by Pierre Fresnay, is a worn, bitterly isolated doctor trying to hide from a troubled past. He finds himself at the center of controversy when anonymous letters circulate accusing him of having an affair with a married woman, selling drugs, and conducting illegal abortions. Others receive similar poison-pen letters. The town, as we soon discover, is filled with men who are mad, perverted and corrupt. Every man is weak and dishonest and, therefore, compromised. A *Movie Gazette* reviewer wrote, "The film's 'hero' is first glimpsed literally with blood on his hands, the community's élite (police, doctors, politicians, treasurers) are at best ineffective, at worst underhanded."[21] Fresnay, who played a popular master detective in pre-war films, is never in charge of this particular situation and fails, in the end, to solve the mystery.

Pierre Fresnay struggles futilely to solve a murder mystery in *Le Corbeau* (1943). This still shows Fresnay and his mistress (Micheline Francey) questioning a potential witness (Ginette Leclerc).

At the center of the film, according to critic Alan Williams, is suffering women. Williams calls it a work "in which the first people we see are old women grieving, and the last image is of the avenging mother walking away down the street."[22] A cancer patient commits suicide after reading another of these letters. The film ends with the cancer patient's mother escaping up a road after having murdered the letter's author. We see her through a window from the perspective of Germain. The woman is dressed completely in black, including a black shawl she has draped over her head. She resembles, in a way, a raven flying off.

The French celebrated their liberation soon after the war with *La Bataille du rail* (1946), which showed the resistance fighters to be brazenly defiant and self-sacrificing in daily confrontations with German soldiers. The film focused on gritty and authentic railway workers. This marked a return of the working class hero that Gabin had popularized prior to the war. The camera comes in tightly on their unaffected faces. These men are sweaty, unshaven, anything but pretty. Their cheeks are smeared with grease, their hair is sprinkled with soot, and their lungs are coughing up dark and gritty smoke. These scenes looked to revive the realism provided by films before the war, except the storytelling was accused by critics of inaccuracy and exaggeration. The filmmakers, in an effort to reclaim the country's lost honor, may have resorted to false bravado.

Passive aggression, a conflict style normally associated with the fairer sex, became pervasive at this time of collaboration and underground resistance. This contrariness, in the form of lies, secrets, manipulation and sabotage, acted as substitute for bloody confrontation. As a resistance fighter remarked in *Laissez-passer*, their job was "intelligence and infiltration, not playing commando."

The most despised of the collaborators were the informants, who could be commonly seen in films of this period. Filmmakers became obsessed with them. In *Laissez-passer*, a producer asks a writer to give him a script that is set in the past and has lots of back streets and peepholes. The informant, a shadowy individual who was often bent forward at keyhole-level, lacked the outsized pride and girth of a true and healthy man. We see this when they turn up in *Le Corbeau, Les Enfants du paradis, L'Éternel Retour, Laissez-passer, Panique,* and *La Kermesse héroïque.* Dwarf men are the informants in *L'Éternel Retour* and *La Kermesse héroïque.* Viewers of *Le Corbeau* are originally made to suspect that a young girl is the culprit behind the poison-pen campaign. A scene is framed in such a way as to create the effect of the girl spying through a keyhole. Jéricho, the informant in *Les Enfants du paradis*, is a ragged, hunched and misshapen wretch who more resembles a rat than a man. In *Laissez-passer*, a man accused of being an informer is unable to stand erect as he lost several toes to frostbite during the war. His bent posture and his name, Softi, suggests this former soldier's collapse into something less than masculine. (At one time, comedy indulged in the grotesque more than drama ever did. In early days of the Commedia dell'arte, comic characters were far from being comely or wholesome. The traditional Pantalone had a hunch just like *Les Enfants du paradis'* repellent informant Jéricho.)

French comedies have long relied on male incompetence as a source of humor. *La Kermesse héroïque*, made five years before the occupation, features Belgian men, unfit and cowardly, going into hiding to avoid Spanish invaders passing through their village. The burgomaster's wife takes charge of the situation, gathering the women to organize a feast to welcome the Spaniards. She ends up wining, dining and bedding a Spanish Duke, who she manages to thoroughly seduce to her advantage. This sort of behavior became a more serious issue during the German occupation. The emasculating effects of defeat and occupation were exacerbated by the knowledge that the wives and girlfriends of French men were having sexual relations with German soldiers. This included the women who were taken by force and those who had willingly gone astray. Outrage over this activity found expression after the war when the government humiliated female collaborators by having them paraded out before an angry crowd, which savagely cheered and jeered as the woman had their hair sheared off.

French filmmakers long avoided the painful subject of the war. In 1957, Stanley Kubrick made the film *Paths of Glory* about French soldiers in the Battle of Verdun. The film questioned the manly principles of loyalty and honor held by the soldiers. It was banned by French officials as a slanderous attack on their country.

After the war, Italy found itself facing its own crisis of masculinity. Filmmakers looked to expose their failings and put them behind them. Director Alberto Lattuada wrote in 1945: "So we're in rags? Then let's show everyone our rags. So we're defeated? Then let's look at our disasters.... Let us pay our debts with a ferocious love of honesty and the world will be moved and join in this great settlement with the truth. This confession will illuminate our secret virtues, our belief in life, our superior Christian sense of fraternity. We will find boundless comprehension and esteem. Nothing reveals the inner resources of a nation better than the cinema."[23] But French filmmakers were reluctant to follow this course.

French filmmaker Claude Chabrol faced up to his country's crisis of masculinity in a later decade. In his 1988 film *Une Affaire de femme*, a prison work camp returns a captured soldier to his wife and children when it is determined that the man is suffering from shell shock and is too weak to work. The man, unable to hold a job, files for veteran disability benefits. In the meantime, he is not much help to his family. He is unable to even control his bowels, which inspires his wife's disdain when it falls to her to hand-clean his soiled shorts. Chabrol noted, "The husband isn't wanted and he sort of senses it." His slack expression, which is maintained throughout the film, conveys a general feeling of impotence. Rosemarie Scullion wrote of this character, "His childlike ineptitude is underscored not only by his steady unemployment and his pajama-clad days spent dillydallying in the house, but also by the endless hours he spends playing cutouts, a hobby whose trenchant features recurrently invoke his own emasculation...."[24] When his wife complains about him spending all day in his pajamas, he asks if she would prefer he dress as a nanny.

The emasculation theme is emphasized by a scene in which the German authorities stage a contest to give the French men the opportunity to win a goose. It is a bloody version of the piñata game. A young man dons a papier-mâché Mother Goose headdress that lacks eye openings and he then takes hold of a long sword, which he is meant to use to behead a goose hanging several yards in front of him. It is, in no way, a manly sport. The man is being momentarily armed with an outdated weapon while being deprived of his sight and being made to wear the head of a silly old woman. The headdress wobbles comically on his shoulders as he stumbles forth and blindly swings his sword. The man manages to kill the goose with a forceful swing, but it remains demeaning that the man had to earn his prize in the absurd disguise of Mother Goose, who is in effect a nanny. Later, a frustrated man remarks, "They cut off our balls."

The shell-shocked husband, Paul, is initially resigned to being a cuckold when his wife Marie starts an affair with the able goose slaughterer, Lucien. Lucien collaborates with the German to improve his lifestyle. He uses his connections to find work for Paul so he can help Marie and, also, get Paul out of the way. The job offered to Paul is that of a security guard who must look out for saboteurs. Paul understands that this job would require him to betray the resistance and cause the death of resistance fighters. He tries to explain to Marie that this is morally wrong and that this is a "filthy job," but he has come to realize by this point that his wife, who is willfully engaging in abortions, prostitution and adultery, has lost all sense of morality. Soon after, she pays the maid extra to have sex with her husband so that she won't have to bother with him.

In the end, Paul decides to report his wife. Chabrol has him nervously hiding in his room to write a letter to the police. He knows what he is doing is appalling, but he has become, as critic John Simon describes it, "demobilized and demoralized,"[25] and he is compelled to do this to restore his power and stability. Before the Vichy government executes Marie, they cut off her hair in the way that female collaborators would have their hair cut off after the war.

Hitler's propagandists had put forth a hypermasculine image. This exaggeration of the male stereotype emphasized physical strength and aggression, reinforcing the association of rugged men and bloody war. In the years that immediately followed the war, French films focused attention more on female characters than male characters. The top male actor was now Gérard Philipe, who had a pretty face and a gentle manner.

French men struggled after the devastation of World War II, in the midst of great social upheaval, to regain and redefine their masculinity. They looked to find balance in themselves and secure relevant masculine virtues, such as initiative, independence and valor. This struggle was never revealed more clearly and forcefully than it was in their country's post-war cinema.

The post-war heroes of French cinema were as flawed and fragile as the protagonists featured in American comedy films of the same period.

5

A Major Minor

Jerry Lewis first achieved fame by running amok like a bratty child during a nightclub act with Dean Martin. Together, Martin and Lewis acted like unruly brats with interviewers, tearing off the interviewers' shirts and cutting their ties in half. But the comedians behaved differently in their films. In the early Martin and Lewis films, Lewis could act just as silly and awkward as a boy, but he was never altogether childlike. In fact, he is often sensible, sensitive and responsible. In *The Stooge* (1952) and *The Caddy* (1953), Lewis is steady and reasonable while the manly Martin is undone by his oversized ego.

Still, apart from his film appearances, Lewis continued in his radio and television appearances to reinforce his image as a bratty boy. It was to exploit this image that Lewis was called upon to play a man masquerading as a boy in *You're Never Too Young* (1955), a remake of Billy Wilder's classic *The Major and the Minor* (1942). But we can see by examining the background of this story that Lewis' casting entirely missed the point of the original film.

In 1920, a period farce named *Little Old New York* debuted on Broadway. Much of the play's charm came from it being set in New York City in 1810. A number of historical figures, including John Jacob Astor, Cornelius Vanderbilt, Peter Delmonico, Fitz Green Halleck and Washington Irving, made appearances.

The plot is set in motion by the death of a millionaire. It is specified in the man's will that his fortune is to go to his closest living male relative. The millionaire's stepson, Larry Delavan (Ernest Glendinning), believes himself to be the rightful heir until he is introduced to a cousin who has just arrived from Ireland. Unknown to Larry, the cousin is a fraud. The millionaire's brother has had his daughter, Patricia O'Day (Genevieve Tobin), dress up as a boy named Pat to fool the executor of the will. The father dies suddenly and Larry must reluctantly take on the role of Pat's guardian. At first, Larry is disturbed by the boy's girlish manners, but he eventually comes to like the boy and even finds himself strangely attracted to him. He is relieved in the end when Pat discloses that she is really a woman. The two profess their love for each other at the closing curtain. Well-received, the play ran on Broadway for 308 performances and then toured with Tobin for two additional years.

In 1921, *The Saturday Evening Post* published a short story by Fannie Kilbourne called "Sunny Goes Home." It was, by 1921 standards, an engaging story. Fresh from high school, Susan "Sunny" Moore travels to New York City to become an actress. The talent agent takes her on as a client due to what he calls "her baby cheek."[1] Kilbourne described this characteristic in particular detail: "[Sunny's cheek] was soft and pink and—this was its real asset—amazingly childlike in its curve. It was a little girl cheek—round, guileless, kissable. Properly played up, it could take an easy nine years off Sunny's nineteen."[2] Also helping make Sunny look younger: she was barely five feet tall in flat-heeled slippers. But playing little girls is not steady work and Sunny decides to give up acting and go home. This would seem to be a reasonable solution to her problem except that she is short of funds and cannot afford the train fare. Sunny figures that she can disguise herself as a child to buy a half-fare ticket. She still has a little girl dress from a failed show and she knows that she can be a convincing preteen in the dress, so she wears the garment to the train station. She makes a point to act shy to avoid attracting attention. Her shy act fools the ticket seller, who never questions her age. Sunny has no problem with the conductor once she is on board the train. Kilbourne wrote, "When [the conductor] spoke to her, she scarcely looked up, keeping her head over a large illustrated copy of *Alice in Wonderland*, her hair shaken forward over her face."[3] She befriends a pleasant-looking young man named Jim Amberly on the train. The couple develop a warm relationship during the trip and, before she arrives at her destination, Sunny admits to Jim that her real age is nineteen. The man is relieved to learn that his attractive companion is a fully mature female and he asks her to run away with him to Mexico, where he plans to pursue a lucrative business opportunity. That's it, that's the story. It's is a playful escapade with no real tension or message.

Playwright Edward Childs Carpenter adapted the story into a Broadway play, *Connie Goes Home*. Of course, he had to expand the story, creating complications and conflict for the heroine. The story starts out the same: Connie (Sylvia Field) has outgrown kid roles on Broadway and is struggling financially. She reaches her breaking point when a rich man proposes that she become his mistress. She decides that the time has come to leave the wicked metropolis and head back to her quiet hometown in Iowa. Unfortunately, she doesn't have enough money to afford a train ticket. An idea comes to her while she is packing her suitcases. She still owns a dress that she wore to play a young girl on stage. She can impersonate a young girl just as she had before and this will allow her to pay the child's fare for her train ticket. She meets a wealthy young man, Jim Barclay (Donald Foster), during the train ride. Love blooms between the young couple by the end of the first act. As the play continues, Connie takes it upon herself to rescue Jim from his fortune-hunting fiancée.

Variety theater critic Jack Pulaski (writing as Ibee) recognized the similarity between *Connie Comes Home* and *Little Old New York*: "Some criticism of the situation having Jim suddenly realizing he loves Connie has been made, but it is not much different from that in *Little Old New York* where the hero becomes smitten with his young ward who has been masquerading as a boy in his teens."[4]

Ageplay masquerades have long appealed to film audiences. In 1917, Billie Rhodes dressed up like a little girl in a Christie comedy, *Kidding Sister*. The film was so well-received that it inspired a sequel (*Just Kidding*, 1917) and a remake (*Kidding Katie*, 1923). A critic with *Motography* magazine was amused by the film's simple premise: "[Rhodes] wears a Buster Brown suit, plays with a Teddy Bear and gets her face smeared with blueberry pie."[5] During this period, it was a stock comic premise for an adult to disguise as a child for one reason or another. In *Billy's Love Making* (1915), a woman dresses her 18-year-old daughter Violet (Violet Mersereau) as a 12-year-old to convince the eligible bachelors at a beach resort that she is younger than she really is. In *The Prize Baby* (1915), Oliver Hardy poses as a baby in order to win the $100 prize in the Best Developed Baby contest.

A 1923 film version of *Little Old New York* produced by William Randolph Hearst's Cosmopolitan Productions turned the stage farce into a melodrama. Screenwriter Luther Reed focused his attention on creating sympathy for Patricia (Marion Davies). When Patricia is introduced, it is shown that she lives with her family in a rundown shack in Ireland. We learn, too, that she is devoted to caring for her sick younger brother. The family is about to be evicted from their home when news comes of their rich uncle's death. Her uncle had risen above his impoverished roots by traveling to America with money borrowed from his brother. The grateful uncle has now left his fortune to his brother's young son. Patricia's father gathers up money so that he and his children can travel to America to claim the inheritance, but the son dies during the voyage across the Atlantic. Patricia is implored by her father to pretend to be her brother so that they can still claim the dead uncle's fortune.

Larry wanted the inheritance so that he could invest in the first steamship, which has been recently invented by his friend Robert Fulton. Although he's disappointed to lose out on the inheritance, he becomes friends with Pat, who he never suspects is a girl. This is not to say that he does not find the cousin's behavior odd at times. For instance, he doesn't think that this fellow looks at all manly strumming on a harp.

Patricia becomes frustrated and unhappy because, although she is attracted to Larry, she is stuck pretending to be her dead brother. The filmmakers played it safe by having Larry show no feelings of sexual attraction for this effeminate boy. He suggests no more than a fatherly affection until he learns that the cousin is female. It is only then that he is permitted to express a physical attraction for her.

Little Old New York was adapted into a second film by 20th Century–Fox in 1940. Strangely, the scriptwriters retained the play's historical aspects but threw out the farcical cross-dressing elements. Instead, Pat O'Day (Alice Faye) becomes a tavern keeper whose sailor boyfriend, Charles Brownne (Fred MacMurray), disapproves of her friendship with steamboat inventor Robert Fulton (Richard Greene).

This finally brings us to *The Major and the Minor* (1942). Billy Wilder and Charles Brackett worked on adapting the forgotten play *Connie Goes Home* into a feature film for Paramount Pictures. The pair did everything they could to exploit the story's comic possibilities. Their script included wit and sophistication that was not present in either the play or the short story. Susan Applegate (Ginger Rogers) visits homes to provide hair treatment and scalp massages for the Revigorous System. Wilder leaves viewers without a doubt that Miss Applegate has sex appeal. He shows her attracting glances from men as she walks past. When she steps aboard an elevator, the operator has an appreciative smirk as he looks her figure up and down. A lecherous middle-aged businessman, Albert Osborne (Robert Benchley), has made it a habit of making passes at young women from Revigorous System. He is particularly pleased when Susan arrives at his apartment. He crudely solicits her and, though she rebuffs him, he continues to make advances. He believes that, if he can ply her with liquor, she will quickly drop her defenses. She becomes infuriated when Osborne grabs her hand. Wilder biographer Gene Phillips wrote, "Susan resists Osborne's blandishments and reads the riot act to him."[6] This "riot act" is a fine piece of writing:

> I'm through. After one year and 25 jobs in New York, Susan Applegate is signing off. Signing off and going right back where she came from. Did you ever hear of Stevenson, Iowa? No, you haven't, Mr. Osborne. Dull. People there just walk around on two feet, and cars have only four wheels, and the grass is just plain green. Who wants that? Who wants a fellow by the name of Will Duffy, who runs a feed-and-grain store? Why not look around? Well, I came and I looked around, from every angle, from the bargain basement to the Ritz Tower. I got myself stared at, glanced over, passed by, slapped around, brushed off, cuddled up against. But, Mr. Osborne, in all that wrestling match, there's one thing they didn't get out of me, not out of Sue Applegate.

Mr. Osborne is unmoved by the speech. "So," he says, "you've got your self-respect, but self-respect isn't everything." Susan doesn't acknowledge him. She is fed up struggling with the lustful men who populate the city. She says that she wants to go back to her small hometown to marry a "plain, honest, slow-witted lug." Presumably, she wants a dull, cool-blooded husband who is not likely to have Mr. Osborne's grabby hands.

Susan figures to disguise herself as a twelve-year-old girl so that she can travel half-fare. She scrubs off the makeup, tapes down her chest, fixes her hair up with pigtails and ribbons, and puts on a big hat. But this still isn't enough. She completes the effect by carrying a balloon, sucking on a lollipop and walking slightly pigeon-toed. By regressing to a twelve-year-old girl, she can now repress her sexuality, which has become an unbearable burden for her. A magazine on display at the newsstand has a curious headline: "Why I Hate Women" by Charles Boyer. One of Hollywood's great lovers seeks to disavow women. Maybe his sexuality has become a burden for him, too. But the problem is that it will take more than pigtails and a lollipop to dampen her sexuality.

Wilder and Brackett changed the heroine's age from 19 to 25. This was possibly to make the character closer to Rogers' age, which was 30 at the time. But it strains credibility to have a 30-year-old actress pass herself off as a child. Amazingly, though, Wilder did not see this as a problem. He said, "It wasn't too difficult for Ginger to imitate a girl of 12, especially in those days. Now it seems a little foolish. To think a 30-year-old could play a 12-year-old girl and be believable! Well, she couldn't, but it didn't matter. The audiences were very generous in those days. They had come to have a good time and they went along with you."[7] Fiction sometimes requires a suspension of disbelief. A pair of eyeglasses is all that is needed to hide the fact that Clark Kent is Superman. Little Red Riding Hood is slow to see through the Big Bad Wolf's grandmother disguise. Consider, too, *Little Old New York*: Marion Davies looks nothing like a boy when she dances a sprightly jig.

The conductor, who is already doubtful about Susan's age, is convinced of her fraud when he steps onto the outer platform of the observation coach and catches Susan casually smoking a cigarette. She runs from the conductor and hides inside a sleeping car occupied by Major Philip Kirby (Ray Milland), an instructor at the Wallace Military Academy for Boys. She amplifies her little girl act, telling Philip that her name is Su-

Ginger Rogers gets half fare on a train ticket by disguising as a 12-year-old girl in *The Major and the Minor* (1942).

su. The kindly major finds her to be delightful and invites her to spend the night in a lower berth. It is established that Philip's vision is impaired in one eye, which helps viewers accept that Philip could fail to recognize Su-su's true age.

During a thunderstorm, Philip seeks to comfort Su-su by holding her tightly in his arms. The queasy look on Susan's face indicates that she is uncomfortable with this sudden attention. In the context of the story, she has a good reason to feel this way. It has to be appalling that, even after she has regressed to a small girl, she still has a man getting grabby with her. The camera is angled down to create a forced perspective, which makes Susan look smaller in Philip's arms than she really is.

Philip's fiancée Pamela Hill (Rita Johnson) and his future father-in-law, Colonel Hill (Edward Fielding), meet Philip at the train station. When Pamela finds Susan in Philip's sleeping car, she assumes that Philip is having an affair. Philip brings Susan to the military school to prove that she is only a twelve-year-old child. After the misunderstanding is cleared up, Philip insists that Susan remain at the school for a few days until someone can escort her home.

Pamela doesn't like Su-su hanging around, accusing her of being an "inflammatory" presence on the military academy. She is, in fact, right. The school's 300 libidinous

5. A Major Minor

young cadets find her irresistibly attractive and she has to fend off their amorous advances. Philip compares her to a light bulb attracting 300 moths. The opposite sex might see Susan as even more attractive now that she appears to lack womanly defenses. This makes her sexually controllable.

Philip is unconsciously repressing sexual feelings that he has for this "child." "She has *something*," he says. But the man is baffled what that "something" is. He tells her, "When I look at you with my bum eye, you look almost grown up." He admits that, in his blurry view of her, she looks like "a knockout." He is, whether he can admit it or not, her biggest admirer on the school's grounds. DVD Savant critic Glenn Erickson wrote, "Milland projects the right blend of decency and farce-approved cluelessness required for the film's pretzel plot."[8] Susan is sad and frustrated because, although she has fallen in love with Philip, she must maintain her charade.

Wilder successfully reworked this story for *Some Like It Hot* (1959). Joe (Tony Curtis) has the misfortune of falling in love with lovely Sugar Kane (Marilyn Monroe) while in disguise as a woman. He is unable to get romantic with Sugar because revealing his true identity would expose him to grave danger with Chicago mobsters, who are determined to murder him and his best friend Jerry (Jack Lemmon). Jerry, too, has disguised himself as a woman. While Joe is chasing after Sugar, the bewigged and skirted Jerry is dating a childishly irresponsible and daffy millionaire, Osgood Fielding III (Joe E. Brown). Libby Hill of *A.V. Club* pointed out that "false-faced love"[9] has been a story device that goes back as far as *Cyrano de Bergerac*.

Joe, snugly disguised beneath a second-hand wig, lavish makeup and a baggy robe, listens intently as Sugar describes her dream man. "I want mine to wear glasses," she says. "Men who wear glasses are so much more gentle, and sweet, and helpless. Haven't you ever noticed it? They get those weak eyes from reading—you know, those long tiny little columns in *The Wall Street Journal*." Gentle, sweet and helpless. She wants a man who is as docile and harmless as a child. Joe, who understands that the only way to approach the skittish Sugar is to fulfill her dream man fantasies, schemes to pose as a mild-mannered, bespectacled millionaire playboy.

Here is an excerpt from the script:

> Joe has come up to a basket chair nearby. Sitting in front of it, sorting sea shells out for a small pail, is a BOY of five. A few feet away stands his mother, calling to him.
> MOTHER: Let's go, Junior. Time for your nap.
> JUNIOR: Nah. I wanna play.
> JOE (out of the corner of his mouth): You heard your mudder, Junior. Scram.
> The boy looks up at him, fearfully.
> JOE (continuing): This beach ain't big enough for both of us.
> The boy scrambles to his feet, and screaming "Mommy," runs off, leaving the pail full of shells behind. Joe settles himself in the chair, peers over his shoulder toward the girls playing ball.

Joe has taken the boy's place on the beach and even adopts the boy's nickname "Junior." Sugar is enchanted when she sees Joe holding the boy's pail of shells. Joe has, to a degree, become the boy.

If Joe can't be the aggressor, he will get Sugar to be the aggressor. He tells her that he has a complex that prevents him from getting excited about women. He says, "When I'm with a girl, it does absolutely nothing to me." He explains that he has been numb since a tragic accident in which his girlfriend Nellie fell into the Grand Canyon while they stood on a high ledge and got ready to kiss. It works. Sugar finds him to be "so cute." Is a manly man "so cute"? Does a manly man walk along the beach collecting seashells? It would not be difficult to argue the point that Sugar wants to mother a boy rather than love a man. It is clear that, from Sugar's perspective, Junior is an anxious and confused young man who is long overdue for his sexual awakening.

As they enjoy a romantic evening alone together on a yacht, Joe pretends to be indifferent to Sugar's kisses. Maintaining his disguise as an impotent millionaire demands that he repress his sexual longing for Sugar. Again, a disguise compels sexual repression. Sugar makes considerable progress once she puts on music and dims the lights.

Some Like It Hot and *The Major and the Minor* have a number of similarities. *Some Like It Hot* features a sexually aggressive bellboy (Danny Richards, Jr.) and *The Major and the Minor* features a sexually aggressive elevator boy (Ken Lundy). The former is billed as "Fresh Bellboy." Both the bellboy and the elevator boy are small-framed and youthful. They look like boys but they express decidedly masculine desires. This fits with a key joke of the films: Men and woman who are childlike (Rogers and Curtis) are, in fact, sexually mature adults. Much like Susan, Sugar is running away from men, whom she refers to as "grabbers" and "bums." She has come to reject manly aggression and develop a preference for a more fragile and submissive type of man. Again, the two romantic leads develop a relationship during a train ride. Also during the train ride, a character remembers crawling into bed with a family member as a child. In *The Major and the Minor*, Philip and Susan find themselves in close proximity in a sleeping compartment of the train. A storm is raging outside. Philip says, "Every time there was a storm at night, I used to crawl in with my Aunt Jenny." Similarly, Sugar and Jerry are lying together in a berth. Sugar says, "When I was a little girl, on cold nights like this, I used to crawl into bed with my sister. We'd cuddle up under the covers, and pretend we were lost in a dark cave, and were trying to find out way out." A child can find comfort and security in sharing a bed with a loved one, but sharing a bed can have an entirely different meaning to an adult.

In *You're Never Too Young*, Jerry Lewis plays Wilbur Hoolick, an apprentice at Francois' Hair Salon. Wilbur figures to fool Francois (Hans Conried) with a disguise, which consists of a wig and beard that he made out of hair clippings, to show him that he can do more than sweep up hair. Viewers who expected to see Lewis disguised as a child must have been surprised to have him introduced in the film disguised as an old man.

A thief, Noonan (Raymond Burr), finds that he is being followed by detectives and hides a stolen diamond in Wilbur's back pocket. Noonan notices a "Private Treatment in Your Home" sign in the salon window, which gives him an idea. He asks Wilbur to go to his home to give his wife, Mrs. Noonan (Veda Ann Borg), a scalp massage. He then lets his wife know that Wilbur is on his way and instructs her to slip the jewel out of his pocket. Mrs. Noonan answers the door wearing an attractive peach-colored satin dress. She speaks flirtatiously to Wilbur. In an effort to get inside his pocket, she keeps groping his backside, which has an unnerving effect on the young man. The same scene was played out 29 years before in Harry Langdon's *The Strong Man* (1926) in which a hostess held Langdon down on a couch and put him in a series of wrestling holds. Mrs.

Veda Ann Borg plies her feminine wiles on Jerry Lewis in *You're Never Too Young* (1955).

Noonan puts on a LP record and forces Wilbur into a series of dance holds. This vertical assault is decidedly less risqué than the earlier horizontal assault. Mrs. Noonan gets her hands into Wilbur's pocket and is relieved to finally remove the diamond. Noonan bursts into the apartment, pretending to be enraged to catch Wilbur dancing with his wife. He frightens Wilbur with a knife and demands that he leave town. After Wilbur has already fled the apartment, Mrs. Noonan realizes that all that she got out of his pocket was a wrapped-up wad of bubble gum.

This scene is less effective than the original. Lewis never expresses the wide-eyed terror that Langdon did in *The Strong Man*. Even before his hostess produced a knife, Langdon looked like he was facing death. He nearly jumped out of his skin when the woman touched his backside. Lewis is a lot more collected. Even less appealing, the "removing the diamond from the pocket" routine is stretched out excessively to the full length of the film (Noonan will still be trying to get into Wilbur's pocket to find the diamond in the third act).

Eddie Cantor, who got laughs with naughty smirks and sexual innuendo, always acted as if he was on the threshold of manhood and was thrilled to be experiencing his first sexual stirrings. Cantor performed a variation on *The Strong Man*'s seduction scene in *Kid Millions* (1934). This time, the seductress (Ethel Merman) is out to steal a will from Cantor's jacket. But Cantor presents a tongue-in-cheek performance, never expecting the audience to believe that he is shy or gullible. He is delighted with being seduced (though he is perhaps not as delighted with the possibility of being robbed and murdered by Merman's hot-tempered gangster boyfriend, Louie the Lug). The shyness and gullibility of Wilbur will similarly come into question in *You're Never Too Young*.

At Union Station, Wilbur tries to buy a train ticket to his hometown, but he finds that he doesn't have enough money. He steals a sailor suit and eyeglasses from a tall twelve-year-old boy so that he can pretend to be a child and purchase a half-price ticket. Wilbur has now regressed from an old man to a young man to a child. Later, he arouses the suspicion of a conductor and must flee to avoid being ejected from the train. He hides in the compartment of Nancy Collins (Diana Lynn), a teacher at a private girl's school. Feeling sorry for this nervous "child," Nancy allows him to remain with her for the remainder of the train ride.

Wilbur's feelings and motivations in this cozy situation are not completely clear. One moment, he expresses distress when Nancy offers to help him button up his pajamas. In the very next scene, he expresses absolute delight when Nancy presses him against her chest to comfort him during a thunderstorm. After she finally relaxes her hold, he pretends to be frightened by a loud crack of thunder so that she will wrap her arms around him again and grip him even more tightly than before. It could be explained that Wilbur's brief encounter with Nancy has brought about a sexual awakening in the young man, causing his shyness to give way to delight. But it's hard to interpret the scene in this way. Wilbur's mischievous smile tells the audience that he knows exactly what he's doing and nothing about this is new or unpleasant to him. He comes across as a knowing manipulator, much like Tony Curtis' character in *Some Like It Hot*. Yet, motives of mischief or manipulation are not supported by the film's denouement, in which Wilbur confesses to Nancy that he has long been incapacitated by his shyness with girls. "I never could talk to girls," he says. "I get very tongue-tied when I'm around girls." That does, in fact, make this a coming-of-age story that focuses on the protagonist's sexual awakening.

The Major and the Minor featured a protagonist driven in the exact opposite direction of Wilbur. The film presented a story of sexual repression, which only worked because Rogers' character wasn't really childlike at all. The tension and humor in *The Major and the Minor* came from a sexually attractive and sexually aware woman dressing up as a little girl. Susan Applegate had been distressed by her sexual experiences and it appealed to her to find temporary refuge in her little girl disguise. Wilbur is presented as a young man whose shyness and awkwardness make him a child even before he puts on his sailor suit. In the end, Wilbur finally achieves his long-delayed maturity. He helps the police to capture Noonan and, with his newfound confidence, he is finally able to graduate from apprentice barber to full-fledged barber.

Lewis more deeply examined his inner child in *That's My Boy* (1951). Junior Jackson (Lewis) is a shy, stumbling and slightly built high school senior getting ready to go to college. His father, former college football hero Jarring Jack Jackson (Eddie Mayehoff), wants Junior to play football at his alma mater, Ridgeville University. Daddy Jack will not allow his son to be soft because he believes that a man needs to have the guts to succeed in life. His overbearing father's philosophy, which author Frank Krutnik called an "obsessive masculine success ethic,"[10] is a source of trauma for Junior. Junior fears that he can never live up to his father's expectations. The stress of dealing with his father causes him to experience low self-esteem and suffer psychosomatic illnesses. Jack arranges for Bill Baker (Dean Martin), a talented quarterback, to make an athlete out of his son. Bill soon becomes the caring and sympathetic father figure that Junior needs.

Problems arise when Bill and Junior are both attracted to a pretty psychology major, Terry (Marion Marshall). The situation gets trickier when Junior, who is unaware of Bill's interest in Terry, asks for Bill's help to romance the young woman. Though Terry loves Bill, she shows Junior affection to give him confidence and make him feel manly. It is similar to the situation that occurs in the far more dramatic *Tea and Sympathy* (1956): Herb Lee (Edward Andrews) wants his seventeen-year-old son Tom (John Kerr) to be manly and fit in with the other boys at his prep school, which isn't all that different than Jarring Jack's objective. Other obvious similarities can be found. Junior is a sensitive boy who wants to devote his life to caring for sick animals. Tom is a sensitive boy who adores classical music and the theater. Both Junior and Tom are criticized for their lack of interest in sports. In *Tea and Sympathy*, Tom develops a crush on Laura (Deborah Kerr), wife of the dormitory headmaster. Laura feels sympathy towards Tom and, to give him confidence as a man, she has sex with him. In *That's My Boy*, Terry agrees to wear Junior's pin. It not exactly the same, but a broad comedy piece could only go so far at the time.

Junior's mother, worried about her son, tells him that he is no longer going to have his father controlling his life. But she herself tries to take control. She demands, "You're going to stop playing football, take up your regular studies, and you're going to shower and have dinner immediately." Junior is unhappy with his mother's efforts no matter

Jerry Lewis is troubled by a loving but overbearing father (Eddie Mayehoff) in *That's My Boy* (1951).

how well-meaning they are. He complains to Terry, "Now I'm being dominated by Mother and she's almost as bad as my father." But he seems, by his tone, to suggest that he resents his mother's control even more.

Junior learns that, to succeed, he must stop thinking only of himself. He must work hard to help his school and his friend Bill. "Stop being self-centered and dependent on other people," Terry tells him. "Get out there and stand on your own two legs." He becomes the star of the football team when he kicks a game-winning field goal. He is ecstatic that he has finally been able to live up to his father's expectations. His proud father exclaims, "That's my boy!" Considering that this is the film's title, it is safe to say that the entire film was leading up to this moment. The film ends without further mention of Junior's lifelong dream of curing sick animals. In this way, the film promotes Jarring Jack's "obsessive masculine success ethic."

Those who study film turn to James Dean's work to support the theory that a masculinity crisis developed in the United States after World War II. The overbearing father (Raymond Massey) in *East of Eden* (1955) also exerts great emotional and mental pressure on his son, Cal Trask (Dean). Wayward Cal wants to find his own identity, but he also wants the affection of his pious, strong-willed father. In *Rebel Without a Cause*

Jerry Lewis is too scrawny to make it on the football field in *That's My Boy* **(1951). The actor who poses as Lewis' teammate in this still is unknown.**

(1955), Jim Stark (Dean) wants to be a man, but he finds his weak-willed father (Jim Backus) to be a poor role model. This father is too hard and this father is too soft. Where is the father who is just right?

Lewis' films no doubt reflect a masculinity crisis. This is especially the case with *That's My Boy*, which established a template for Lewis. In *The Caddy* (1953), Lewis is again intimidated at the prospect of following in the footsteps of his sports champion father. In *The Disorderly Orderly* (1964), Lewis lacks the confidence to become a doctor like his esteemed father.

Writer-director Frank Tashlin emphasized the childlike qualities of Lewis in *Artists and Models* (1955). Eugene Fullstack (Lewis), a clumsy and excitable young man, is obsessed with comic books. A psychologist suggests that this has stymied Eugene's development.

Artists and Models casts Lewis as a character more dysfunctional than usual. He desperately clings to his childhood. It's not only the comic books. He has been devoted to his best friend, Rick Todd (Dean Martin), since he and Rick were small boys. The pair still abide by the fellowship oath of the Kangaroo Patrol: "Pals forever," they chant in unison before they perform a silly ritual in which they shake hands, hop up and down, and bump backsides.

Eugene and Rick live together and work together. Their latest job has them setting up billboards. When the film opens, Rick has just finished painting a billboard of a woman smoking a cigarette. Eugene has to activate a machine that will release steam into a tube and force it out of the woman's mouth. Eugene is so preoccupied reading a comic book that he pulls the wrong lever on the machine and *he* gets sucked down inside the tube.

The comic books overstimulate Eugene's imagination, making him act unhinged during the day and causing him to have frightening dreams at night. Rick, who sees commercial value in his roommate's gory and surreal nightmares, takes notes while listening to Eugene talk in his sleep and later sells the nightmare scenarios to a comic book publisher.

The idea of arrested development being linked to a childhood trauma is rarely examined in stories of the comic man-child. But childhood trauma is touched on briefly in *Lars and the Real Girl* (2007). The film's protagonist, Lars Lindstrom (Ryan Gosling), feels nervous around people and prefers to be reclusive. We later learn that Lars has intimacy issues because his mother died while giving birth to him and he was left in the care of his hopelessly heartbroken father. The childhood trauma gives a serious foundation to the story, but the film's humor comes from this socially inept young man developing a passionate relationship with a sex doll. This is a reoccurring issue in man-child comedies. *Artists and Models* features no sex doll, but Eugene does developed a hopeless crush on a cartoon character, a female superhero named The Bat Lady.

A man can avoid sexual intimacy by focusing his erotic desire on an idealized woman that he can never have. This is a form of sexual repression. This occurs in *Hollywood or Bust* (1956) when Lewis becomes fixated on Hollywood sex symbol Anita Ekberg. In *Tramp, Tramp, Tramp* (1926), Harry Langdon falls in love with a model's image on a billboard. Harry has just finished throwing kisses at the image when he turns around and discovers the actual model, Betty Burton (Joan Crawford), standing behind him. Startled, he doesn't know how to react. He buckles at the knees. The image had become so real to him that he struggles to understand how one person can be in two places at one time. He is confused and frantic as he is caught between this lovely pair. James Neibaur wrote in *The Silent Films of Harry Langdon (1923–1928)*, "He backs up, sits on the bench, gets up, moves slowly towards Betty, rushes back again, hides behind a tree, comes back out, sits again, gets up again, and so on."[11] He finally settles down, accepting it as a miracle that the woman he has adored from afar is suddenly standing in front of him.

Something reminiscent of Harry's encounter with the billboard model occurs in *Artists and Models*. The comic book–obsessed Eugene, who has trouble separating fantasy from reality, becomes unnerved when he encounters an artist's model dressed as the Bat Lady.

The protagonists of Lewis' solo films were far more neurotic. Their fears and sensitivities were greatly exaggerated. In *The Disorderly Orderly* (1964), Lewis' character, Jerome Littlefield, never makes it onto the football field at Quimby High School, but he makes himself useful during games by shaking pom-poms and singing the school's fight song. The scene has a direct connection to *That's My Boy* in that Lewis reworked the Ridgeville College fight song into the Quimby High School fight song. Jerome shares Junior's dreams of healing the sick, but he flunks out of medical school due to a pain phobia that makes him squeamish around sick people.

In *The Ladies Man* (1961), Lewis is so traumatized after seeing his college sweetheart kiss a football player that he swears off women. Film critic Zach Lewis wrote, "This [betrayal] reverts him to a childlike state of sexuality, horrified at even the slightest touch from a woman."[12] *That's My Boy* ended with Junior learning that the girl he loved was in love with quarterback Martin, but he managed to handle the situation in a confident and mature way. Herbert lacks that confidence and maturity. He runs off to California, where he gets a job as a houseboy at a boarding house. The twist is that, unknown to Herbert, the boarding house is occupied by dozens of young women. The revelation is sudden and dramatic. He is forced to confront his greatest fear when, at daybreak, a horde of women is roused from sleep and crowd into the dining room for breakfast. The owner of the boarding house, Helen Wellenmellen (Helen Traubel), persuades Herbert to stay by offering to help him overcome his shyness with women. Zach Lewis described Herbert as being "emasculated and an object of willing servitude."[13]

Lewis is as physically uncoordinated as a toddler. Geoff King wrote, "Lewis is one of the most crazily infantile of comedian stars, his performances built to a large extent out of childish mannerisms and incapacities. The speech of his characters lapses frequently into screeches, screams or incoherent and childlike stammering and burbling."[14] Lewis stammered and burbled worse than Langdon, which is saying a lot.

Lewis typically refers to his screen persona as "the nine-year-old kid." This character is front and center in the films that the comedian made during the period of 1957 to 1964. Lewis never looked more childlike than he does in *The Ladies Man*. This is especially evident when he sits in a high chair while a kind-hearted maid (Kathleen Freeman) spoon-feeds him pabulum. The film itself depicts, according to film critic Kevin B. Lee, "childlike free play."[15]

The "nine-year-old kid" persona is fully on display in *The Bellboy* (1960). Lewis' bellboy, much like Jacques Tati's Mr. Hulot, has a boyish curiosity that often gets the better of him. Mr. Hulot is at his most curious when confronted by a highly noisy and highly baffling gadget. Technology is also an attraction for the bellboy. When he boards a jet to retrieve a suitcase for a hotel guest, he becomes mesmerized by the sight of the pilot's control panel. The next thing we see, the jet is taking off. After he makes a mess of things, the bellboy is willing to steal away from the scene before someone has time to notice. We can see him cringing with fear and embarrassment as he quickly tiptoes away. He is a naughty child afraid to get a spanking. Tati is also unwilling to answer for

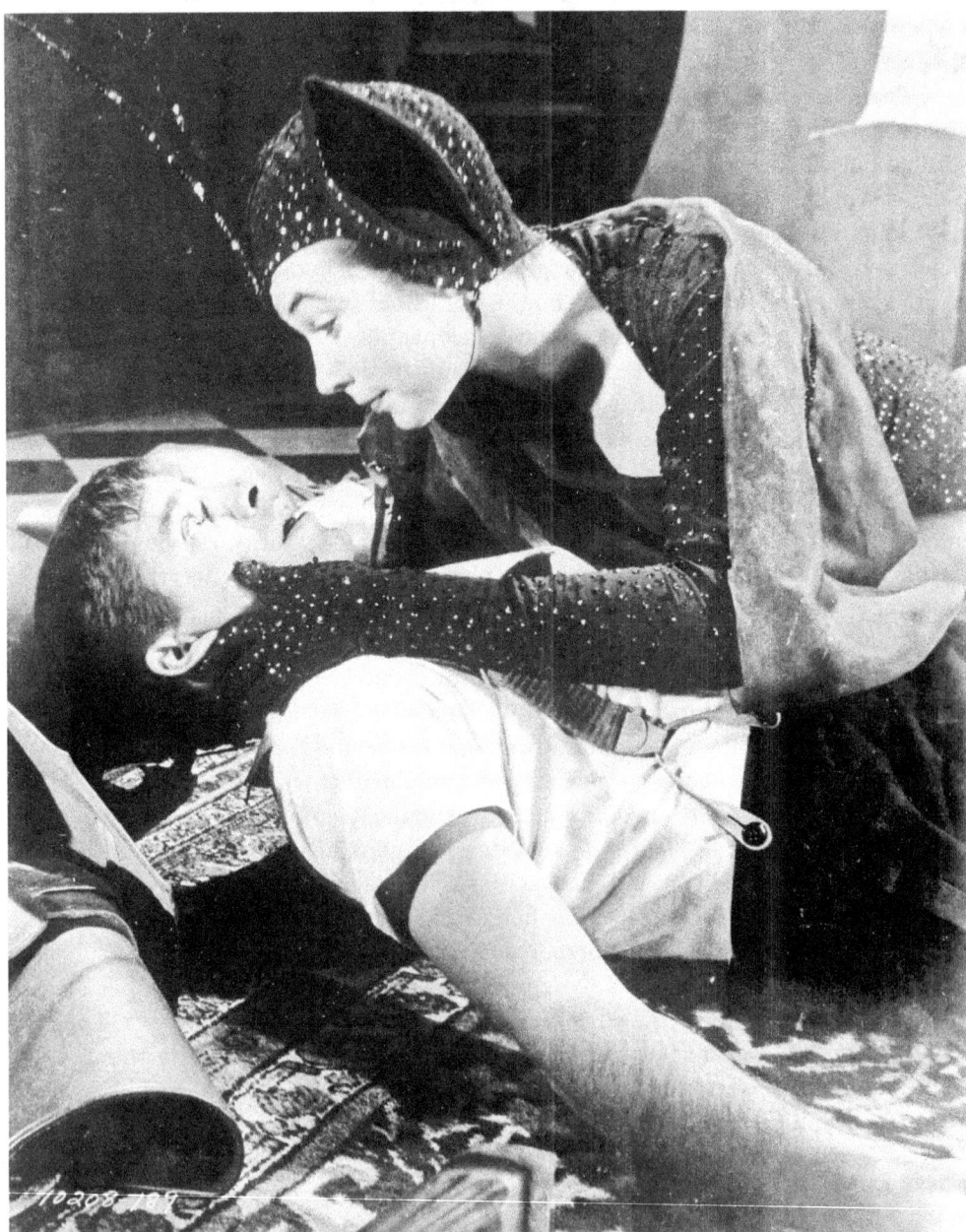

Comic book fanatic Jerry Lewis is shocked to meet his idol, The Bat Lady (Shirley MacLaine), in *Artists and Models* **(1955).**

his actions. He is expressionless as he saunters away from a scene, acting as if he was in no way involved and doesn't even known that something has gone wrong.

In *You're Never Too Young*, Mrs. Noonan wants to get inside Lewis' pants to grab hold of his jewel. It's not too subtle what's going on here. Lewis took this situation to a surreal extreme in *The Ladies Man*. He stumbles into the forbidden room of Miss Cartilage (Sylvia Lewis). A lone drumbeat signifies his beating heart. Miss Cartilage

Kathleen Freeman cradles Jerry Lewis like a baby in *The Ladies Man* (1961).

descends from the ceiling on a long black thread. She is wearing a black leotard and her face is covered in vampirish white makeup. Zach Lewis wrote, "Cartilage swings and sways her way around his body, tantalizes him on the bed, and stands in the way of his escape."[16] The rumba record is now replaced by a full live orchestra conducted by Harry James. The orchestra members, dressed in dazzling white tuxedos, are incredibly revealed when a wall of the bedroom rises. It isn't long before Herbert flees the fantastic room screaming, "*Maaaaaa!*" The *You're Never Too Young* seduction scene is recalled a second time. In this instance, Herbert becomes alarmed when movie actor George Raft puts on a record and asks that he join him in a tango. These are sexual fears expressed in a bizarrely dreamlike way.

Sexual repression is also a prominent feature of *The Nutty Professor* (1963). A serum unleashes a chemistry professor's sexual desires. Jerry Agonistes wrote in *Enfant Terrible!: Jerry Lewis in American Film*, "[I]n *The Nutty Professor* [Lewis] is Buddy Love and Julius Kelp, Don Juan and his desexualized opposite."[17]

Lewis' *The Patsy* (1964) opens with news of a plane crash. The crash receives special coverage because one of the dead passengers is famed comedian Wally Brandford. Unwilling to give up their lucrative jobs, members of the comedian's management team are determined to find a nobody who they can turn into a star. They set their sights on a clumsy bellboy, Stanley Belt (Lewis). The film, in effect, involves a committee of fathers who are ruthless in their efforts to mold and refine Stanley. Their makeover, unlike Jarring Jack's makeover in *That's My Boy*, is devoid of love. It is motivated purely by greed and self-interest. Film scholar Angelos Koutsourakis wrote, "[A]t the end of *The Patsy*, after his success, Stanley Belt has become a new person. The old, charming, bumbling kid has become slick and self-assured. In one expressive, low-angle shot, we see that he *has* been made over; his innocence is lost."[18] It was good to see Keaton emerge as a man following his father's makeover in *Steamboat Bill, Jr.*, but it is disappointing to now see Lewis undergo the same transformation. At this point in Lewis' career, we want to see Lewis in the role of the awkward man-child.

Lewis would only make one more film in which he played the "nine-year-old kid" character. He was simply getting too old to play the part. The innocence had, unfortunately, been lost.

6

Further Post-War Immaturity

Though Americans emerged from World War II as the victor, American masculinity fell into a turbulent state after the war. After the chaos of the Great Depression and World War II, the idea of the man as the breadwinner was reestablished. The new consumerist society demanded that a man earn a good salary to maintain his family in an affluent lifestyle. Men were expected to conform to a group design. They were made to become corporate clones or "yes-men." Men struggled to live up to this ideal. Philip Wylie wrote in *The Abdicating Male* of men's natural desire to battle against "conformity, togetherness [and] anonymity."[1] The increasing domesticity of men inevitably led to a troubling decline in traditional masculinity. Men were long told that they must be strong-minded and set themselves apart from their family, particularly their mothers. This established self-determination and individuality as masculine qualities. But the role of men, especially in times of war and post-war, can be determined by national purpose. Even though the modern world of togetherness, suburbs and mass culture was feminine, it was a sign of immaturity and low moral character for a man to perceive the family life as a trap that must be avoided.

The pressure exerted on a man to be a breadwinner is evident in *The Yellow Cab Man* (1950). Our accident-prone hero, Red Pirdy (Red Skelton), is deeply ashamed that he is unable to hold a job. In the end, he succeeds in the corporate world by selling his unbreakable glass invention, Elastiglass. All is now well in his life.

It was all too complicated in this new world. Robert Young was perfect as the new suburban father in *Sitting Pretty* (1948). Young's Harry King is a beleaguered lawyer working for an oppressive law firm. He fails to get a raise that he expected, which puts a strain on his family's household finances. Harry and his wife, Tracey (Maureen O'Hara), are unable to control their three rambunctious sons and desperately seek outside help. This is when we are introduced to a pompous, know-it-all efficiency expert named Lynn Belvedere (Clifton Webb).

Belvedere can, in many crucial ways, be regarded as well-developed. He is proud, confident, and self-reliant. He has a strong work ethic. He assures the Kings of this when he tells them, "I've never been an idler or a parasite." He is certainly well-developed compared to Clarence Appleton (Richard Haydn), a mama's boy and local gossip who acts as Belvedere's principal adversary in the film. Doug Johnson of Alt Film Guide wrote, "Appleton spends his time lifting pollen specimens from his neighbor's yards when he is not snooping (sometimes with his mother)."² As far as we know, Appleton has lived with his overbearing mother for his entire life. An overbearing or overindulgent parent has much to do with creating a man-child. This is evident in films as diverse as *The Secret Life of Walter Mitty* (1947) and *The Waterboy* (1998). This can make one feel

Clifton Webb travels to the suburbs to provide domestic assistance to married couple Robert Young and Maureen O'Hara in *Sitting Pretty* (1948).

sympathy for Appleton, who was never allowed the opportunity to develop into the model family man. Uninterested in a wife and children, Appleton has turned to pollen collection as his own unique way to distribute seed for reproductive purposes. He shows himself in this one distinctive way to be like Belvedere, who similarly lacks interest in marriage and offspring. Belvedere specifies that he dislikes all children intensely.

Johnson was highly critical of the King family in his analysis. He wrote, "[The family] has broken down into disorder. Harry and Tracey King exhibit no parental control."[3] Belvedere, who believes that Yoga meditation is more satisfying and productive than the family's frantic suburban lifestyle, is able to calmly restore order in the home. Tracey and the children are quick to adapt to his philosophies, but Harry is too set in his manly ways to cooperate.

Belvedere has little respect for Harry. He sizes up Harry as a typical suburban husband, which he describes in short as "stupid and stuffy." He accuses Harry of behaving in a helpless manner in his own home. Harry has no way to defend himself against this criticism. Cultural analyst James J. O'Meara wrote that Henry King is "a king in name only; his children run wild, his dog jumps on his back, and he is forced to all but kowtow to his boss, including taking his wife to his boring bridge evenings...."[4] Harry is no more affectionate in his opinion of Belvedere, who he resents for having usurped his authority in his own home.

The cruelties of war left men with disturbing memories and it is believed by some historians and sociologists that it created a post-war gloom. *The Best Years of Our Lives* (1946), which won nine Academy Awards, focused on the social readjustment of World War II servicemen. The film was followed three months later by *Buck Privates Come Home* (1947), which also dealt with the social readjustment of World War II servicemen. But *Buck Privates Come Home* did not show us war-scarred veterans. The film's service veterans, Slicker Smith and Herbie Brown (Bud Abbott and Lou Costello), are not missing body parts and do not suffer nightmares about combat experiences. They are the same characters that they were six years earlier in *Buck Privates* (1941). They are older but no wiser. The plot is only slightly more developed than the spare plot of *Buck Privates*. A U.S. troop ship arrives in France to transport soldiers home. Slicker and Herbie smuggle Evey, a six-year-old war orphan, aboard the ship. After enduring many problems on the voyage home, Slicker and Herbie bring Evey to the French consul in New York to apply for adoption, but Herbie is told that he needs to be married and employed before the consul can approve his request. This sets up serious goals for Herbie, but then the story veers off in an entirely different direction and these goals are quickly forgotten. Slicker and Herbie befriend an aspiring race car designer, Bill Gregory (Tom Brown). Gregory's fiancée, Sylvia Hunter (Joan Shawlee), cares for Evey while the men try to obtain financing to build a prototype of Gregory's racing car. In the end, an automobile magnate orders a large number of the cars from Gregory, which assures a steady income for Gregory and his wife-to-be. Gregory and Sylvia, who have developed an attachment to Evey, successfully petition the consul to adopt her.

It wasn't really a surprise that Herbie didn't become a husband and father. *The Kid* (1921) did not end with Charlie Chapin getting to keep Jackie Coogan. Laurel and Hardy had to give up their ward (Jacquie Lyn) before the end of *Pack Up Your Troubles* (1932).

The last that we see of Stan and Ollie, an angry cook is chasing after them with a butcher knife. This was not the victorious conclusion that had been refined and patented by Harold Lloyd. The Tramp is not the Tramp unless he remains rootless and alone. Laurel and Hardy are not Laurel and Hardy unless they remain childish fools. The point, presumably, is that perpetual comedy produces perpetual immaturity. Some comedy stars are stuck in amber and never meant to improve.

Bob Hope, a top comedy star of this period, did well without contending with modern-day realities. Soon after the war ended, he had great success with *Road to Utopia* (1946), *Monsieur Beaucaire* (1946), *Road to Rio* (1947) and *The Paleface* (1948). Period costumes and oversea locales had nothing to do with the post-war American male's relationship to family, country or career. The royal court of *Monsieur Beaucaire* and the Alaska gold mine of *Road to Utopia* were far away from the troubles of the American man.

In the "Road" series, Hope and Bing Crosby certainly behaved childishly. A well-known running gag of the series involved the children's game pat-a-cake. When menaced by brawny thugs, Hope and Crosby would abruptly face one another and play pat-a-cake. This bewildered the thugs, who couldn't decide how to react. Before they could resolve their confusion and respond, Hope and Crosby would swing into action, segueing from pat-a-cake claps to hard-knuckle sucker punches.

Hope achieved great success with the western spoof *The Paleface*. Hope plays a novice correspondence school dentist named "Painless" Peter Potter. Potter makes a poor western hero. He is afraid of Indians and outlaws and he is inept at shooting a gun. The traditional western hero has the virtue of modesty. His actions bespeak his worth. But Potter is a braggart and show-off. He talks tough even though he is really not tough at all. Despite many attempts, he isn't even able to consummate his marriage with Calamity Jane (Jane Russell), who only married Potter to conceal her identity as a government agent.

In a 1957 survey, more than 2,000 Americans were asked a series of questions designed to reveal their behavior and attitudes about work, family, self-definition, satisfactions, dissatisfactions and personal crises. The survey was conducted by the Survey Research Center at the University of Michigan under the direction of the Joint Commission on Mental Illness and Health. The survey showed that Americans reacted with suspicion and hostility to people who avoided marriage and parenthood. More than half of those surveyed in 1957 viewed a man or woman who did not want to march down the aisle as selfish, peculiar, or morally flawed. The general idea was that a person was obligated to commit to marriage and take steps to assure their ability to support a family. It was important for a person to obtain an education and establish themselves in a career because, otherwise, they would be unable to set up an appropriate household where children could be raised.

The Seven Year Itch (1955), Billy Wilder's witty adaptation of George Axelrod's risqué Broadway farce, makes the point that the social order would not exist without the calming influence of a wife. It is made clear in its prologue that, while a wife is away, her husband will be inclined to "run wild," meaning that he might drink alcohol, eat ulcer-inducing food, and chase women. The theory is put to the test with a milquetoast

Bob Hope is eager to learn about romancing women in *Road to Morocco* (1942) (courtesy www. doctormacro.com).

family man, Richard Sherman (Tom Ewell), during a steamy summer in Manhattan. Sherman remains in town to work while his wife (Evelyn Keyes) and son (Butch Bernard) vacation in Maine. He is referred to by another character as a "summer bachelor." He is determined that, when his wife is away, he will be mature and responsible and resist the many sexual temptations that surround him. But he's not sure if he can do this or if he wants to do this. The filmmakers might not be sure about this either. It is suggested in the film that, by repressing powerful urges in men, marriage and parenthood turn men into bland and dispirited creatures. Sherman is certainly not a proud or vigorous specimen of a man. His droopy shoulders and hangdog expression say as much. He is constantly lighting a cigarette or pouring himself a drink to settle his nerves. He is, in every way, a hopeless sad sack.

It isn't unusual for one of Wilder's male protagonists to be unmanly. Tasha Robinson, editor of *The Dissolve*, described Wilder's male protagonists as the director's "usual batch of saps and sinners."[5] These men are, according to Robinson, "weak, easily led, confused, or struggling men."[6] She wrote, "His dramatic protagonists are often beaten down by life, or manipulated by a woman with an agenda, or just tempted beyond their moral boundaries by the promise of some gain. His comic protagonists are often baffled and hapless and trying to keep up."[7]

The film raises the question, would society benefit from returning to a freer and more primitive state? A waitress talks to Sherman about a nudist camp fund, which she insists is a "worthy cause." She says, "We must bring the message to the people. To unmask our suffocating bodies and let them breathe again. Without clothes, there'd be no sickness and no war. Can you imagine two armies on the battlefield ... no uniforms, completely nude? No way of telling friend from foe, all brothers together." Perhaps, as these remarks imply, inhibitions can make men miserable and mean. It seems reasonable that, if social order perverts us, it is best to discard it. This is reminiscent of *I'm All Right Jack* (1959); film critic Wheeler Winston Dixon wrote of that film's ending, "[B]oth labor and management are shown to be interested only in their own ends, often to absurd degrees, and when Stanley makes a televised statement exposing bribery, slacking off at work, price gouging and extortion by all the principals involved, he is banished from 'polite' society. When last seen, Stanley is ensconced in a nudist colony, trying (literally) to escape from all the trappings of a social order that has broken down at every level."[8] We were nude as innocent babies. We were nude at our creation in the Garden of Eden. Only adults in the corrupt modern world are obsessed with the modesty and markings of clothing.

Sherman snatches a bottle of soda out of the refrigerator and, to pry loose the cap, he jams the mouth of the bottle into a cabinet handle. He says aloud in a feminine voice, "Use the bottle opener, Richard." Clearly, he is mimicking his wife's voice, which has taken residence in his brain as the voice of his superego. As this dominant woman has left him alone in an empty home, he feels compelled to speak in her voice and carry on her duty to protect him from his gender's iniquitous ways. He is Norman Bates with a few less bats in the belfry. But Sherman has even more in common with Walter Mitty. Like Mitty, he is an imaginative editor of pulp novels who is plagued by vivid daydreams. The big difference, though, is that Sherman's daydreams are lusty and wicked. He imagines his secretary, Miss Morris (Marguerite Chapman), pushing him down on his desk and kissing him.

Without his wife and son around, Sherman gets into the habit of talking to himself a lot. He talks at length about his wife. He says, "She probably figures she isn't as young as she used to be. She's 31 years old. One of these days, she's gonna wake up and find her looks are gone and then where will she be? Well, no wonder she's worried. And especially since I don't look a bit different than I did when I was 28. It's not my fault that I don't. It's just a simple biological fact. Women age quicker than men. Yeah, probably won't look any different when I'm sixty. I have that kind of a face. Everybody will think she's my mother." His wife *already* acts as if she is his mother. She tells him as her parting words at the train station to "eat properly," which is something that a mother tells her child. Sherman's delusion about his youthful appearance reveals a man with a Peter Pan syndrome. He fantasizes never getting old and remaining wild and free.

In his daydreams, Sherman is strong and self-assured as he sets out to seduce his upstairs neighbor, blonde bombshell Marilyn Monroe (known in the film only as "The Girl"). He settles down at his piano and provides a magnificent rendition of Rachmaninoff's Piano Concerto #2. But, in real life, all that he can manage to play on the piano is the childishly simplistic "Chopsticks." Monroe is the shapely blonde that tempts Sherman just as Janet Leigh will one day be the shapely blonde who tempts Norman Bates.

Sherman finds that his sexual fantasies are taking on a dark aspect. He imagines his wife bursting into his apartment and shooting him dead. Sexual desire leads only

Tom Ewell is delighted to test his seduction techniques on Marilyn Monroe in *The Seven Year Itch* (1955).

to murder just as it would in *Psycho*. Sherman becomes so fearful that he turns down an opportunity to have sex with The Girl. But this was a change that the censors demanded. In the play, Sherman goes through with the sex act, fulfilling his adulterous desires. This changes the Sherman character significantly. The fact that he looks upon a beautiful woman with a mixture of fear and attraction makes him analogous to a pent-up virgin adolescent with first-time jitters. He is not much different than Jerry Lewis' women-phobic character in *The Ladies Man*.

We know that Sherman has finally abandoned his childish ways when he punches his wife's brawny ex-beau, Tom McKenzie (Sonny Tufts), who he thinks is still interested in his wife. McKenzie drops to the floor unconscious and Sherman stands above him as a proud victor. The only way for him to assert his masculinity is to commit an act of violence. He has restored social order by becoming a warrior and protecting what is his. After all, social order is largely about boundaries, possessions, and war. It doesn't seem to matter to the filmmakers that McKenzie was not actually making advances to Sherman's wife.

The same year, *Mister Roberts* (1955) focused on a group of U.S. Navy men who have no way to assert their masculinity. They are separated from their families, which means they cannot fulfill their duties as husbands or fathers; they are stationed on a cargo ship outside the war zone, which means that they cannot fight to defend their country; and they are denied contact with women, which means that they cannot indulge their sexual desires. How can they not act like children? No crew member acts more like a child than Ensign Frank Thurlowe Pulver (Jack Lemmon), an idle young man. He spends most of his time hiding in his cabin to avoid Lieutenant Commander Morton (James Cagney), who he clearly sees as a formidable father figure. While in his cabin, he usually lounges in his bunk and mouths off about brave acts that he will one day accomplish. The brave acts that he describes are nothing more than childish pranks that he has concocted, like plugging up the captain's toilet line. He is anxious to please

Ensign Pulver (Jack Lemmon) prepares to toss a homemade firecracker under the captain's bunk in *Mister Roberts* (1955) (courtesy www.doctormacro.com).

Lieutenant Roberts (Henry Fonda), who acts as a big brother, but Roberts has no respect for him. He tells Pulver that he is hapless, lazy and disorganized. He says, "Have you ever in your life finished anything you started out to do?" Roberts' rebuke provokes Pulver to destroy the ship's laundry with a giant home-made firecracker (the cardboard center of a roll of toilet paper filled with mercury). What can be more childish than blowing up something with a firecracker?

Like *Hail the Conquering Hero*'s Woodrow Truesmith, Roberts is desperate to get into battle to show his mettle. The problem is that Morton, a vainglorious man determined to earn a promotion, believes that Roberts plays an indispensible role in the operation of his ship and he fears that his (Morton's) promotion will be jeopardized if he approves Roberts' request to be transferred to a destroyer. Determined to help their beloved officer, crew members risk court martial to forge Morton's signature on transfer papers. This succeeds in finally obtaining Roberts' transfer. Unfortunately, it isn't long after the transfer that Roberts dies in the Battle of Okinawa. It takes news of Roberts' death to give Pulver the courage to finally stand up to Morton. It is at this moment that we are led to believe that Pulver has transformed from a firecracker-exploding child to an assertive adult.

Roberts expresses a burning desire to get into the fray. Only an obsessed man would submit transfer requests week after week even though he knows that they will be rejected. At the time, American servicemen were motivated to get revenge for Japan's sneak attack on Pearl Harbor. It is reasonable to assume that, as friendly and honorable as Roberts may seem, he is a man compelled by bloodlust to kill Japanese soldiers. During this same period, the bloodlust of a military career officer was criticized in *The Bridge on the River Kwai* (1957). Major Shears (William Holden) tells Major Warden (Jack Hawkins), "You make me sick with your heroics! There's a stench of death about you. You carry it in your pack like the plague.... You and Colonel Nicholson, you're two of a kind, crazy with courage. For what? How to die like a gentleman, how to die by the rules, when the only important thing is how to live like a human being."

Others called for men to act in peace. Psychologist Wilhelm Stekel wrote, "The mark of the immature man is that he wants to die nobly for a cause, while the mark of the mature man is that is wants to live humbly for one."[9] In *The Americanization of Emily* (1964), Lt. Cmdr. Charles E. Madison (James Garner) is an avowed coward who declares,

> Cowardice will save the world. War isn't hell at all. It's man at his best—the highest morality he's capable of. It's not war that's insane, you see. It's the morality of it. It's not greed or ambition that makes war: it's goodness. Wars are always fought for the best of reasons: for liberation or manifest destiny. Always against tyranny and always in the interest of humanity. So far this war, we've managed to butcher some ten million humans in the interest of humanity. Next war it seems we'll have to destroy all of man in order to preserve his damn dignity. It's not war that's unnatural to us, it's virtue. As long as valor remains a virtue, we shall have soldiers. So, I preach cowardice. Through cowardice, we shall all be saved.

A gung-ho attitude towards war continued through much of the 1960s. Take, for example, the family film *The Incredible Mr. Limpet* (1964). A mild-mannered husband,

Henry Limpet (Don Knotts), feels unmanly when he is turned down by the Navy during World War II. But then he is magically transformed into a fish and finds that he now can produce a powerful underwater roar, which enables him to sink German U-boats. It takes Limpet becoming a fish to become a man.

Cultures channel masculine qualities to serve the benefits of the society. It is an important tenet of the man code that a man be willing to sacrifice his life for family and country. This requires him to accept that he is expendable.

Alfred Hitchcock's semi-comic *North by Northwest* (1959) featured a perfect postwar man-child, Roger Thornhill (Cary Grant). The opening scenes of the film are specifically designed to bring Thornhill's many flaws front and center. Thornhill is not a firm, well-centered model of maturity. His fast-talking ways make him come across as a rambunctious little boy. He is cocky, brash, shallow, and self-absorbed. Film director Guillermo Del Toro described him, bluntly, as being "full of himself"[10] and acting essentially as a "stunted child."[11] It is not surprising then that the main woman in his life is his mother.

Screenwriter Ernest Lehman specifically made Thornhill an ad man because he wanted a character whose life was centered around deception. We see that he is deceptive as he leaves his office with his secretary, Maggie (Doreen Land), on his way to a business luncheon. Without a moment's thought, he steals a cab from a man by claiming that his secretary is ill and he needs to get her to a hospital. Maggie is uncomfortable with him lying. "Ah, Maggie," he says, "in the world of advertising, there's no such thing as a lie. There's only the expedient exaggeration. You ought to know that." Thornhill smiles like a naughty boy as he says this.

Thornhill tells Maggie that he intends to drink martinis at lunch and he expects that his mother will sniff his breath for alcohol when she sees him later. This is the first of many references to Thornhill's drinking habits. Thornhill apologizes for arriving late to his lunch meeting, but he assures the others that the head start they've gotten with their cocktails "won't last long." The cocktails are prominently displayed in the frame. The amber-colored whisky in the glasses catches the light in a way that makes the drinks glow. Hitchcock no doubt wants the drinks to leave an impression.

Thornhill is abducted by spies that have mistaken him for a CIA agent. The spies figure to get rid of Thornhill by filling him with liquor and letting him drive down a dangerous mountain highway. Thornhill amazingly survives the ride, but he is unable to get anyone to believe his story about murderous spies. No one, not even his own mother (Jessie Royce Landis), believes him. Film critic Justin Price wrote, "[H]is mom especially is skeptical because of his propensity for drink and history of stretching the truth."[12] We now see the way that his flaws can work against him. Thornhill's childish ways prevent others from taking him seriously. But, as the man-child film works, these bad ways are bound to change. Film director and Hitchcock fan Christopher McQuarrie said, "You're watching a man learn responsibility in his life and, over the course of the film, [he] comes to the point where he's willing to sacrifice his own life for someone else's [life]."[13] He is willing to sacrifice his life for family and country. He is especially protective of CIA operative Eve Kendall (Eva Marie Saint), to whom he proposes marriage while he rescues her from a precarious cliff edge. We are distinctly reminded of the United States' interests at the film's climax, when Thornhill and Kendall engage in a deadly showdown with the foreign spies against the backdrop of the Mount Rushmore National Memorial.

Brett McKay wrote in his essay "Where Does Manhood Come From?," "Men who lived the code, men who were good at being men, gladly chose a potentially shorter life full of risk, danger, excitement, adventure, and glory over a life that was longer and safer but infinitely duller. Thus when a modern man evinces a casual indifference to prolonging his life, we instinctually feel he'd be the kind of guy we'd want on our team when guarding the perimeter—the kind of man who'd run towards the danger instead of seeking out the safest place to hide."[14] Pulver spends most of the film hiding from danger, which makes him the opposite of Roberts. But, to our joy, Pulver is still alive at the end. The character's survival allowed him to be the central character of the film's sequel.

Another seaman who allowed his obsession with revenge to send him to a watery grave was *Moby Dick*'s Captain Ahab. If Roberts was Ahab, then Pulver was Ishmael. Jack Murnighan, the author of *Beowulf on the Beach: What to Love and What to Skip in Literature's 50 Greatest Hits*, wrote,

> [T]he narrator, Ishmael, is an irreverent wisecracker, forever making jokes at the expense of landlubbers, society, religion, his fellow sailors and himself. He's a terrible shipmate, falls asleep on watch in the crow's nest, is always about to tumble overboard, generally gets in the way of the killing of the whales, and is invariably more involved in his own ruminations than in the spume and storm around him. Ishmael is like Shakespeare's clowns: equal part comedian and tragedian, philosopher and cutup, always ready with the barbed aside or incisive aphorism.[15]

Ishmael is the only member of Ahab's crew who survives the battle with the great white whale. Maybe the fool is no fool. Courage alone does not signify manliness. It is more important for a man to have wisdom to foresee when a course of action will doom himself and others.

Other films of the 1950s interestingly explored the issue of immaturity. In *The Ladykillers* (1955), a gang of ruthless criminals plot a heist at a quiet boardinghouse. The guilty men behave like naughty boys in the presence of the stern and unsuspecting little old lady who owns the home. They live in abject fear of this mother figure learning of their mischief. At one point, they hang their heads like truant children when the little old lady scolds them for bad behavior. In the end, greed and distrust turn the criminals into petty children and lead them into a deadly squabble. The film makes it clear that criminals are poorly developed, dysfunctional adults. They are children in adult bodies, which makes them dangerous. As Rousseau said, an adult possesses strength that needs to be curbed.

Jacques Tati's popular alter ego, Mr. Hulot, is in every sense a child. We can see this clearly in *Mon Oncle* (1958). He is dreamy, frivolous and, most of all, unemployed. He has never reached the higher stages of psychosocial development, including intimacy and industry. His sister and her husband put pressure on him to marry and get a job. His brother-in-law gets him a job in a factory that manufactures plastic hose. Of course, he fails dismally at the task.

Tati had no interest in plots or dialogue, which he felt interfered with his comedy. He produced loosely connected gag sequences enhanced by music and sound effects. Tati was influenced by silent film comedians, including Charlie Chaplin, Buster Keaton and Harold Lloyd, but he did not follow their example in relation to plot elements, including character development and conflict resolution. The goals and obstacles in his films are small and fleeting. Tati chose to focus on gags and routines rather than story. Film critic Roger Ebert wrote, "Hulot doesn't find himself starving, hanging from clock faces, besotted with romance or in the middle of a war, but simply puttering away at life, genial and courteous, doing what he can to negotiate the hurdles of civilization."[16] Hulot's sister says outright, "What my brother needs is an objective." But Ebert disagreed with this assessment, writing, "[An objective] is precisely what Hulot does not need. He simply needs to be left alone to meander and appreciate, without going anywhere or having anywhere to go."[17] Meandering is all that can be accomplished by comedians who reject plot and character development, as we have seen with Abbott and Costello and the Three Stooges. Meandering is what children do. Like a child, Hulot observes the world with great curiosity and frequent bewilderment. He studies other people in an effort to conform to social norms. The whole time, he shows no self-consciousness.

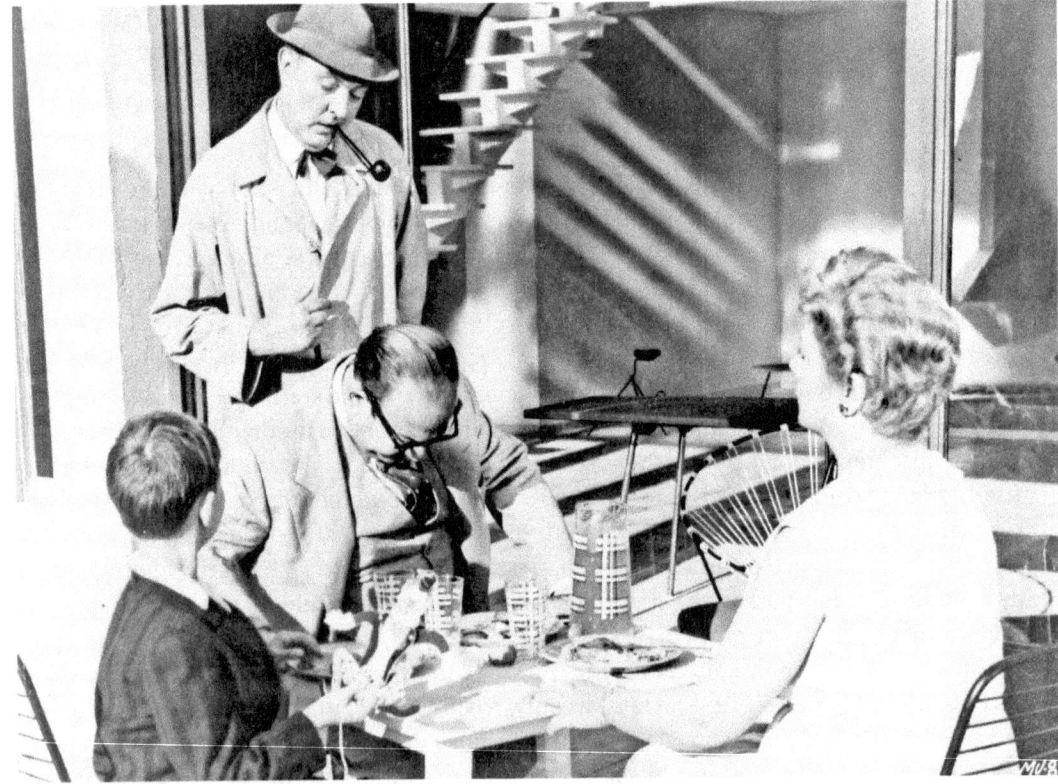

Jacques Tati cannot adapt to family life in *Mon Oncle* (1958). The other actors in this scene are, from left to right, Alain Bécourt, Jean-Pierre Zola and Adrienne Servantie.

Jürgen Martschukat of Germany's Erfurt University examined the post-war American man in "Men in Gray Flannel Suits: Troubling Masculinities in 1950s America." He focused attention on Tom Rath, the main character of Sloan Wilson's novel *The Man in the Gray Flannel Suit*: "Tom perfectly incorporated the 1950s' male dilemma of opposite demands. On the one hand, he lived his life according to the familial imperatives of the postwar world, and yet, on the other hand, he was grayish, conformist, not in control of his own existence, subordinated, and consequently considered 'no man at all' (Gerald Weales, 'Life in Modern America')."[18] Martschukat wrote in reference to the film version of Sloan's novel, "Betsy complains about her husband having lost his drive and his self-determination. She wants a good father for her children, a good provider, and 'a real man' at the same time. In one of their countless debates she gets to the point by saying, 'I wanted you to go out and fight for something *again*—like the man I married [before the war]. Not to turn into a cheap, slippery yes-man.'"[19] A dichotomy no doubt existed. Martschukat wrote, "[T]his hegemonic white middle-class man had to be a family man who at the same time was willing and able to take his life into his own hands—a man who was caring and responsible as well as free and forward-moving."[20]

Men desperately wanted to have something else in their lives. Hugh Hefner understood men's fantasies. Martschukat wrote, "*Playboy* nourished the dream of owning a fast sports car instead of a station wagon, of living in an urban skyscraper playboy penthouse instead of a suburban ranch-style family home, of wearing elegant silk instead of gray flannel, and of loving pretty young bunnies instead of their wives."[21]

A man who influenced men as much as Hefner was John F. Kennedy. Martschukat wrote,

> Kennedy took the American public by storm by uniting the seemingly antagonistic masculine stereotypes. After the Democratic Convention at Los Angeles in July 1960, author Norman Mailer was stunned and boasted that "superman comes to the supermarket." Kennedy blemished the "softness" and "corrosion" of the 1950s consumer society, and he demanded a revitalization of the American "pilgrim and pioneer spirit of initiative and independence." He generated himself as forward marching, powerful, and energetic explorer with, according to Mailer, "savvy and go-go-go," and he was a womanizer par excellence. At the same time, JFK presented himself as family man, as husband of a beautiful wife and as father of two wonderful children, playing in the Oval Office of the White House while father was taking America to new frontiers.[22]

American literary scholar Morris Dickstein described maturity as "the albatross of the postwar generation."[23] A new type of man was introduced in highly acclaimed novels of the period, including *The Adventures of Augie March, On the Road, Catcher in the Rye* and *Rabbit, Run*. These men, which the *New York Times*' A.O. Scott described as "a new crop of semi-antiheroes in flight from convention, propriety [and] authority,"[24] behaved impulsively, indecisively and promiscuously. Was this new freedom a good thing? Take, for instance, *On the Road*'s Dean Moriarty. Ross Posnock, a professor of American literature at Columbia University, observed of this character, "In his openness and immunity to inhibition, Dean's consciousness is rapturous, pure, sensuous receptivity. But, finally, for all his energy, an air of futility surrounds him, exhausting [his friend] Sal and everyone else. The painful ending, when a desperate Dean arrives impromptu in New York to see his old friend only to be turned away, expresses Kerouac's own unease with Dean's empty freedom."[25]

Comedy films of the 1960s focused on libidinous men as the brave pioneers of the sexual revolution. Confirmed bachelors were free to play the field, but cheating husbands also got in on the girl-chasing action. The indulgence of lustful desire was an effective way for a man to remain unsocialized. Films that displayed this new frontier included *The Apartment* (1960), *Boys' Night Out* (1962), *Come Blow Your Horn* (1963), *Under the Yum Yum Tree* (1963), *Goodbye Charlie* (1964), *How to Murder Your Wife* (1965), *A Guide to a Married Man* (1967), *How to Save Your Marriage and Ruin Your Life* (1968) and *Cactus Flower* (1969).

In *The Secret Life of Walter Mitty* (1947), Danny Kaye was able to use his childlike imagination to create adventure stories for a pulp magazine. In *Artists and Models* (1955), Jerry Lewis used his childlike imagination to create stories for comic books. But men who cling to childish things, even if those childish things afford them a good living, can still come across as faulty and dysfunctional. Surprisingly, this was not the case with the eminent cartoonist at the center of *How to Murder Your Wife* (1965). Stanley Ford (Jack Lemmon) writes and illustrates a popular newspaper comic strip about a secret agent named Bash Brannigan. Instead of having models strike static poses in his studio, Ford has his valet Charles (Terry-Thomas) take photographs while a troupe of actors perform Brannigan's brisk adventures at various locations around New York City. Ford himself plays the role of the glamorous Brannigan. It could certainly be construed as childish for Ford to make use of costumes and props to play-act secret agent fantasies. But let us take a closer look at Ford. He has not embraced the cherished traditions of marriage and family, but he seems in every way self-assured and content. He delights in the bachelor life. He gets all the care and support that he needs from his faithful valet. But all of that changes when he attends a bachelor party and becomes smitten by a beautiful stripper (Virna Lisi). After getting drunk, he goes off with the stripper and marries her. It isn't long after they have exchanged vows that he turns into a fat and miserable husband, referring to himself as a "hen-pecked boob." He becomes disgusted with himself and infuriated by the situation. He disputes marriage being a normal way of life: "Marriage is not a basic fact of nature. It is an invention." He sees no value in a man having a wife, insisting, "Too long has the American male allowed himself to be bullied, coddled, mothered, tyrannized and, in general, made to feel like a feeble-minded idiot by the female of the species." The film was written by George Axelrod, the author of *The Seven Year Itch*. This time, Axelrod was more open about his disdain for marriage.

The shortcomings of marriage would remain an issue decades later in *Old School* (2003). Bernard Campbell (Vince Vaughn) resents his wife, who he sees as judgmental and controlling. He is even less happy with the concept of monogamy. He sounds defeated when he grumbles to his friends, "You get only one vagina for the rest of your life." In *The Hangover* (2009), Phil Wenneck (Bradley Cooper) complains a great deal about the responsibilities that he has as a husband and father. He expresses this at first during the drive to Las Vegas.

PHIL WENNECK: Look, I left my wife and kid at home so I could go with you guys to Vegas. Do you know how difficult that was?
ALAN GARNER: That's really sweet, Phil.
DOUG BILLINGS: Yeah.
PHIL WENNECK: Dude, I was being sarcastic. I fucking hate my life. I may never go back. I might just stay in Vegas.

These husbands are just as angry about marriage as Lemmon was in *How to Murder Your Wife*.

In Billy Wilder's *The Apartment* (1960), Bud Baxter (Lemmon, again) works as an anonymous clerk in a massive insurance company. Like Harold Lloyd in *Safety Last*, he is desperate to stand out from the crowd and advance in the company. But Baxter has no opportunity to perform a spectacular climb up a building. He has found a different way to gain favor with his immediate superiors: He routinely loans out his apartment to the men for extramarital affairs. It is an obvious irony that, to climb the social ladder, he must descend to filthy depths. Lemmon recognized this point very clearly. He said, "I always felt that Billy Wilder grew a rose in a garbage pail with this one."[26]

Fran (Shirley MacLaine), who operates the elevator in the building, is having an affair with personnel manager J.D. Sheldrake (Fred MacMurray). On Christmas Eve, she accompanies Sheldrake to Baxter's apartment. She is despondent because Sheldrake will not commit to leaving his wife for her. After Sheldrake leaves Baxter's apartment, Fran attempts suicide by swallowing a bottle of sleeping pills. When Baxter returns home, he finds her passed out on his bed. He tries to wake her, but she won't respond. Then he finds the empty sleeping pill bottle beside her and he realizes what she has done. He rushes into the hallway to find his neighbor, Dr. Drey-

Jack Lemmon is sorry that he lent his apartment key to his boss (Fred MacMurray) for an illicit affair in *The Apartment* (1960) (courtesy www.doctormacro.com).

fuss (Jack Kruschen). He desperately pounds on Dreyfuss' door. When the doctor answers, Baxter grabs him by the shirt and tells him that a girl in his place has taken sleeping pills and he can't wake her up.

Dreyfuss has continually overheard the executives' sexual exploits through the wall and has assumed that all of this commotion came from Baxter trying to satisfy a monstrous sexual appetite, and assumes that it was Baxter's mistreatment of Fran that drove her to attempt suicide. He feels obligated to vehemently denounce this lady-killer. He tells him, "Why don't you grow up, Baxter? Be a mensch! You know what that means? A mensch—a human being!"

Being an adult is about being a human being. The executive are not human beings. Their shallowness and uncontrolled appetites make them bratty children dressed up in tailored business suits. They do not feel the slightest bit of guilt or shame. How can they possibly call themselves human? It makes it worse that these immoral men are childishly gleeful about their naughty escapades. No one conveys that childishness better than Ray Walston, who plays Administration manager Joe Dobisch. At one point, Dobisch lets out a giddy laugh as he tells Baxter that his latest pick-up looks like Marilyn Monroe. He is so excited at the prospect of getting this woman into bed that he can barely contain himself. It is worth pointing out that Dobisch, whose uncontrolled appetites also led him to drink to excess, is in a blotto state when we first meet him. It has to be difficult for Dobisch to wipe the sozzled naughty boy smirk off his face whenever he has to return home to his wife.

Fran looks like a frightened child when Baxter tells her that Sheldrake is on the phone and he wants to talk to her. Baxter senses her nervousness and decides that he should give her privacy. He places the phone on the table and excuses himself to go to the store. Wilder frames the scene so that the phone is in the foreground as Fran slowly approaches it. This forced perspective trick makes Fran look like a child in comparison to the phone, which appears much larger than it really is. (The ominous phone in the foreground trick was spoofed in Zucker, Abrahams and Zucker's *Top Secret!* [1984], in which the phone surprisingly turns out to be as large as it looks.)

Fran finally takes hold of the receiver and presses it to her ear. Sheldrake does not hesitate to scold her. "Why did you do it, Fran?" he asks. "It's so childish and it never solves anything. I ought to be very angry with you, scaring me that way." He has assumed the tone of a stern father to outright accuse Fran of being a child. The truth is that everyone playing a role in this sordid affair is childish.

The only models of maturity in the film are Dr. Dreyfuss and his wife Mildred (Naomi Stevens). Dr. Dreyfuss is honest, humane, upright, and competent. We see much less of his wife, but she clearly shares her husband's virtues. Baxter is surprised to find that Mrs. Dreyfuss is aware of Fran's suicide attempt. She tells Baxter, "From me the doctor has no secrets." This is an interesting line of dialogue as so many people in the film have secrets. When Sheldrake arranged the tryst, he was extremely cautious about keeping the matter confidential. "Now remember, Baxter," he said, "this is going to be our little secret."

Baxter is no manly figure when the story begins. He is too meek and too compliant. But, still, Lemmon projects an appealing vulnerability that makes the audience care about the character and hope that he will become stronger as the story progresses. This is, in fact, what happens. Baxter changes as he becomes intimate with Fran and helps her to recover from her drug overdose. He dedicates himself to protecting Fran from Sheldrake even though it means standing up to Sheldrake and quitting his job. He comes to display honor and compassion, qualities that ultimately show him to be a fine and well-developed adult.

The sex comedies continued throughout the decade. In *Boys' Night Out* (1962), Cathy (Kim Novak) is a sociology student writing a doctoral thesis titled "Adolescent Sexual Fantasies in the Adult Suburban Male." She takes a job as a housekeeper for four businessmen who have taken to sharing a midtown apartment for potential assignations. The four men each try to seduce the beautiful housekeeper, but she is able to deftly deflect their advances. It doesn't matter much to these inhibited men, who are more interested in having a kept woman who is understanding and will listen to them talk about their problems. The film is *The Apartment* without the sex.

It is odd that, three years after making *The Apartment*, Lemmon starred in the smutty sex comedy *Under the Yum Yum Tree* (1963). The film is, in many ways, the anti–*Apartment*; it's the type of film that Ray Walston's giddy, sex-crazed Joe Dobisch would have made if he ever got out to Hollywood. Lemmon plays a swinging bachelor landlord named Hogan, who only rents apartments to lovely single women, who he has every intention of seducing. In the film's trailer, the announcer describes Hogan as "the love-happy landlord who specializes in luscious tenants." A blogger at Crazy for Cinema was more blunt, calling the character "a pathetic shell of hormones."[27] *New York Times* critic Bosley Crowther wrote, "[T]he whole thing is in faintly malodorous taste. [Lemmon has] got to be lovable but lecherous, innocent but full of guile, comical but rapacious, a Peter Pan and a Peeping Tom." Lemmon was later embarrassed to have made the film. He said, "I was unhappy with myself and the character, a lecherous nut who acted more like a leering kid than a grown man." This role is especially shallow when compared to Lemmon's sensitive character in *The Apartment*.

New ideas of maturity were taking hold in the 1960s. *A Hard Day's Night* (1964) showed its protagonists as being delightfully young and free. Among the film's iconic images was the image of cool rock star John Lennon playing with a toy boat in the bath. This was a revelation: An adult could play with toys and remain an admirable and glamorous figure. It was an even more appealing notion that an adult could find comfort from the stresses of this new world by playing with toys.

The Producers (1968) introduces us to a mismatched pair of men, neither of whom has a wife or children or expresses the least interest in a wife or children. Are these men immature? Leo Bloom (Gene Wilder), a high-strung accountant who settles his nerves by pressing a little blue blanket to his cheek, certainly does not come across as mature. Max Bialystock (Zero Mostel) is a washed-up, aging Broadway producer who romances wealthy old women for financing. He is hardly mature. The story offers the men no love interests with whom they can become intimate. Bialystock no longer cares about intimacy, generativity, or integrity. He is a bitter man who only cares about money, which can bring him security and pleasure. The only two woman prominent in the film are a frisky 84-year-old dowager (Estelle Winwood) and a tall, gorgeous Scandinavian blonde secretary (Lee Meredith). Meredith, who has much more screen time than Winwood, is nothing more than a sex object from an adolescent's daydream. This type of woman is often the focus of the man-child. We have already seen her in *The Seven Year Itch* and *Hollywood or Bust* and we will see her again in *The Heartbreak Kid* (1972) and *10* (1979). Writer-director Mel Brooks said that Max was the Id and Leo was the Ego. Maturity is provided by the Superego, which Brooks left out of this partnership.

The protagonist of *The Heartbreak Kid*, Lenny Cantrow (Charles Grodin), sets out on his honeymoon doubting his decision to marry needy and unsophisticated Lila (Jeannie Berlin). Through charm, deceit and determination, he manages before the honeymoon ends to leave his newlywed wife for another woman (Cybill Shepherd). It goes without saying that Lenny is a self-absorbed man-child whose actions are impulsive and reckless. Not surprisingly, he seems at his most comfortable when he is sitting at a kid's table at his wedding and conversing with a group of children. Jake Cole of Spectrum Culture wrote, "*The Heartbreak Kid* serves as a blistering response to *The Graduate*. Nichols intended Benjamin Braddock to be the subject of critique, but the lad emerged sympathetic enough to became a rallying point for the sort of nebbishy, entitled post-grad he was meant to spoof. May does not leave room for misunderstanding. Charles Grodin's Lenny is an oblivious, repellent mess of a human being who unfailingly mistakes his id for his superego."[28]

The same year, *Play It Again, Sam* (1972) presented another nebbish man-child in search of the perfect mate. But this young man, Allan Felix (Woody Allen), was less repellent than Lenny. Allan feels out of his depth in the dating world and fears that he is not masculine enough to attract a woman. Like Sherman of *The Seven Year Itch*, he finds himself preoccupied by sexual fantasies. He has even more than this in common with Sherman. At one point, Sherman envisioned his wife sitting on a chair across from him. She laughed derisively at his fantasies and expressed disbelief that the women in his fantasies would find him attractive in real life. "You're attractive to me," she said, "but of course I'm used to you." In much the same way, Felix is pestered by visions of his ex-wife Nancy (Susan Anspach), who does nothing but mock Felix for his sexual inadequacies. Trying to overcome his insecurity with women, Felix looks to Hollywood for a model of masculinity. He imagines Humphrey Bogart, who he sees as "a perfect image." Felix depends heavily on this imaginary father figure to help him to navigate through the tricky adult world of dating. But he doesn't find love until he finally stops emulating Bogart and learns to be himself. The problem is that he finds love with his best friend's wife, Linda (Diane Keaton). Consumed with guilt, he doesn't know what to do. In the end, Felix finds that Bogart can still be useful to him as a role model. He uses Bogart's closing speech from *Casablanca* to convince Linda to return to her husband.

Television was competing with films during this period, presenting Baby Boomers with many childlike characters: Ralph Kramden, Gomer Pyle, Jethro Bodine, Maxwell Smart, Herman Munster, and Mork. These were simple characters to whom children could relate.

The best shorthand to indicate that a character was childlike was to show the person sleeping with a teddy bear. It was done with Radar O'Reilly on *M*A*S*H* and Rowan

Atkinson's Mr. Bean. Despite his perennial teddy bear, Mr. Bean is more bizarre than childlike. At a department store, he plays mischievously with the figurines in a Nativity scene. He eventually brings into the scene other toy figures, including a plastic Tyrannosaurus that attempts to eat Baby Jesus. Fortunately, this impromptu playtime does come to a happy conclusion: Mr. Bean brings along toy tanks just in time to shoot down the toothy beast. Then he has a battery-operated helicopter airlift the sacred infant to the safety and comfort of a Barbie Dreamhouse.

The Television Tropes & Idioms website identified many other childlike characters on television. The site points out that Lenny and Squiggy from *Laverne and Shirley* "often do childish things like drinking chocolate syrup and watching cartoons."[29] Spencer, a character on *iCarly*, according to the website, makes "whimsical and sometimes weird sculptures that usually end up catching on fire or exploding before being perfected. He loves light-up socks, has a pet goldfish (that he often forgets to feed, resulting in another pet goldfish), and once went to law school for three days."[30] Tom Baker's Doctor Who (The Fourth Doctor) "offers everyone sweets, plays with children's toys, doodles cartoons of people he dislikes, loves playing and running around and getting attention, [and] tends to sulk when he can't get his way.... He absolutely detests authority and is willing to go anywhere, do anything to avoid taking orders...."[31] Vince in *The Mighty Boosh* "is constantly eating sweets, writes in crayon and has an imaginary friend made out of bubble-gum called Charlie."[32]

By the 1970s, the rejection of adulthood was no longer seen as a dysfunctional act. Being an adult meant living a conventional life, which was repressive and boring. This bred disdain for older models of maturity. At the time, a person could inspire admiration for successfully avoiding the burdens and grief of adult life. Comedy of the 1970s was largely presented by the young, who made a point to mock the values of their elders.

Remember the University of Michigan's 1957 self-perception survey, which was discussed earlier? Joseph Veroff, a research scientist at the Institute for Social Research, initiated a project to follow up to the 1957 University of Michigan self-perception survey in 1976. In an effort to trace the changes in American values, he arranged for a matched sample to be asked the very same questions that the original sample had been asked. The changes they found were extensive. The study showed a relaxation of the traditional definitions of work, marriage, parenthood and self.[33] Society was changing.

Anti-establishment youth could enjoy a film like *Lifeguard* (1976). R. Emmet Sweeney examined this film's anti-establishment message in his article "The Outsiders":

> Rick (Sam Elliott) is an aging well-tanned lothario, closing in on a decade-long career as a lifeguard. While all his old friends have become salesman of insurance or luxury cars, he still spends his days at the beach and his nights with stewardesses. He has successfully avoided the responsibilities and stresses of adult life, content with staring at the ocean instead of his bank account. His apartment is a bachelor pad par excellence, festooned with surf posters and shag carpet, while he spends his free time on the highway in his Corvette Stingray. His parents fret about when he will settle down and stop wasting his life.... *Lifeguard* is an understated and wise film about the rejection of adulthood. Director Daniel Petrie lets the story develop its own shaggy tempo, and elicits a grounded, engaging performance from Elliott. He exudes a bodily calm, his gestures an extension of his surfer-Buddhist ethos."[34]

Rick is like Mr. Belvedere, who cherished solitude and self-improvement and found that it was more important to find inner peace than engage in the chaos of family life.

Young people rebelled against the gender roles that society prescribed for them and, in their minds, this rebellion would allow them to fully express their desires and realize their true selves. A man needs to strive to find form and definition, but this sort of self-development can have the unwanted effect of diminishing his natural powers. Posnock wrote, "Maturity is ... artifice—to be a man is to imitate being a man—a coerced condition produced by the social imperative of adaptation."[35] Peter Christopher Kunze wrote in his essay "The Tears of a Clown: Masculinity and Comedy in Contemporary American Narratives," "Scholars of masculinity contend that men now are starting to see masculinity as an unattainable ideal that restricts, oppresses, and frustrates them.... [Comedy] functions as a viable way for men to redirect and sublimate the fear, anxiety, and anger they experience as men."[36]

Had the time come to laugh off the traditional ideals of masculinity?

7

Forever Young

Filmmakers of the 1970s presented without shame overt examples of the manchild. It wasn't difficult for overindulged Baby Boomers to relate to characters who were hesitant to leave behind the security and comfort of childhood.

The maladroit and pampered rich man, previously on display in *The Navigator* and *Battling Butler*, continued into the 1970s with *A New Leaf* (1971). This is even a darker look at the subject than *Battling Butler*. Indolent trust fund playboy Henry Graham (Walter Matthau) has run through his entire inheritance. He has never cared about work or intimate relationships. He admits that he has no skills or ambitions to establish himself in a career and provide for himself. He says, "All I am, or was, is rich, and that's all I ever wanted to be." He is dependent on his valet, Harold (George Rose), who tries his best to be Henry's moral conscience even as he takes care of his master's physical needs. When Henry kneels on a broken wine glass, Harold is there with tweezers and a magnifying glass to meticulously pluck out every last shard of glass.

Henry decides to marry a rich woman and then murder her to inherit her money. He realizes that he has found the perfect victim when he encounters the clumsy and socially inept Henrietta Lowell (Elaine May).

On the wedding day, Henry is so fearful of walking down the aisle that he can't move his legs. As guests gather at his home for the wedding, he becomes upset to see a young girl examining one of his abstract art pieces. He shrieks to his valet, "I will not have her touching my things." He worries that, once he and Henrietta move in together, she will be touching his things, too. He rages as he falls down on his bed and kicks out his legs. It seems that, at any moment, he will burst out in tears. This is a child having a tantrum. His valet tries to comfort him, explaining that he and his wife will learn to share things. "I don't want to share things!" he shouts.

The marriage is not as terrible as Henry expected. He finds in Henrietta a person even more helpless than he is and, surprisingly, he comes to enjoy taking care of her. Before she leaves the house, he makes sure to brush off the crumbs from her last meal and cut off any price tags that may be dangling from her latest outfit. Harold observes that, in coping with her helplessness, Henry has shown himself to be a competent spouse. It makes Henry feel good to be useful and causes him to abandon his plans to kill Henrietta. To the contrary, he rescues his bride from drowning just as Keaton once saved his bride-to-be in *Steamboat Bill, Jr.* In the closing moments of the film, Henrietta makes a loving and tender appeal for Henry to teach history at the local college. Henry thinks about it and he seems to like the idea. His transformation from bratty child to productive adult is complete. It simply took Henry learning to care for another person and finding a purpose in life. This represents Erikson's intimacy and generativity stages.

Significantly, the marriage remains unconsummated at the film's end. Throughout their marriage, husband and wife have slept in separate beds and they have never gotten physically intimate with one another. This arrangement is, by every indication, acceptable to both parties.

In the wedding scene, when it came time for Henry to exchange vows with Henrietta, he was ready to call off the ceremony because he feared that Henrietta would fall into the habit of touching his things. Without getting too Freudian, it sounds like he really fears his new wife touching one particular *thing*. Harold is trying to calm Henry and get him dressed. Then, just as Henry falls back on his bed, the girl who was touching his abstract art piece suddenly enters the room. "Oh," she exclaims, "I thought this was the bathroom!" Henry becomes even more upset. He shouts that he will not get dressed in front of a woman. He goes into a rant. He calls the little girl a "spy," and bellows, "This is what it will be like, isn't it, Harold? She'll be everywhere, touching things, poking her nose into where it doesn't belong, pretending that she's looking for the bathroom." The girl has become a stand-in for his wife-to-be. In his mind, she has come into his bedroom on false pretenses so that she can catch him half-dressed in bed.

We are not given the slightest indication that this wealthy single man has ever cared at all about dating women until he came up with his marriage scheme. A friend tells him, "You know, Henry, I never thought you were terribly interested in women." His first date is with Sharon Hart (Renée Taylor), the rich widow of a cattle baron. Sharon is not unattractive. They lounge beside a pool in her backyard. Sharon declares to Henry the importance of sexual desire. She is about to remove her bathing suit top when Henry panics. "No," he screams, "don't let them out!" He runs off into the woods, where he falls into a poison ivy bush and contracts a bumpy, inflamed rash as a result. The rash, which resulted from his running away from a sexual encounter, is in a way a sexually transmitted disease.

The title character of *Arthur* (1981), Arthur Bach (Dudley Moore), is a mirthful, drunken playboy who regularly makes a spectacle of himself in public. His loving valet, Hobson (John Gielgud), is careful to look after him and keep him safe and content. He reminds Arthur to wash under his arms and sit up straight. He smacks him in the back of the head whenever he needs a sharp reminder to behave himself. Arthur's room is decorated with children's toys: a basketball, model cars, a train set, and a rocking horse. He sings a children's song, "Santa Claus Is Coming to Town," while he takes a bath. *New York Times* critic Vincent Canby referred to the Arthur character as "a sprite."[1] But he's not an impossible creature like Harry Langdon's Little Elf. The film succeeds in creating sentiment because, no matter how silly he acts, Arthur remains a believable human being.

Arthur's family, desperate for him to grow up, pressures him into marrying a dull socialite, Susan Johnson (Jill Eikenberry). He meets with Susan's father, Burt Johnson (Stephen Elliott), who insists that Arthur come to work for him after he marries. This means that Arthur will, in one day, gain a wife and a job. His family leaves him with no

Walter Matthau is terrified at the prospect of marriage in *A New Leaf* (1971), but marrying a shy and clumsy heiress (Elaine May) is the only way that he can maintain his extravagant lifestyle after depleting his family fortune.

choice. His grandmother, Martha Bach (Geraldine Fitzgerald), tells him, "You're too old to be poor. You don't know how." This is similar to Henry Graham saying that he didn't know how to be anything other than rich. Arthur's father, Stanford Bach (Thomas Barbour), does not temper his words. He tells Arthur, "You are the weakest man I have ever known. I despise your weakness."

Arthur shows signs of maturity once he falls in love with a waitress, Linda Marolla (Liza Minnelli). She accepts him for the way he is. She enjoys herself when Arthur takes her to a game arcade on their first date. This, again, represents the protagonist achieving intimacy.

Dudley Moore plays a drunken millionaire in *Arthur* (1981).

A turning point of the film occurs when Arthur learns that Hobson is fatally ill. When Hobson is hospitalized, Arthur lavishes him with a variety of toy store gifts. It is hardly practical for Arthur to give a dying old man a basketball and a toy train, but the items do lighten Hobson's mood for a bit. The inevitable death of Hobson completes Arthur's transformation, spurring him to stand on his own two feet and make his own decisions.

Arthur's father, grandmother and Susan's father have bullied Arthur into showing up at the church to marry Susan, but Arthur decides to stand up to them. Mr. Johnson, a man devoid of compassion and understanding, wallops Arthur in an alcove of this solemn cathedral. Linda throws herself in front of Mr. Johnson to stop him from hurting her man. But Mr. Johnson is not going to be stopped. He roars, "Is this the slut that you disgraced my daughter for?" Arthur steps forward to defend Linda against the insult. This is the moment for Arthur to fight back and tear apart this person who has been bullying him. Buster Keaton did it in *Battling Butler*. Harold Lloyd did it in *Grandma's Boy*. But Arthur only gets beaten even more badly for his effort. Having heard the ruckus, Arthur's grandmother bursts into the room. She is not as passive as Lloyd's grandmother in *Grandma's Boy*. She smacks Mr. Johnson in the face. "Don't screw with me, Burt," she tells him.

In the end, Grandmother can't bear the idea of a member of her family being poor. She consents that, as long as Arthur is willing to produce children to carry on the family name, he can marry Linda and keep his fortune. He doesn't need to change at all. This ending may have seemed silly at the time, but it was in fact a bold statement: hedonism is good, adulthood is bad. The 2011 remake didn't dare end in this way. The new Arthur (Russell Brand) ends up devoting his time and energy to managing a charity.

Astoundingly, the Arthur character became even more childish in the remake. The original film opened with Arthur inviting a prostitute into his limousine. The remake opened with Arthur dressed up as Batman and driving around in a costly reproduction of the Batmobile.

Other "Arthur types" turn up in modern comedy films even though the comic valets are virtually extinct. A man-child does not have to be as rich as Arthur to live a life of leisure. In *Big Daddy* (1999), Adam Sandler subsists on a generous settlement that he was awarded for a minor injury that he suffered when a cab ran over his foot. In *About a Boy* (2002), Hugh Grant is able to live off royalties from a successful Christmas song that his deceased father composed. In *Knocked Up* (2007), Seth Rogen lives off funds that he received as compensation for an unnamed injury.

It makes perfect sense for the man-child comedy to feature a bride at some point in the story. To a man, a bride represents intimacy, commitment and responsibility. In *Run, Fatboy, Run* (2007), Dennis Doyle (Simon Pegg) has a panic attack while in his bedroom getting dressed for his wedding. His anxiety is especially high as the lovely bride-to-be, Libby, is in an advanced stage of pregnancy. Dennis sprawls out on the bed. He sweats profusely. He bangs his head on the floor. He mumbles incessantly to himself, "I don't wanna, I don't wanna!" This infantile refusal cannot be mistaken for healthy youthful rebellion. Unfortunately, he has no valet to calm him. Finally, he climbs out a window and flees the premises. Dennis later realizes that he should have confronted his fears rather than run away. He must learn courage and perseverance if he wants to be accepted as an adult. He decides to prove himself to Libby and son Jake (Matthew Fenton), now five years old, by running in a marathon. Dennis continues in the race even after he injures his leg. He falls to the ground as he nears the finish line, but he sees Libby and Jake calling out to him from the finish line and this inspires him to stand up and conclude the race. This is similar to the climax of *Battling Butler* except here the protagonist must battle his own pain and exhaustion rather than a bullying foe. Films are visual, which means that obstacles are often expressed in a tangible form. A character's fears and hindrances can come across clearly if externalized in the form of a bully or rival. But Dennis' romantic rival, Whit (Hank Azaria), is not relevant to the climax. Dennis has already beaten out Whit, who collapsed from exhaustion early in the race.

The promotional material for *The Longest Week* (2014) refers to protagonist Conrad Valmont (Jason Bateman) as "affluent and aimless." Film critic Nathan Rabin described the character as a "quasi-intellectual, quasi-artistic playboy leading a life happily devoid of substance and actual accomplishments."[2] Conrad is a 40-year-old man who has never done a day's work in his entire life. The one thing that Conrad takes seriously is his psychotherapy sessions with Dr. Barry (Tony Roberts). He claims to suffer from separation anxiety, abandonment issues, and an inferiority complex. But his mental ills do not stop him from enjoying sex with a steady stream of beautiful young women. Conrad's greatest confidante other than his psychiatrist is his chauffeur Bernard (Barry Primus), who functions to an extent as the valet of *Battling Butler* and other past comic valets.

Problems arise when Conrad's aloof and largely absent parents abruptly evict their useless son from his hotel suite and cut off his financial resources. Conrad moves in with his friend Dylan (Billy Crudup), hoping that he can figure a way out of his predicament. But he never focuses for too long on possible solutions. He instead falls in love with Dylan's new girlfriend, Beatrice (Olivia Wilde). He keeps the relationship secret from Dylan, who unknowingly furnishes Conrad with money to take Beatrice on dates, and he desperately conceals from Beatrice the fact that he is broke. Conrad can imagine spending the rest of his life with Beatrice. He has come to the conclusion that, at 40, it is time for him to "ease into adulthood." It is inevitable, though, that his lies will be exposed and he will have to face the consequences. Beatrice is furious to learn that Conrad has been lying to her. She tells him, "You have just managed to coast through life without worrying about money or anything else pertaining to reality. You are just a philandering narcissist who is so afraid of being alone because, when you are alone, you going to realize how empty your life is."

In *Battling Butler*, Keaton never had to confront his wife about his deception. He never had to respond to accusations that he coasted through life, avoided reality, and led an empty existence. But it doesn't matter. Though those accusations may have applied to him in the opening parlor scene of the film, they no longer applied in the final scene of the film. He has proven his love, faithfulness and grit, which is all that should matter to his wife. In contrast, Conrad never takes action to prove himself and, worse, he acts childishly when Beatrice finally confronts him. Rather than tell her he loves her and admit that he was wrong, he lashes out at her, telling her that all she ever cared about was his money. This is the real reason that Beatrice becomes furious with him.

Conrad's parents restore their son to his old status after a week. Conrad has the opportunity to return to his old indolent ways, but his sad and bitter breakup with Beatrice prompts him to pursue his lifelong dream of becoming a novelist. To redeem himself with Dylan and Beatrice, he reunites the couple by sending each of them a ticket to the same social event. Conrad believes that being without money for a week entirely changed his perspective on life and caused him to appreciate his wealth. He achieves success as an author and finds pride and satisfaction in himself. The narrator says at the film's close, "At the ripe old age of 42, Conrad Valmont is finally growing up."

Delayed gratification means resisting a small, immediate reward in order to receive a larger and more enduring one at a later time. College students must learn to delay gratification. At times, they must set aside youthful play for serious study so that they will eventually earn a degree and be able to pursue a desirable career. But the fraternity slobs of *National Lampoon's Animal House* (1978) do not possess self-discipline and do not know how to delay gratification. Michael Arbeiter, staff writer of Hollywood.com, wrote in "A History of Slackers in Movies" that *Animal House* "was one of the earlier movies to not only not demonize, but to actually celebrate the ideas of debauchery, laziness and rejection of all things otherwise. The faculty, ambitious students, and the military were all villainized in this light of slacker appreciation. And the heroes didn't even turn it around in the end. When faced with the penalty of expulsion, they didn't say, 'All right, guys. It's time to pass this final test so we can stay in school,' like so many films prior and since have done. Instead, they just ruined a parade."[3]

The members of the Delta House fraternity are not people that you would enjoy having around in real life. Nathan Rabin of The Dissolve wrote, "[The Deltas] aren't in favor of anything beyond serving their own needs at all times, no matter the consequences...."[4] It was a sign of the times. It didn't matter to the Deltas if other people enjoyed having them around. According to Veroff's study, the growing shift away from social integration meant that people were less concerned with being liked by others.[5]

English satirist Tony Hendra was impressed by John Belushi for his "total commitment"[6] to acting like a "big baby"[7] in *Animal House*. He referred specifically to Belushi falling down and doing nothing right. Hendra believed that comedians strive towards capturing the openness and innocence of children. He said, "[T]he better a comedian is, the more he approaches a childlike state ... a childlike form of behavior, a childlike

English satirist Tony Hendra enjoyed seeing John Belushi act like a "big baby" in *Animal House* (1978) (courtesy www.doctormacro.com).

openness to statement."[8] Belushi was, in his childlike state, rude and crude. Rudeness was wielded by Belushi like a weapon against conformity. Posnock acknowledged that rudeness could be used effectively to oppose "the socializing forces bent on exacting obedience, restraint and repression—basic constituents of mature adulthood."[9]

A less boisterous member of the film's notorious frat house is Boon (Peter Riegert), the one character in the film who experiences conflict. Boon is always eager to have fun with his friends, but his girlfriend Katy (Karen Allen) disapproves of the fraternity's wild and reckless extracurricular activities. Allen said that she very much sympathized with her character, who she realized was just "trying to pull Boon out of that madhouse."[10]

Immaturity is central to the plot of *Being There* (1979). The main character, Chance (Peter Sellers), is a simple-minded middle-aged gardener in a townhouse in Washington, D.C. We learn as the story progresses that, throughout his life, Chance was strictly sheltered within the confines of the townhouse by a reclusive millionaire. The millionaire, who Chance calls "The Old Man," never let Chance leave the home and left him to spend his days watching television and working inside a walled garden plot. The relationship of Chance and "The Old Man," is never clarified. The Old Man dies and the estate lawyers who attend to his property and possessions have no record of Chance's existence. Chance could have been a servant's baby who was adopted in the same way that Mortimer was adopted by the master of the house, Mr. Brewster, in *Arsenic and Old Lace*.

Chance is calm and detached. This, coupled with the fact that he is well-groomed and dresses in the Old Man's tailored suits, makes him seem like a mature and dignified gentleman to people who do not know him. We, the audience, are led to make this same assumption when we are first introduced to him. But his calmness comes from the fact that he is needy and helpless and his dependence on his caretakers has required him to adopt a docile manner. He acts detached because he lacks the maturity to develop close personal relationships. All the viewer needs to know about Chance can be found in an early scene in which Chance becomes transfixed watching a puppet sing on *Sesame Street*.

The estate lawyers inform Chance that they are closing the townhouse and he must pack up his belongings and leave. This means that Chance will need to discover the outside world for the first time. The premise of an ill-prepared young man being forced into the world has been regularly employed by film comedians. For years, it was a favorite premise of Lloyd Hamilton. It is, in fact, an old story that can be traced as far back as Voltaire's 1759 novella *Candide, ou l'Optimisme*. The idea is, without a doubt, a reliable basis for comedy. Within months of the release of *Being There*, it turned up as the premise of two other popular films, *Up in Smoke* and *The Jerk*.

Man needs an extended term of development to adapt to the variability and complexity of adult society. This prolonged period of immaturity and dependency allows him the time to develop into a responsible, moral and skilled individual. But so much can go wrong during these years of development.

Being There was adapted from Jerzy Kosinski's novel. It was established in the novel that Chance was largely raised by Louise, the Old Man's black cook. In the film, Louise approaches Chance in the garden to say goodbye. She acts caring towards Chance but, at the same time, she cannot help but express exasperation and even contempt towards this hopelessly inadequate man-child. The whole time, Chance is oblivious to the fact that they are going their separate ways and they are not likely to ever see each other again. He just keeps tending to his flowers and plants. Louise says, "You're gonna need somebody, someone's gotta be around for you. You oughta find yourself a lady, Chance. But I guess it oughta be an old lady, 'cause you ain't gonna do a young one any good, not with that little thing of yours. You're always gonna be a little boy, ain't you?" By now, she has reached out and put her hand on Chance's shoulder. Chance reacts with a smile, but he fails to understand the significance of this gesture and he goes back to working as if this was any other day. Louise kisses him on the cheek and tells him goodbye. Louise establishes in this dialogue that Chance is stunted mentally, emotionally and physically. The point will be made repeatedly in later scenes that Chance, with his childlike personality and his underdeveloped sexual apparatus, does not have the faintest interest in sex. He simply never got beyond the pre-sexual stage of development.

As he wanders aimlessly through the city, Chance stops a heavyset black woman (Alfredine Brown) to tell her that he is hungry and ask her if she could give him lunch. If he was an actual child, it is likely that the woman would have been willing to help him, but having a well-dressed middle-aged man beg her for something to eat unnerves the woman, who moves away from him as quickly as she can. It is significant that this encounter happens outside of a strip club. Standing near the entrance of the club is a female mannequin dressed in pasties and lingerie. Director Hal Ashby precisely sets up within the frame the motherly woman, who stands on Chance's right side, and the sexy mannequin woman, who stands on his left side. A large man, whose job it is to solicit passersby to come inside the club, stands directly beside the mannequin. The man calls out to Chance, "It's an all-girl show, sir. Come right in." Chance glances apprehensively at the mannequin before he hurries away. The mannequin frightens him as much as he just frightened the heavyset woman. Chance desperately wants a woman to act as his mother and feed him. He does not have the slightest interest in a pretty young woman who is willing to get naked to indulge a man's sexual desires.

This scene is reminiscent of a scene from the Harry Langdon vehicle *Soldier Man* (1926). Langdon plays an American soldier roaming aimlessly through Europe, in danger of starving to death. After hiking across fields and pastures, he stumbles into the kingdom of Bomania. It just so happens that Langdon resembles the country's drunken, war-mongering King Strudel. Langdon encounters the queen, who assumes Langdon is her wicked husband and approaches him with the intent to knife him in the back. *Time* magazine critic Richard Corliss wrote, "[The Bomanian queen] caresses [Harry] with one hand, holding a dagger behind him with the other. But Harry is so obsessed with eating that he takes forever to plant one on her. When he does, the innocent impact is so strong that she drops the dagger and crumples in dazed ardor to the floor. Harry's response to this display of royal passion? He gets more food."[11] Harry engaged in these ill-fated seduction scenes for years. His character seems to have a basic understanding of sex and has resolved himself to protect his sexual innocence. As the story progresses, the prime minister (Vernon Dent) has this unwary innocent pretend to be the king to get a peace treaty signed and end a civil war.

Kerr singled out a favorite scene from *Soldier Man*:

> Harry, newly made king for reasons that are entirely confusing to him, is asked if he has any orders to give. Eager to cooperate, and with a daze in his eyes giving way to a sneaky appreciation of his new powers, he suggests that it would be nice if a fellow who has been pestering him could have his head cut off. As his prime minister departs, ostensibly to do his bidding, Harry cocks his head slightly in deep concentration, blinking slowly once or twice. Then the sweet smile forms. Suddenly, hands gripping the arms of the throne and feet shooting high in air, he is rocking wildly back and forth, whistling infant monarch on his hobby-horse.... I never knew a child who didn't delight in decapitation.[12]

Harry's reign as king proves to be a dream. Harry wakes up in bed with a wife (Natalie Kingston) and attempts to embrace and kiss her in the same way that he embraced and kissed the queen. Kerr wrote, "His wife shoos him off, impatient as she would be with a five-year-old." This isn't entirely accurate. The wife tells Harry, "Be Yourself!" The film ends with the wife lacing up Harry's boots as a mother would lace up the boots of a child.

Chance also stumbles into a royal court and is drafted as a presidential candidate to end a political crisis. Chance is like Langdon in many ways. It is most obvious that, like Langdon, he is blissfully ignorant. Like Langdon, he is guided and protected by a benevolent fate, a divine force that favors him with an unimaginable series of opportunities. Corliss described Langdon's two essential traits as his infantilism and his passivity. This description can easily be applied to Chance.

At the end of the play *Peter Pan*, Wendy wishes she could hug Peter, but Peter draws back from her. She says resignedly, "Yes, I know." She knows, in fact, that Peter lacks the maturity to handle physical affection from a girl. In *Boobs in the Woods* (1925), Harry gets a job at a lumber camp and develops a relationship with a waitress (Marie Astaire). When the waitress purses her lips for a kiss, Harry raises an axe to defend himself. Kerr described a scene in *Saturday Afternoon* (1926) in which a young woman gets flirtatious with Harry and "fingers the straps of his overalls."[13] Harry, as usual, panics.

Harry was in a constant struggle to protect his sexual innocence. No better example can be found than a memorable scene in *The Strong Man* (1926). A femme fatale (Gertrude Astor) sets out to retrieve a roll of cash that she has secretly hidden inside of Harry's coat. After tricking Harry into coming into her apartment, Astor knocks her naïve guest unconscious by smashing a vase over his head. Harry reacts like a small boy taking a nap: He happily curls up on a bed and shuts his eyes. Astor wrestles Harry onto his back and roughly gropes him in search of her money. It is not surprising that Harry is unable to remain asleep throughout this violent frisking. Harry, who believes that he is being molested, becomes frantic and does everything he can to resist Astor. Frustrated, Astor takes a knife in hand. When she has Harry in her clutches, she jerks him forward and poises the knife to his throat. Harry believes that it is time to acquiesce and give this seductress the kiss that she so desperately wants. During the kiss, Astor manages to get to the roll of money. It is at this point that Astor, who has no more need of Harry and is probably exhausted from having chased him around the room, pretends that Harry's kiss has taken her breath away and collapses on the bed. Harry is stunned to think that his kiss had such a powerful effect. Astor hands over the key to her front door, and Harry is free to leave her lair. Harry is so ashamed of the incident that he covers his face as he walks out into the hall. But then Harry walks into an art studio, where he encounters a naked woman posing for a sculptor. A wicked fate has intervened, forcing upon Harry the very sight that he so desperately struggled to avoid. Harry, understandably alarmed, erupts in a frenzy and storms out of the room. Not looking where he is going, he flips over a banister and somersaults down a staircase.

It could be argued that, because Harry is married and has a job in other films, his sexuality is ambiguous. He is a blending of man and child, alternately displaying sexual anxiety and sexual longing. Kerr wrote,

> A five-year-old and not a five-year-old. A twelve-year-old and not a twelve-year-old. A full-grown functioning male and not a full-grown functioning male. Langdon was and was not all three at once, with nary a seam showing. There was no nailing him, no naming him, no insisting that he settle down and be this or that. He was called "the baby" for convenience, but "baby" doesn't precisely describe the remaining two thirds of the incredibly imagined contradiction.... He is up there on the screen an incontestable whole—not a collection of mismatched gags but an organic impulse charting its own unthinkable flight; and the fact that we cannot define him, pigeonhole him, teach him to see reason, becomes his tantalizing hold on us.

David Kalat, who produced *The Harry Langdon Collection: Lost and Found*, addressed this issue informally, but astutely, in an Internet forum:

> I see *Long Pants* as the first volley of a trilogy of films exploring Langdon in adult relationships. In the first of these, *Long Pants*, he's an adolescent overwhelmed by hormones and looking for love in the wrong places, as adolescents are wont to do. Thus the title, the transition from boyhood to manhood, aka teenager Harry. Then in *Three's a Crowd* he's more grown up, and longing not for sex but for a family, a domestic life. In the final film of the trilogy, *The*

Harry Langdon in *The Strong Man* (1926) (courtesy www.doctormacro.com).

Chaser, we get a married but unhappy Harry longing for the freedom of adolescence back again.[14]

Problems came for Langdon when, as Kerr described it, "[t]he ambiguity dissolved."[15] Film critic Justin DeFreitas wrote, "Langdon no longer walked the line but stepped right over it, even going so far as to portray himself as an actual child, at one point peering out from a baby carriage. The character was no longer ambiguous and intriguing; it was grotesque and absurd."[16]

In *Being There*, Chance follows the example of people on television to figure out how to act with others. While watching the antebellum drama *Jezebel* (1938), he sees a carriage driver tip his hat to a lady. This inspires him to tip his hat to a lady in the following scene. He sees news footage of the president exchanging a two-handed handshake with a foreign leader and he immediately adopts this handshake as a way to greet people. Does this make him peculiar or dumb? Other protagonists who we *wouldn't* consider peculiar or dumb have also relied on television and movies to learn how to act. This type of modeling is a natural part of growing up. In *Sherlock* Jr. (1924), Buster Keaton took cues from a movie hero to romance a lovely lady (Kathryn McGuire). Woody Allen did the same in *Play It Again, Sam* (1972). Still, it is somewhat different with Chance. He hugs and kisses a woman not because she arouses him, but because he is watching a man and woman on television and he wants to play-act their relations. Chance comes across as an alien life form adapting to life on Earth. Television could offer many examples of human behavior to a visitor from deep space. In *Starman* (1984), an alien who has assumed human form (Jeff Bridges) learns how to kiss by watching television (specifically, *From Here to Eternity*). Unlike Chance, the Starman at least has a basic understanding of love and intimacy. We can see this, too, when *Sherlock Jr.* ends with a similar scene. It is clear that Keaton has an ardent interest in the woman. Chance has no such interest at all.

Cheech and Chong's *Up in Smoke* (1978) was yet another story of the man-child trying to find a place for himself in an adult world. Anthony "Man" Stoner (Tommy Chong) spends his days getting high smoking marijuana. His parents are fed up taking care of him and demand that he get a job by sundown or they will send him off to military school. He takes to the road after he is unable to find a job and he unwittingly becomes involved in a plot to smuggle a van constructed of marijuana from Mexico to Los Angeles. The film ends with Man and his friend Pedro (Cheech Marin) driving away triumphantly from a Battle of the Bands competition (the audience responded blissfully to their band's performance because the marijuana van caught fire and the smoke fumes drifted into the club). Man tries to pass a joint to Pedro, but he accidentally drops the joint into Pedro's lap. Pedro panics, swerves the car, and nearly crashes. We now know, as smoke from the exhaust rises up in the frame and the credits roll, that these two men have not come out of their experiences as viable adults. More important, their fans don't care.

The protagonist of *The Jerk*, Navin R. Johnson (Steve Martin), was raised by poor black sharecroppers. He doesn't realize that he's not black, but knows that he is different from the rest of his family because he lacks the rhythm that the other family members demonstrate whenever they play blues music. *The Jerk* brings to mind *Battling Butler*, which introduced wealthy parents who had sheltered their son to the point where he can't function on his own. *The Jerk* shows that a family with*out* wealth can shelter a son just as much as a family with wealth.

Like Chance of *Being There*, Navin is able to draw the support and affection of others through his likable and non-threatening nature. Like *Being There*, *The Jerk* is set in motion when the protagonist leaves his home and family. Navin has come to the conclusion on his eighteenth birthday that he needs to leave home to discover the world. The 33-year-old, silver-haired Martin hardly looks like an 18-year-old man. So, no matter what the script says, Navin comes across as a dire example of the late bloomer. While it is unfavorable for an 18-year-old man to act in a juvenile manner, it is much worse for a 33-year-old man to act in a juvenile manner. He is not much better than the silver-haired Chance, whose mismatched appearance and manner sent at least one woman fleeing in terror.

Navin is introduced to sex by a daredevil biker, Patty Bernstein (Catlin Adams). The aggressive Patty takes complete control of the situation, wrestling Navin down on a bed much like Astor had once wrestled Harry down on a bed. Patty has no problem seducing Navin, who is too naïve to know what she is planning to do with him. It is implied that Navin has a large penis, what the black woman who raised him called his

Steve Martin runs a kiddie ride at a carnival in *The Jerk* (1979).

"special purpose." This is the direct opposite of the scene in *Being There* in which the black woman who raised Chance calls Chance's penis "that little thing of yours." This may be the reason that this lovemaking session turns out more successfully than the sex scene in *Being There*. Patty enjoys having sex with Navin. Navin enjoys having sex with Patty. No one struggles. No one panics.

Later, Navin's beloved Marie (Bernadette Peters) reluctantly leaves him because she realizes that, due to his lack of skills, he will never achieve financial security. Several other people understand the young man's shortcomings and accept him unconditionally.

Businessman Stan Fox (Bill Macy) is the one person who has complete confidence in Navin's abilities. Navin volunteers to repair Fox's eyeglasses so that they stop sliding down his nose. He adds a handle and a nose brake onto the bridge of the slippery spectacles. Fox thinks that Navin is a genius. He is so thrilled with this invention that he mass-produces this unique style of eyeglasses under the name Opti-Grab. The product is highly profitable at first, but Fox realizes he made a mistake when the people who wear Opti-Grab eyeglasses become cross-eyed and file a class action lawsuit against his company.

The film has a happy ending despite the fact that Navin has lost all of his money in the lawsuit. Navin shows in the closing scene that he has gained a small token of maturity: perfect rhythm.

We live in a society that produces an overabundance of stress and a scarce amount of compassion. This is the point of Neil Simon's *Prisoner of Second Avenue* (1975). Mel Edison (Jack Lemmon) unexpectedly loses his job, which sends his life into a downward spiral. Mel is, in ways, the broken husband in *Une Affaire de femme*. After he loses his job, he sits around his apartment in his pajamas while his wife Edna goes out to work. Through much of the film, Mel behaves like a petulant child. Upset that his stewardess neighbors are having a noisy party in the middle of the night, he gets into a heated argument with the neighbor on the phone. The neighbor becomes irritated with Mel and bangs on the wall. This rouses the otherwise morose Mel, who has Edna bang back. The neighbor bangs again. Mel forces Edna to bang even harder in response. The fact that the argument has quickly devolved into a tit-for-tat banging on the wall makes Mel look childish. But Mel, who smiles gleefully during the banging, is unaware that this is not a mature way to resolve a conflict. He doesn't even show compassion when his wife hurts her hand banging on the wall. His brother, Harry (Gene Saks), later tells him, "I don't think you can handle emotional problems. You're a child, a baby, a spoiled infant."

The bungling, self-important Inspector Clouseau (Peter Sellers) continually demonstrates childish behavior as he investigates crimes in *The Pink Panther* (1964), *A Shot in the Dark* (1964), *The Return of the Pink Panther* (1975), *The Pink Panther Strikes Again* (1976) and *Revenge of the Pink Panther* (1978). Psychologist David F. Bjorklund wrote, "[I]t seems obvious that an overly self-centered perspective and the state of being out of touch with one's cognitive abilities is generally maladaptive."[17] It is extremely absurd when these maladaptive traits hinder a figure of authority who is responsible for solving a murder case.

A timid man can assume adult responsibilities to a narrow extent. He can create a safe and tidy island for himself and then seal off his personal island from the troubled world. But this safe life is merely another form of childhood. F. Scott Fitzgerald was identifying this type of strategy when he wrote, "It is much easier to skip [adulthood] and go from one childhood to another."[18] A man can function adequately in this way, but he can never evolve into a fully formed adult.

A worse problem with this timid seclusion strategy is that the messiness of the outside world can sometimes seep through the cracks. This is evident in the plot of *The In-Laws* (1979). A rogue CIA agent (Peter Falk), possibly insane, gets an anxious, mild-mannered dentist (Alan Arkin) swept up into highly dangerous international intrigue. The dentist goes through a wacky rite of passage, which transforms him into a self-assured and self-satisfied adult. For sure, he comes out financially richer with the money that he and Falk are able to scam from a demented South American dictator. Masculinity is clarified by a man's ability to provide for his children. Arkin is an outstanding provider now that he is able to give his daughter a million dollars as a wedding gift. Janet Maslin of *The New York Times* said that, like *The Producers* (1968), this was the story of "milquetoast meets entrepreneur."[19] In this case, the milquetoast benefited from being pushed out of his safe little world by the entrepreneur.

It is hard to imagine a mama's boy lasting very long in the ancient world, which presented so many serious challenges to a person's survival. But we are introduced to a mama's boy in the Biblical spoof *Life of Brian* (1979). In the first century a.d., a hapless young man named Brian is mistaken for the Messiah. Brian's mother, Mandy, tells her son's followers, "He's not the Messiah. He's a very naughty boy!" Brian comes to the window to speak to his followers, but his mother interrupts him by dragging him off by his ear. Mandy is not the only person who treats Brian like a child and yanks his ear. A centurion who catches Brian writing a protest message on a palace wall is upset by grammatical errors in the message. He acts as a cross teacher, twisting Brian's ear as he forces him to remember the correct forms for words in his message. (Brian has a particular struggle with a pattern of Latin conjunction called *third person plural present indicative*.)

John Kennedy Toole's 1980 novel *A Confederacy of Dunces* anticipated the coming wave of man-child characters. The novel's lead character, Ignatius J. Reilly, is a blustery, vulnerable mama's boy. The sheltered young man fears journeying outside his hometown of New Orleans. Ignatius believes that he does not belong in the world and that his numerous failings are the work of a higher power. He is not Langdon's divinely protected innocent. A small boy is quick to interpret bad luck as divine punishment for something that he did wrong. Ignatius, recognizing that he is a weak specimen, says, "I suspect that I am the result of particularly weak conception on the part of my father. His sperm was probably emitted in a rather offhand manner." For more than thirty years, filmmakers have tried and failed to adapt the book into a motion picture. During this period, Hollywood has had no shortage of comedians who could play a barefaced man-child, including John Belushi, John Candy, Chris Farley, John Goodman, Will Ferrell and Zach Galifianakis.

8

Young Again

Regression involves a person returning psychologically to a younger age. It brings about within a person awkward and uncontrollable changes in behavior and mood, which ideally serves the purposes of a comedy film.

We discussed the 1914 comedy *Uncle's Finish*, in which a man who drank from the Fountain of Youth turned into a monkey. More monkey business occurs in a youth elixir comedy called, appropriately enough, *Monkey Business* (1952). A lab chimp that belongs to research chemist Dr. Barnaby Fulton (Cary Grant) randomly mixes a beaker of chemicals, then pours it into a water cooler. The chimp's mixture just happens to have amazingly powerful properties. Anyone who takes a drink from the water cooler begins immediately to act like a child. This regression is, according to *New Yorker* critic Richard Brody, "exhilarating and destructive."[1] Barnaby's wife Edwina drinks from the water cooler, providing her husband with his first human test subject. At first, the formula energizes Edwina and causes her to lose her inhibitions. Later, though, the fun ends. Edwina becomes overemotional, abruptly bawling that she misses her mother. Then she becomes enraged for no good reason and gets into a nonsensical argument with Barnaby. She shrieks long suppressed grievances and batters her husband repeatedly with a pillow. The strangest effect of the mixture is that Edwina becomes squeamishly shy when her husband begins to undress for bed. The scene mirrors the train compartment scene in *The Major and the Minor* in which Rogers was shy about getting into her pajamas in front of Ray Milland.

Under the influence of the formula, Barnaby and Edwina react to conflict with primal violence. Edwina shoots people with a slingshot. Barnaby drags Edwina by the hair. The bickering couple grab paint brushes and slather each other with paint. Barnaby applies Indian war paint to his face and subjects his wife's former flame, Hank Entwhistle (Hugh Marlowe), to a drastic haircut (which he describes as a "scalping"). Barnaby's boss, Oliver Oxly (Charles Coburn), suggests that, stripped of his adult qualities, Barnaby has become insane. Children can convey a range of qualities other than sweetness. The ferment and flurry of children can reach a level of outrageousness and madness. Later, Oxly and various scientists unknowingly consume the formula, which causes them to swing on chandeliers and spray each other with water. The message of the story is delivered by Barnaby in the closing moments of the film. He explains, "Youth is a word you keep in your heart, a light you have in your eyes, someone you hold in your arms." Barnaby represents youth as something beautiful and romantic, which is odd considering that nothing beautiful or romantic came out of the characters' youthful behavior. In the *Peter Pan* novel, J.M. Barrie described children as "innocent and heartless." Maturity is what really has been idealized by the events of the film. Its message should be that it is maturity that makes us selfless, committed, reasonable and loving. At best, youth is a vital life force that should remain as a glowing ember cautiously contained within our breasts.

Thomas C. Renzi wrote in *Screwball Comedy and Film Noir: Unexpected Connections*, "[The screwball heroine] can punch the male on the jaw (*Nothing Sacred*, *Breakfast for Two*), close the door on his nose (*Mr. & Mrs. Smith*), drop an apple on his head (*The Lady Eve*), and humiliate him in public (*Adam's Rib*).... [W]e recognize these assaults as childish pranks that disguise the true feelings of an innocent boy and girl who like each other."[2] By now, the heyday of the screwball comedy was over. Audiences expected more mature behavior from romantic couples. Howard Hawks, who helped to popularize the screwball comedy trend with *Bringing Up Baby* (1938), was now the main creative force behind *Monkey Business*. He had to update the formula to suit modern times. Renzi wrote, "The couple ... reverts to their younger, less inhibited selves in which state they can resume their childish battle of the sexes. That is, the screwball

Cary Grant is determined to create a youth formula in *Monkey Business* (1952) (courtesy www.doctormacro.com).

couple can no longer behave like the classical screwball couple without help from science.... So the former vivacious, dynamic screwball couple represents what most (all?) married couple are couple to become—contented, tolerant, stodgy, and inert.... [T]he staid married couple represents all the aged screwball characters who have matured and moved beyond their former reckless and riotous selves to become model members of conventional society."[3] Mature individuals are dull and uninspired in the context of a screwball comedy. In real life, though, mature individuals are dynamic and inspirational in their various achievements.

Author Anaïs Nin believed that we grow up "unevenly" and "partially." She saw it as possible for a person to be mature in one part of their life and be childish in another. She recognized that past events, present circumstances and future goals can "pull us backward, forward, or fix us in the present."[4]

The stages of development are never orderly or stable. Marriages fall apart. Jobs are lost. This can cause a backslide to an earlier state. It is difficult for a mature person to maintain calmness or steadiness after they have been thrown into the middle of a crisis. A divorce causes instability in *The Odd Couple* (1968). Unemployment causes instability in *Lost in America* (1985). The psychological effects of middle age cause instability in *10* (1979). Instability is induced by less ordinary crises in other comedy films, including *It's a Mad Mad Mad Mad World* (1963) and *The In-Laws*. *It's a Mad Mad Mad Mad World* involves a group of strangers who become involved in a frenzied race to find a dead gangster's buried loot. The promise of wealth releases the avarice and wantonness that resides deep inside the competing treasure hunters and it is these urges that bring about appallingly childish and petty behavior. In film comedy, childish behavior is usually associated with property destruction. That association can be seen clearly in any Three Stooges comedy. But no film offered more property destruction than *Mad Mad World*. This became a bone of contention for the film's detractors, which include Wheeler Winston Dixon. Dixon complained in his article "Dark Humor in Films of the 1960s" that *Mad Mad World* was a "mind-numbing orgy of violence and destruction."[5]

The Odd Couple sheds light on the disintegration of the American family. Oscar Madison (Walter Matthau) divorced his wife, who then took their children three thousand miles away to California. Oscar, who is defined by his poor handling of money, excessive gambling and messy house, is an unruly big kid. We are appropriately introduced to this big kid as he hosts a poker game for his friends. It is like many of the modern comedies that feature the protagonist contently playing video games with his friends. Boys love their games and they love their friends. But we have no idea if Oscar was always like this or if he went astray after his divorce.

Oscar's roommate, Felix Unger (Jack Lemmon), is so despondent over his breakup with his wife that he has lost his sexual desire. He acts like a lost child while sitting with the attractive Pigeon sisters, Cecily and Gwendolyn. In contrast to his sexually aggressive roommate, Felix has regressed to an asexual stage of development. He tells Oscar, "Funny, I haven't thought of women in weeks." He is vulnerable and weepy and the women want to mother him. Cecily says, "He's so sensitive. So fragile. I just want to bundle him up in my arms and take care of him."

8. *Young Again*

Jack Lemmon becomes helpless and weepy after his wife throws him out of their home in *The Odd Couple* (1968). Lemmon is comforted in this scene by Carole Shelley and Monica Evans as a mortified Walter Matthau looks on.

Felix takes on the wife role when he moves in with Oscar. It makes sense. He is more responsible when it comes to budgeting household funds, planning healthy meals, and performing household chores. This point was emphasized in the film's poster, which showed Felix wearing an apron and brandishing a feather duster. This hardly presented Felix as a masculine figure.

Felix throws temper tantrums. Oscar throws temper tantrums. In an angry fit,

Oscar throws a plate of linguine against a wall. Is this how adults act? *The Dissolve*'s Tasha Robinson definitely saw Felix as childish. She could not conceal her loathing when she wrote, "[Felix] is self-pitying and selfish, infuriatingly oblivious to any needs but his own."[6]

Psychologists claim that regression comes in many forms. They could say that Felix's excessive tidiness is the result of a regression to the anal stage and Oscar's yelling and overeating is the result of a regression to the oral stage.

The goal of the regression character is to reject the stress and misery of adulthood and reclaim their laid-back youth. Who could not support this goal? In *10* (1979), a popular songwriter, George Webber (Dudley Moore), is depressed by the advent of his 42nd birthday. Webber manages in his distress to act impulsively, irresponsibly and unpleasantly. His writing partner, Hugh (Robert Webber), complains that he is behaving like "a spoiled child." His girlfriend breaks up with him for making an insensitive comment. This man who produces elegant music is not showing much elegance; he is behaving like an overheated adolescent, engaging obsessively in voyeurism and sexual fantasy. He takes multiple opportunities to peer into a telescope to spy on his porn producer neighbor's sexual antics. Later, he becomes infatuated with Jenny Miles (Bo Derek), a beautiful newlywed. Like Monroe in *The Seven Year Itch*, Derek proves in the end to be a false ideal.

In films, an overactive imagination usually prevents a young man from becoming a sober, steady adult. Danny Kaye has a childish fascination with daydreams in *The Secret Life of Walter Mitty* (1947). Mitty seeks in his fantasies the respect and excitement that he is denied in his real life. Though this may provide Mitty with transient satisfaction, it is generally regarded as an immature tendency to escape into fantasies rather than face up to reality.

The *Twilight Zone* episode "The Incredible World of Horace Ford" (1963) is not a comedy, but it is relevant in the many ways that it recalls *Mitty*. Mitty, a writer, made a living turning his boyhood adventure fantasies into gripping pulp stories. In much the same way, Horace has managed to channel his boyhood love of toys into a respectable profession as a toy designer. But his job has become stressful and he has little time to have fun. Horace becomes obsessed with happy, carefree memories of his childhood. One day, he visits his old neighborhood and is amazed to find that it has remained exactly the way that he remembers it. He recognizes boyhood friends, who have not aged at all. He repeatedly returns to the neighborhood and stays slightly longer each time. Finally, one night, he lingers longer than usual to pursue his old friends. He suddenly finds that he has become transformed into a small boy again. His friends, who are angry that his mother didn't invite them to his birthday party, surround him and beat him. Horace awakens with his clothes mussed and his face bruised, but at least he has returned to his adult form. He decides that his childhood was not as pleasant as he remembered and commits to living in the present. This was a remake of a 1955 episode of *Westinghouse Studio One*. In the original version, Horace never returned home. The moral of the story was that a wistful man can become lost in his own past. In the new version, the man learns to commit to leaving behind his past and becoming an adult.

Children need to be children and adults need to be adults. It serves no purpose to pervert the natural order. Philosopher Jean Jacques Rousseau saw no benefit to providing the world with "young doctors and old children."[7] This happens to be the exact premise of *Like Father, Like Son* (1987), in which a doctor (Dudley Moore) swaps bodies with his teenage son (Kirk Cameron). This was part of a trend of body swap comedies, which also included *Freaky Friday* (1976), *Vice Versa* (1988), *Dream a Little Dream* (1989), *18 Again!* (1988) and *Detention* (2011).

Sometimes, regression comedies have nothing at all to do with being irresponsible and having fun. These films have to do with regrets, missed opportunities, and unfulfilled yearnings. In *Damn Yankees* (1958), Joe Boyd (Robert Shafer) is a middle-aged fan of the Washington Senators baseball team. He is so desperate to see the team win the pennant that he says aloud he's willing to sell his soul to the Devil in exchange for their success. The Devil suddenly appears in the guise of suave con man Mr. Applegate (Ray Walston), eager to accept Joe's offer. Joe's true desire comes out in the following dialogue:

> APPLEGATE: Your secret yearning all your life has been to be a baseball player yourself.
> JOE BOYD: I wasn't so bad in high school.
> APPLEGATE: Not so bad? They were scouting you for Kansas City. You still got your spike shoes and your glove up in your bedroom.... I'm offering you a chance to be something that you've wanted to be for all of your life.

A deal is struck: Applegate transforms Joe into a young champion player so that he can lead the Senators through a winning season. Everything goes as Applegate promised, but Joe misses his wife Meg. In the end, he takes advantage of an escape clause in his contract with Applegate to skip the final game of the season and return to his wife as his old self.

Elements of *Damn Yankees* turn up in *17 Again* (2009). The film's main character, 37-year-old Mike O'Donnell (Matthew Perry), regrets that he gave up a basketball scholarship to marry his pregnant high school sweetheart. That regret eventually turned him into a bitter husband, which eventually compelled his wife to leave him. Mike wants to go back to his youth so that he can start again and follow a different path in life. A mysterious janitor (Brian Doyle-Murray) transforms Mike into his 17-year-old self. The janitor is presumably a guardian angel, which makes his intentions very much different than the intentions of the devilish Applegate. Mike's problem, though, is that he can't give up his adult responsibilities. He continues to look after his son and daughter, who are students in the same high school he attends. In both *Damn Yankees* and *17 Again*, fidelity to family members is more important than being a star athlete.

The plot of *Momma's Man* (2008) is simple: A man visits his parents and refuses to leave. *Boston Globe* film critic Ty Burr wrote, "*Momma's Man* is dedicated to the proposition that in every man's heart lives a homesick little boy, and if he's very unlucky his childhood bedroom is still waiting for him. Complete with glow-in-the-dark stars on the ceiling."[8] The son, Mikey (Matt Boren), has come to town on business, but he suddenly finds himself terrified to leave the safety and security of his parents' loft. The loft, warm and cluttered, is the perfect cave in which a man can hide. Mikey tells his parents that he has gotten bumped from his flight, but he is vague about the details. He outright lies to his boss, telling him that he has to delay his return home because his mother is in the hospital. He later informs his parents that he is working when he's really reading comic books and going through his old Garbage Pail Kids trading card collection. Mikey is in bliss as he rummages through boxes of childhood mementos. He smiles as he unfolds a superhero cape. He ties the cape around his shoulders and stretches out his arms as if he is preparing to take flight. He is able to revisit his teen years when he finds song lyrics that he scribbled in a high school notebook. He gets out his guitar and plays the long-forgotten song. Burr wrote, "The angry yet satisfied expression on his face when Dad tells him to keep the music down says it all: This is his last teenage rebellion, and he wants it to last forever."[9] He calls his wife Laura (Dana Varon) every day with a new explanation for his continued absence. She senses something's wrong and, not knowing if he's *ever* coming home, becomes distraught. She phones Mikey in tears, but Mikey shows no emotion. He is monotone. "I'm just gonna stay a little bit longer, okay?" he says. "Just a little bit longer." He looks quite content sitting quietly on a park bench. This is not something he probably has time to do during a normal work day. His mother is deeply concerned about him, but he refuses to discuss his feelings with her. His father asks, "Do you need to get back to your family and to your work?" He gets defensive. Burr wrote, "Days turn into weeks, and Mikey clings, barnacle-like, to the flotsam of his childhood.... After a while, he turns off his cellphone so he can't hear his wife's pleas to come home. Anyway, he is home."

It is clear that Mikey is suffering. He cannot articulate what he's feeling. Whenever he tries, he chokes up and tears well up in his eyes. He doesn't break free of his inner turmoil until he sits on his mother's lap and cries. It is the catharsis that he so desperately needed. A similar scene was featured in *The Freshman* (1925). Harold Lloyd is devastated when he learns that his classmates have been making fun of him behind his back. His caring girlfriend, Peggy (Jobyna Ralston), holds out her arms to him. In response, he lays his head down on her lap and weeps. Lloyd's granddaughter, Suzanne Lloyd Hayes, said, "My grandfather decided in the 1960s that he didn't like what he called 'the crying scene,' and he took it out. After much discussion we recently reinstated it, because it creates such a lovely emotional bond between Harold and the girl." Lloyd was likely worried that the scene made the character look weak. But the crying has the opposite effect: It makes the character stronger. By dropping his defenses, he is now able to stop putting on an act and be himself.

Momma's Man, which presents a realistic and relatable story, gets to the sad and desperate core of regression. Its potent message is that being an adult can be a deeply painful experience.

Momma's Man is more subtle and real than Albert Brooks' *Mother* (1996). Brooks' protagonist, John Henderson, is as neurotic as the comedian's previous characters. He believes, based on the failure of his two marriages, that he never bonded properly with his mother and this prevented him from developing into a stable and secure adult. He gets the idea that, to make himself into a better man, he needs to go back and start again. So he moves back in with his mother (Debbie Reynolds), occupying the same bedroom that he had as a child. Mikey avoided talking to his warm and caring mother, but not John. John talks incessantly to his mother. He sees her as taciturn and unsupportive and is desperate to get her to open up and say something helpful. Mikey wanted

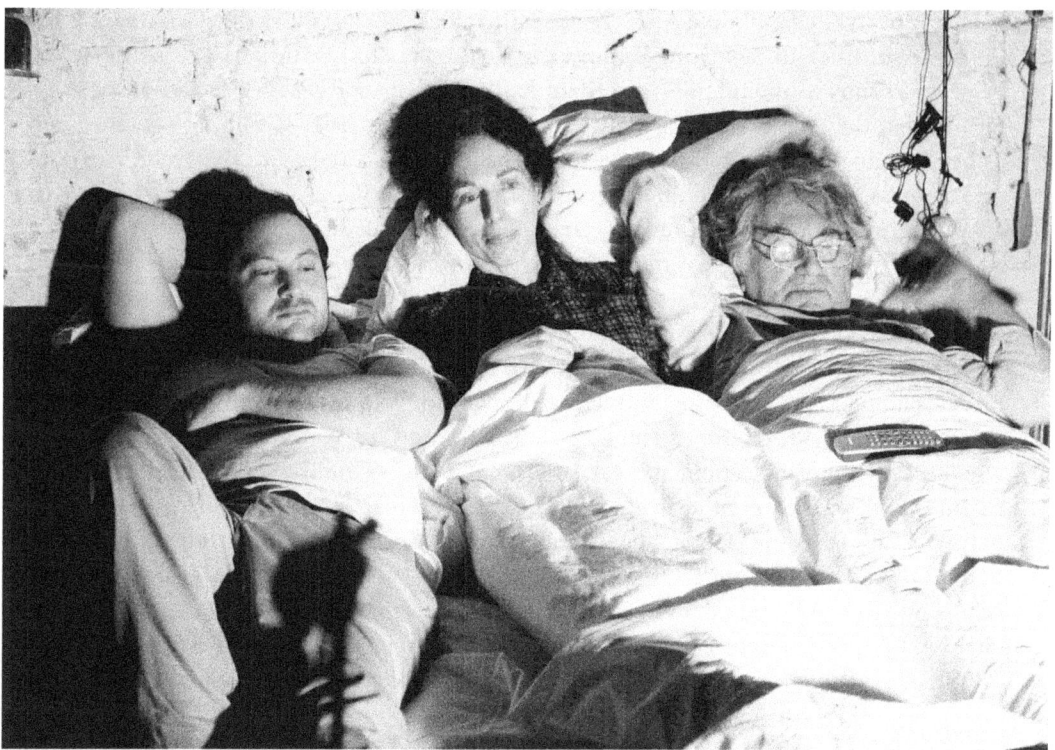

Momma's Man (2008) is a quieter, more profound meditation on the man-child dilemma. A 30-something man (Matt Boren) has become so overwhelmed by his responsibilities as a father and husband that he clings desperately to the safety and comfort of his parents' home. Pictured in the scene, from left to right, are Boren, Flo Jacobs and Ken Jacobs.

to return to his childhood because his mother was so good to him. John wants to return to his childhood because his mother was so bad to him. Mikey, who slips into his regressive state without planning or control, is in the end a more sympathetic character than self-conscious and self-absorbed John.

The *Mother* premise is handled more crudely in *Dickie Roberts: Former Child Star* (2003). Dickie Roberts (David Spade) is a washed-up ex–child actor making a living as a parking valet. He gets an opportunity to appear in a major film, but the role calls for him to be a normal person and the director has doubts that Dickie knows how to be normal. Dickie gets the idea to pay a family to "adopt" him so that he can relive his youth and learn the way that normal people live. He calls this "Operation: Redo Childhood." The problem is that simple childhood skills prove difficult for Dickie to master. He tries to learn to ride a bicycle, but he crashes into a garbage pail and runs into a road sign. His efforts to slide on a Slip'n'Slide end up with him slamming headfirst into a fence. He goes as far as having the mother push him around in a stroller, which of course attracts strange looks from passersby. It was an old surefire vaudeville gag to have a comedian brought on stage in a baby buggy.

The Hangover (2009), which Chris Herrington of Memphis Flyer called "a midlife crisis binge-drinking film," involves the drug-induced regression of four men during a bachelor party. The childlike Alan (Zach Galifianakis), who is more imp than man, leads his future brother-in-law Doug Billings (Justin Bartha) and Doug's friends astray when he secretly slips rohypnol pills into their drinks. The drug frees them of all of the inhibitions that they have developed as adults. But in the end, these inhibitions are treated as neurotic hang-ups rather than reasonable social constraints. Stu (Ed Helms) in particular finds the experience liberating and realizes that he no longer wants his mean-spirited girlfriend, Melissa (Rachel Harris), to control his life.

Alan is a unique sort of man-child. In *Animal House*, Bluto is angered to hear a young man play a sappy folk song on his acoustic guitar. He snatches the guitar and smashes it against a wall. Alan, a namby-pamby man-child, lacks the aggressiveness of the guitar-smashing Bluto. He is earnest and innocent. This, however, is not to say that he is a safe person to have around. He is dimwitted, helpless, and possibly insane.

Alan futilely attempts to emulate Doug's friend Phil Wenneck (Bradley Cooper), who presents himself as bold and self-assured. Of course, neither of these men is really mature. Phil, a discontented teacher, acts smug and insincere as he dismisses his students for the weekend. His insincerity extends to him stealing the students' field trip donations so that he can have money to gamble in Las Vegas. As soon as he leaves the school for his weekend getaway, he regresses to an unapologetic adolescent. He gets charged up when he sees Doug drive up to his school in a classic 1969 Mercedes-Benz 280SE convertible. He sees this car for what it is—a big toy. He doesn't bother to open

Bradley Cooper, Ed Helms and Zach Galifianakis are undone by a drug-fueled Las Vegas spree in *The Hangover* (2009).

the car door to get inside. He hops into the back seat, ignoring Doug's plea that he not get his dirty shoes on the leather upholstery. He is loud and insulting during the trip. Stretched out in the back seat, he guzzles a beer in a defiant, I-do-what-I-want manner. He nags Doug to let him drive: "I drive great when I'm drunk," he insists.

A person who longs for their earlier days will be motivated to seek out the Fountain of Youth or, at least, they will be motivated to consume large amounts of drugs and alcohol in Las Vegas. The rohypnol pills might as well be the youth elixir from *Monkey Business*.

Regression stories can become pitch-black when approached from a dramatic standpoint. A 2013 drama, *The Lifeguard*, is a good example. The film involves news reporter Leigh London (Kristen Bell), who becomes disillusioned with her life and moves back to her childhood home in Connecticut. She becomes a lifeguard at the community pool, the same job that she had while she was in high school, and spends most of her time after work hanging out with teenagers and smoking pot. She is attracted to the maintenance man's teenage son, Jason, and begins having sex with him. She disrupts the life of family and friends in her desperate effort to return to her younger days. An old friend, Mel (Mamie Gummer), joins Leigh in her carefree activities, which ends up jeopardizing her job and her marriage. Leigh's mother becomes furious with her, but Leigh is quick to defend herself. She tells her mother, "I'm allowed to be confused and stumble once in a while." Leigh would no doubt defend Mikey taking time off to hide out in his parents' loft or a group of men abandoning responsibility for one wild weekend in Las Vegas. Indirectly, Leigh's selfish and inconsiderate actions cause Jason's best friend to hang himself. It is then that she realizes that she needs to go back to her adult life.

Robin Williams, whose breakout role was the childlike Mork on TV's *Mork and Mindy*, played characters with varying degrees of childlike qualities in numerous feature films, including *Survivors* (1983), *Moscow on the Hudson* (1984), *The Fisher King* (1991), *Toys* (1992), *Mrs. Doubtfire* (1993), *Jack* (1996) and *Patch Adams* (1998). In *Patch Adams*, Williams greets an old woman while hanging upside down from a lamppost. A person cannot do more than this to display a child's playful and uninhibited nature. But the actor explored the subject more deeply in other films.

The title character of *Jack* is Jack Powell (Williams), a ten-year-old boy who has a bizarre disorder that makes him age four times faster than a normal child ages. It is difficult for Jack to handle this outlandish disparity: His body matures astonishingly fast while his emotions and intellect mature at the normal rate. Like Josh in *Big* (1988), he is truly a boy trapped in a man's body. This presents a particular problem when the boy develops sexual feelings for his teacher, Miss Marquez (Jennifer Lopez). Jack asks Ms. Marquez out, but the teacher explains that she cannot date a student. Undeterred, Jack later meets up with a classmate's mother (Fran Drescher) at a bar. His natural physical drive overrides the uncertainty and shyness that he feels for the opposite sex. He does not follow Harry Langdon's example of fleeing from women. Rather, he rushes in headlong.

Regression therapy involves a person reliving earlier experiences to resolve a problematic psychological condition. This was the essential idea behind *Hook* (1991). Staid businessman Peter Banning (Williams) undergoes an intense and unplanned form of regression therapy when he suddenly learns that, in his youth, he was the mythical Peter Pan. During the course of the story, Peter must regain his youthful spirit to rescue his son and daughter from the villainous Captain Hook. He also recognizes the need to reconnect with his family, from whom he has become isolated, and restore their confidence in him. The film shows that a person can be corrupted by the formal trappings of the adult world—contracts, schedules, meetings, paychecks. From Peter's perspective, social conflict does not need to be resolved with patience, compassion, debate and compromise. When Captain Hook (Dustin Hoffman) expresses fiery indignation at Peter's long-ago act of cutting off his hand, Peter simply whips out his checkbook and a pen. "How much?" he asks. Captain Hook shoots a hole through the checkbook.

Peter has lost the boyish attributes that once made him a legend in Neverland. Both Captain Hook and Lost Boy Rufio (Dante Basco) define Peter Pan's greatest abilities as follows: fight (physical strength and courage), fly (agility and free spirit) and crow (pride and confidence). Peter's past with Wendy and the Lost Boys eventually comes back to him. During a visit with an aging Wendy, Peter fell in love with Wendy's granddaughter Moira and decided to remain in London with her. He willingly made this choice even though he knew that, by failing to return to Neverland, he would grow up and grow old. He tells Tinker Bell, "I know why I came back. I know why I grew up. I wanted to be a father." Peter maintains that it was worth forsaking his eternal youth to have a family. In the end, Peter regains his ability to fight, fly and crow and he defeats Hook in a lively sword battle. Bilge Ebiri of Vulture.com wrote, "*Hook* is about one final go-round as a child before finally saying good-bye to it forever. It's an elegy, but it's also a kind of exorcism."[10] Still, Peter comes to appreciate his old qualities and has no wish to exorcise them. He vows to

Robin Williams suffers an unusual aging disorder in *Jack* (1996).

now approach life as an adventure, relying on the support of his family while he bravely and enthusiastically stands up to life's challenges. Cary Grant's message at the end of *Monkey Business* is more appropriate for this film: "Youth is a word you keep in your heart, a light you have in your eyes."

Williams' character in *Good Will Hunting* (1997) spoke out against the callousness of immaturity. The actor plays a no-nonsense psychologist, Dr. Sean Maguire (Williams), who is called in to provide guidance to a wayward young man, Will Hunting (Matt Damon). Sean challenges Will's childish obstinacy. He tells Will, "I doubt you've ever dared to love anybody that much. And look at you. I don't see an intelligent, confident man. I see a cocky, scared-shitless kid." Cockiness only exists to hide fear and need and it must be abandoned along with other youthful qualities to progress to a more substantial stage of life.

Regression involves a retreat to a safer and more pleasant time. Regression could be simple and fleeting. It could be a troubled man sleeping with a stuffed animal because it reminds of his childhood. It is understakable for a person to retreat from a grim life into a world of childlike frivolity.

In general, people do not mature in a linear way. Periods of improved self-control are followed by periods of less self-control, but we should eventually move with all of our stops, starts and backups to an adult level.

9

"I know you are but what am I?"

In 1980, comedies did well at the box office. Seven of the year's top ten moneymakers were comedies. This included *9 to 5, Stir Crazy, Airplane!, Any Which Way You Can, Private Benjamin, Smokey and the Bandit II* and *The Blues Brothers.* Contemporary Hollywood hasn't been able to get seven live-action comedies into the top ten box office rankings in the entire last decade.

Characters in comedy films of the period often had childlike qualities. In *9 to 5*, bad boss Dabney Coleman behaves like a screaming, greedy, self-centered infant. An immature person is, above all else, self-centered. He expects special treatment, contributes little to the lives of those around him, and complains when others do not satisfy his demands. He will whine and cry to get what he wants and he will manage through destructive behavior to harm those upon whom he depends the most. In *Amadeus* (1984), Wolfgang Amadeus Mozart is portrayed by Tom Hulce as a man-child—rude, crass, arrogant, volatile and cackling. In *Beverly Hills Cop* (1984), Detroit cop Axel Foley (Eddie Murphy) is playful and at times reckless in his investigation techniques. His way to stop two men from following him is to sneak behind their car and stick bananas into their tailpipe. He not only accomplishes this prank, but he is childish enough to taunt the men about it before he climbs into a car and drives off. In *Ghostbusters* (1984), misfit parapsychologist Dan Aykroyd is gleeful to be able to slide down a fire pole, which is more openly childish than Coleman's whining, Mozart's cackling or Murphy's pranks.

In films, comedy characters became increasingly immature in the 1980s and 1990s. At the start of this period, *Stripes* (1981) established itself as a trend-setting film in the man-child film genre. A pivotal scene occurs when John (Bill Murray) has to tell his girlfriend, Anita (Roberta Leighton), that he quit his job as a cabdriver. Anita, who is tired of John being unable to hold a job, becomes enraged. She calls out her boyfriend on his idle ways.

> ANITA: "You sleep in till noon, then you watch *Rocky and Bullwinkle.* Then you drive your cab, what, a couple hours? You come home, you order out food ... and then you play those stupid Tito Puente albums until two in the morning!"
> JOHN: "Tito Puente is gonna be dead, and you'll say: 'I've been listening to him for years. He's fabulous.'"

ANITA: "Then you watch movies until dawn, and then ... then you come to bed with me."
JOHN: "You don't think that takes energy? You're a sexual dynamo. Most guys couldn't even handle you. I've been reading books on the outside so I can keep up with you."
ANITA: "It's not funny. You're going nowhere, John. It's just not that cute anymore."
JOHN: "It's a little cute. Come on. I'm part of a lost and restless generation. What, you want me to run for the Senate?"
ANITA: "I don't know what I want. I just know that I don't want you."

John jokes that he's going to find a sharp knife so that he can kill himself. Anita still doesn't find him funny. She insists that their relationship is not going to work. "I like you," she says. "but I need something more. I need somebody who's going to develop with me and grow."

John gets on his knees as he begs Anita not to leave. He says, "Who could grow more than me? Talk about massive potential for growth. I am the little acorn that becomes the oak."

The man-child dilemma is outlined distinctly in this scene. A lazy and unambitious man who can find nothing better to do with his time than watch cartoons and listen to records is not a model adult and, by no means, an adequate partner. He does not look like someone who can be relied upon to one day focus, develop, and attain oak-like sturdiness. Murray makes his character's slacker nature evident with his loose limbs, floppy gait and droopy posture. He can barely hold himself up through the opening scenes of the film.

Murray's John is surrounded by decor that offers convincing evidence of his fun-loving childlike attitude. Of course, he has his television to watch *Rocky and Bullwinkle* cartoons and a stereo system to play Tito Puente records, but we also see that he has equipped his living room with a golf green and a basketball court. He has set aside his entire living space for play. This tells us, in a simple way, everything that we needed to know about Murray's character.

The *Stripes* scene was later reworked by Adam Sandler for *Big Daddy* (1999). Sandler's surreal factory-turned-loft included a pinball machine, a golf green, a dart board, and a "Live Nude Girls" neon sign. The most notable difference between the *Stripes* scene and the *Big Daddy* scene is that, in the former scene, the girlfriend character is presented in a sympathetic manner. We see that this breakup is difficult for her and we see that her useless boyfriend has left her no choice. *Big Daddy* wants us to believe that the girlfriend is a horrible person for rejecting Sandler's charming man-child. The Sandler films wanted audiences to believe that the man-child trend was an enchanting and admirable new stage in the evolution of man.

Four years later, the era's man-child was already in full bloom in *Pee-wee's Big Adventure* (1985). Pee-wee Herman demonstrates a playfulness and mischievousness in every aspect of his daily life. He has reshaped the world around him to serve his childish desires and fascinations. He asserts a childlike capacity to find play in a routine as mundane as making breakfast. He activates a Rube Goldberg–type breakfast-making machine that has more entertainment value than practical value. He giggles continually as he watches the contraption operate. Gadgets like Pee-wee's breakfast-making machine were introduced in silent comedy films by Buster Keaton, Harold Lloyd, Snub

Pollard and Charley Bowers. But these gadgets, regardless of their fanciful design, were used strictly for the purpose of efficiency. Pee-wee's gadgets are playthings that exist mostly for their user's amusement. Pee-wee is joyous in his appreciation of his toys and he delights in the wildly imaginative amusement park design of his home. It is certainly a sign of immaturity that Pee-wee likes his bicycle more than anything else in the world. Baby Boomers love Pee-wee. Baby Boomers want to *be* Pee-wee.

The forerunner to Arthur's bedroom and Pee-wee's bedroom was Norman Bates' bedroom in Alfred Hitchcock's decidedly unfunny *Psycho* (1960). The viewer is able to examine Norman's bedroom from the perspective of Lila Crane (Vera Miles), who has snuck into Norman's home for clues regarding her sister's disappearance. A creepiness is conveyed as Lila discovers that this bedroom of a fully grown man is filled with children's playthings. A worn plush rabbit sits alone on a single unmade bed. Its right ear is awkwardly bent. A ribbon around its neck is frayed. The doll has a downturned grin that suggests the joylessness of the place. Film critic Joseph W. Smith III observed, "The script indicates that the bed is 'far too short' for Norman, 'yet the rumpled covers indicate that it is in this bed that Norman sleeps.'"[1] We see a painting of a sailboat, another a painting of a boy on a pony, and a third painting of a little girl in a Victorian dress. We see a schoolboy globe, circus wallpaper, a baby doll, a toy train, a Teddy bear, a portable record player, and a model truck. The only things missing to make this an ideal boy's bedroom are a catcher's mitt and a coloring book. Pee-wee's bedroom includes many similar items, including a Howdy Doody doll, a toy train, a portable record player, a globe, and multiple toy trucks. Pee-wee's wallpaper also has a children's theme, featuring tableaus of a 19th century Indian village. The room does not have a plush rabbit in plain view but it does have a plush ostrich. Can we reasonably regard Norman's bedroom as joyless and unsettling while we regard Pee-wee's bedroom as wondrous and charming?

Pee-wee is defiantly sexless, wanting nothing more than platonic friendships with women. This is made clear in his relationships with Dottie (Elizabeth Daily), who has a crush on Pee-wee, and Simone (Diane Salinger), an unhappy waitress who receives comfort and advice from Pee-wee.

The film is a fantasy by the simple fact that it shows Pee-wee living in his dream home even though he has no visible means of support. Matt Singer of *The Dissolve* wrote, "Pee-wee has no parents, no job, and no responsibilities. He's free to crack silly jokes, goof off, get into adventures, make new friends, and finally get revenge on the snooty neighborhood brat. To a child, all that craziness seems perfectly logical: Of course you'd chase your bicycle across the entire continental U.S. if it got lost. What could possibly be more important than getting back your beloved bike?"[2] The ending of the film is even more unrealistic. Executives at the Warner Brothers movie studio pay Pee-wee to turn his adventures into a James Bond–style action film.

Pee-wee's Big Adventure has been singled out by critics for its unique story structure. Scott Tobias of *The Dissolve* wrote that Pee-wee "manages to win everyone over without having to change a bit. That separates [*Pee-wee's Big Adventure*] from other films about man-children, which usually force them to grow up in the third act."[3] Similarly, *Dissolve* critic Nathan Rabin wrote, "[T]he film doesn't push a maturation arc on

Paul Reubens is content and comfortable in his perfectly designed boy's bedroom in *Pee-wee's Big Adventure* (1985).

a character who doesn't need one, in part because the world of *Pee-wee's Big Adventure* is one where you don't have to grow up or be burdened by the responsibilities of adulthood to have an awesome life."[4] The film took the same position as *Arthur*, which also did not require its childish hero to change.

The film is unique in the way that it presents the world from a child's perspective. Rabin wrote, "On paper, *Pee-wee's Big Adventure* has laughably low stakes: Pee-wee's bike is stolen, and he sets out to retrieve it. But Burton and company do such a great job of getting audiences inside his myopic, childlike sensibility that the loss of his bike assumes a life-or-death importance."[5]

Albert Brooks didn't need Pee-wee Herman's red bow tie and white loafers to play a man-child in *Modern Romance* (1981). Film critic Jay Carr wrote, "Brooks encompasses comedy's three Ns—neurosis, narcissism and neediness."[6] Brooks has the self-absorbed perspective of a child. Everything that happens to him is epic in scale because, of course, it happens to him. At one point, he equates his troubled relationship with his girlfriend Mary Harvard (Kathryn Harrold) with the Vietnam war. Carr describes Brooks' character as "whiny and impossible."[7] This neurotic young man is insecure, obsessive, possessive, and irrational. He is desperate for attention and approval. He is, in other words, a child.

In *Three Men and a Baby* (1987), three happy bachelors have their lives suddenly disrupted by a baby girl who shows up on their doorstep. Domesticity does not make

Pee-wee Herman (Paul Reubens) looks small and helpless compared to jealous boyfriend Andy (Jon Harris) in *Pee-wee's Big Adventure* **(1985).**

these men fat and cranky as it did to Jack Lemmon in *How to Murder Your Wife*. The baby easily draws out maternal instincts in these manly men, which is the thin joke on which the entire film is built. Like Keaton's *The Navigator*, the film shows foolish men who are able to tap into powerful inner resources to handle sudden responsibilities.

Big (1988) presents a man who has a legitimate reason to be immature. A 12-year-old boy, Josh Baskin (David Moscow), attends a carnival with his family. He happens to meet up with Cynthia, a pretty classmate he likes. As they get on line for a ride, Josh and Cynthia are joined by Derek, a strapping sixteen-year-old boy who is dating Cynthia. Josh feels small and inadequate alongside Derek, but he feels even worse when the ticket taker stops him from getting on the ride because he is too short. Dejected, Josh puts a coin into a wish machine called Zoltar Speaks and makes a wish "to be big." He wakes up the next morning and finds he has become a six-foot-tall, 185-pound adult (Tom Hanks). By this time, many films had involved a man who acted as if he was a boy trapped in a man's body. This time, a boy has *actually* become trapped in a man's body. Josh's mother panics to find this strange man in her home and, when she screams for help, Josh sees no option other than to run away.

Josh needs to get a job while he and his best friend, Billy Kopecki (Jared Rushton), try to locate the wish machine and undo its spell. He gets a job as a data entry clerk at MacMillan Toys. The president of the company, Mr. MacMillan (Robert Loggia), has a chance encounter with Josh in the world-famous FAO Schwarz toy store and he is immediately impressed with Josh's contagious enthusiasm and his insight into toys. He quickly promotes Josh to vice president of product development. Josh's office becomes cluttered with the prototypes of various toys. When Billy asks him what his job is, he says, "I play with all this stuff and then I go in and I tell them what I think." This, of course, is a dream job for a boy.

The film is, in many ways, a lighter and more charming version of *Being There*. Josh is favored by a high-powered businessman known as "The Old Man," who mistakes his naïve statements for something more profound.

> MACMILLAN: You can't see this on a marketing report.
> JOSH: Um, what's a marketing report?
> MACMILLAN: Exactly!

His new salary allows him to upgrade his lifestyle. He obtains a roomy loft apartment, which he furnishes with various playthings: a basketball hoop, an inflatable dinosaur, a Pepsi machine, a skateboard ramp, a pinball machine, a Gumby lounge chair, a trampoline, a dart board, and a fluorescent lamp in the shape of the Empire State Building. He rivals Arthur and Pee-wee for his decorating sense.

The film portrays the adults in the corporate world as immature, which enables Josh to comfortably fit within his work group. Immaturity is never more evident than when a rival executive, Paul Davenport (John Heard), has a tantrum upon learning that Josh has a bigger office than he does. Similar to a subplot of *Being There*, Paul has an investigation conducted to find out where Josh came from and he can't believe it when he's told there's no record of this mysterious man.

Josh develops a romantic relationship with a co-worker, Susan Lawrence (Elizabeth Perkins). This is the cornerstone of the film. Like Eve in *Being There*, Susan is perplexed trying to find a way to get Josh to become physical with her. Josh simply isn't ready for sex. He has the following exchange with co-worker Scotty:

> SCOTTY: See that girl over there in the red? Say "hi" to her and she's yours. She'll have her legs around you so tight you'll be begging for mercy.
> JOSH: Well, I'll stay away from her then.

Of course, Josh must have *some* sexual interest as it was an attraction to a pretty girl that got him to wish for his transformation.

Josh's boyish curiosity is aroused when he gets to ride in the back seat of a stretch limousine with Susan. He plays with the electric door locks, checks for a dial tone on the car phone, flicks the light switches on and off, changes the channels on the radio, and finally sticks his head out the sun roof. This is different than the way that the more passive and slow-witted Chance reacts to his first ride in a limousine. Chance is content to play with the remote control of the limousine's television. As a normal and well-adjusted boy, Josh is excited to discover this new world.

It is only a matter of time before this eager, curious boy explores the new and exciting world of sex and romance. In *Arthur*, Arthur and Linda's first date was at a game arcade. Josh and Susan's first date is at an amusement park. To a boy, these are perfect places to go to have fun. Josh and Susan's date is filled with play. The couple first express love for one another while bouncing together on a trampoline. It's no wonder, under the circumstances, that Josh is able to bring out the young girl in Susan. She abandons her back-stabbing corporate shark ways and becomes kind, open, and loving. She, in turn, brings out the man in Josh. He learns romance, passion, confidence, sensitivity, and responsibility. He works hard to act like an adult around Susan. He waits until she's asleep to play a video game. This is amusing when you consider how, today, men openly play video games. The film shows that children and adults both have valuable qualities and that a person can find happiness by combining the best qualities of both life stages.

As the relationship develops, we never again see Josh's loft. The couple is only seen together in Susan's stylish and practical apartment. Josh's love of Susan has caused him to become lost in the adult world. Romance and sex have, in this instance, proven to be the death of childhood.

When he finally locates the wish machine, Josh has to decide if he is willing to give up a successful career and a loving girlfriend to become a boy again. He visits his old neighborhood. He sees children playing baseball, riding bicycles, and jumping around in leaves. He sees Cynthia and her friends piling into a car. This last sight makes him aware that, by restoring his youth, he can look forward to the joys and thrills of his imminent teenage years. What should he do? It's a difficult question to answer and it is doubtful that every viewer can agree with the choice that Josh finally makes.

An important part of becoming an adult is conquering fears that can prevent you from functioning in the wide world. This is the initial question posed in *What About Bob?* (1991). Bob (Bill Murray) is afraid to leave his apartment, ride a bus, or get into an elevator. His new psychiatrist, Dr. Leo Marvin, tells him that he is "an almost paralyzed multi-phobic personality that is in a constant state of panic." The doctor applies his "Baby Steps" philosophy to treating Bob. He tells Bob to take small steps in making his way through the world. This means that, due to his anxieties, Bob must begin moving with short, unsteady steps like an overgrown toddler.

Bob can be slightly manipulative, like a child. This is most obvious when he has a sobbing fit to get his way with Dr. Marvin. But he is, for the most part, guileless. Dr. Marvin becomes incensed when this neurotic nuisance follows him to his vacation home and befriends his family. The situation keeps getting worse and, finally, Dr. Marvin is driven to a nervous breakdown. The film ends with Bob marrying Dr. Marvin's beloved sister, Lily. To Dr. Marvin's horror, the endlessly irritating Bob is now his brother-in-law. But does Bob's marriage mean that Bob possesses a mature sexual desire? We never see him kiss Lily or hold her tightly. His sexual desire is not evident in the film, but the script included a closing scene in which Bob and Lily become the proud parents of triplets.

Murray was back playing a different sort of man-child in *Groundhog Day* (1993). The film introduces us to a decidedly unpleasant man, Phil Connors (Murray): miserable, arrogant, self-centered, insincere, and caustic. The film explores the way the character changes when he becomes stuck in a time loop and has to live the same day over and over. At first, Phil exploits the fact that he can do anything without worrying about

Top and above: Tom Hanks and Elizabeth Perkins gradually get to know one another in *Big* (1988).

the consequences. He engages in gluttony, philandering, and general bad habits. In a memorable moment, Phil stuffs creamy pastries into his mouth while his lovely co-worker Rita (Andie MacDowell) looks on in disgust. Next, Phil engages in thrilling, high-risk activities. In one scene, he drives down railroad tracks towards an approaching train. He smiles gleefully just before he swerves to avoid an imminent collision. He is chuckling as he announces, "I'm not going to live by their rules any more!" But eating pastries and cheating death gets to be boring after awhile. He comes to desire more depth and substance from his strange new existence. He realizes that the time loop has given him a chance to become a better person. He cares for a dying homeless man, he catches a boy falling out of a tree, he performs the Heimlich Maneuver on a choking diner, and he counsels a young couple who are having doubts about their pending nuptials. He learns to play the piano, speak foreign languages, and create beautiful ice sculptures. Best of all, he falls in love with Rita. Rita, who recognizes that he has changed, feels love for him, too. The fact that he has learned to care about others and be generous to them is what finally frees him from the time loop. He has developed into a mature person and can now go out into the wide world. Danny Rubin, who wrote *Groundhog Day*, said, "One of the takeaways for people is just the realization that this first day that he experienced, that was so awful, that was so terrible, that was the worst day of his life ever, was the same day that he experienced at the end, the same day that was presented to him, that turned out to be the best day of his life. And the only thing that changed was him."[8]

A major part of maturity is socialization. This becomes obvious in *Ace Ventura: Pet Detective* (1994). Ace (Jim Carrey) is clever and responsible, but it is debatable if he is mature. His vulgarity and flamboyance alienates him from civil adults. He can socialize better with animals than with people.

It is easy to confuse stupidity and immaturity. But the fact is that virtues of maturity, including responsibility, strength and stability, are not dependent on intelligence. Carrey's other big hit of 1994, *Dumb and Dumber*, is overwhelmingly a film about stupidity. The fact that the main characters, Lloyd (Carrey) and Harry (Jeff Daniels), are immature is secondary to the character's experiences. Of course, this is not to say that the characters do not display undeniably childish behavior at times. Restraint and prudence, which are key elements of maturity, are shown to be lacking in Lloyd and Harry. King wrote,

> Sent out to buy "just the bare essentials" with the last of the principals' limited cash, Lloyd emerges from a shop wearing a ludicrous giant Stetson and carrying two cases of beer and a bunch of plastic windmills. Stumbling later across a fortune they intend to restore to its owner, the pair blow it recklessly on a flashy hotel room, a Ferrari and absurdly loud clothes. Playing in the snow in a would-be lyrical interlude, Harry demonstrates an infantile lack of perspective, hurling snowballs with excessive force and generally demonstrating a lack of understanding of the acceptable boundaries of play.[9]

We skip ahead 16 years to a film that ideally clarifies the immaturity versus stupidity debate. *Grown Ups* (2010) is supposed to be about adults acting like children, but children never really act like these adults do. A man shoots another man in the foot with an arrow. A man trips and falls into mud. A man runs into a tree branch. A man swings

Andie MacDowell is appalled by Bill Murray's gluttonous eating habits in *Groundhog Day* (1993).

on a rope swing and slams into a tree trunk. A man slaps another man with a piece of fruit. A man accidentally urinates on another man. Is the average child anywhere near as dumb as this? A young boy at least knows how to control his urine stream.

Critic Michael Arbeiter ideally summed up the slacker characters who populate *Clerks* (1994):

> The depressed, ambitionless Dante, a convenience store clerk, felt the world had nothing to offer him, and vice versa. The indignant Randal, clerk of the partnered video store, was actively rejecting anything thrown his way. Then there was a band of misfits who hung out around the stores, led by delinquent drug dealers Jay and Silent Bob. Smith's film was definitively slacker not only in its characters, but in its mood. It never left the convenience store parking lot setting, never promised anything to Dante or Randal, never even promised much to its audience. It meant to honestly chronicle a day in an increasingly empty life. Very slacktastic.[10]

Matty Show of the Campus Socialite website identified *Billy Madison* (1995) as the keystone to the movie man-child revolution. Billy (Adam Sandler) is a rich and overly pampered 27-year-old twit who, according to Gregory P. Dorr of DVD Journal, maintains a "death-grip on adolescence."[11] Dorr wrote, "[Billy] spends his days drinking, leafing through porno mags, and chasing hallucinatory man-sized penguins."[12] He hangs out for most of the day in a tent set up outside his mansion. This is probably because he doesn't want to be house-trained, preferring to live as an untamed savage amid the foliage and shrubbery of the estate. He is somewhat like Huck Finn, who would rather sleep in the woodshed than in his home. He devotes himself to frivolous interests. Lying out by the pool, he draws a smiley face on his chest with sunscreen. Billy has turned his lavish estate into a giant playground. This surpasses Pee-wee Herman's home in length and breadth. The larger scale is especially evident when Billy merrily drives a golf cart into a set of giant inflatable bowling pins. Show wrote, "The whole movie is about [Billy] going back to grade school—he fits right in there."[13]

Critic J.R. Jones noted that, in Sandler's early films, he "oscillat[ed] between boyish mania and worldly wisecracks."[14] Sandler's crowd-pleasing performance in *Billy Madison* was quickly followed by Chris Farley's equally childish antics in *Tommy Boy* (1995). It is not surprising since, together, Sandler and Farley had perfected their gleefully juvenile ways on NBC's *Saturday Night Live* series.

In *Big Daddy* (1999), Sandler plays Sonny Koufax, a man who has spent years refusing to take on adult responsibility. Koufax is adequately described by Wikipedia as follows: "[He] is an unreliable, unmotivated 32-year-old bachelor.... He has a degree in law but has chosen not to take the bar exam.... He is employed, on a part-time basis only, as a toll booth attendant, and more or less does this job just to get out of the apartment once in a while."[15] Sonny's efforts to care for an abandoned young boy inspire him to become responsible. We find in the final scene of the film that the newly mature Sonny has achieved success as a husband, a father and a lawyer.

Who is the real childish fool of *The Dinner Game* (1998)? A group of friends com-

Adam Sandler is comfortable as an elementary school student in *Billy Madison* (1995).

pete to find the stupidest person and bring that person to a dinner. Pierre Brochant (Thierry Lhermitte) could not be more pleased when he finds François Pignon (Jacques Villeret), whose hobby is constructing elaborate replicas of famous landmarks out of toothpicks. Pignon fails the maturity test due to his lack of social skills and his poor perspective of social situations. CNN film critic Paul Tatara wrote, "[Pignon's] core stupidity bubbles to the top during his inept stabs at intelligent conversation. He thinks he's much more clever than he is, can't keep his mind on the subject at hand and laughs at highly inappropriate times."[16] But is Brochant any better? Mocking those less fortunate than you is childish. It has also proven to be the case that an inflated sense of your own value can bring about a negative outcome. Pride goes before a fall.

Brochant, who is athletic, graceful and handsome, is outwardly superior to Pignon, who is overweight and lacks physical grace. But during a casual round of golf, Brochant throws out his back. Pignon now appears fit and vigorous compared to Brochant, who spends the remainder of the film unable to stand upright. The fact that he is physically helpless leaves him vulnerable to Pignon, whose efforts to help him do nothing but create calamity. Through a series of gaffes, Pignon inadvertently exposes Brochant as an adulterer to his wife and a tax evader to a tax auditor. But the simple fact is that Brochant has made himself vulnerable. His terrible secrets have rendered him weak and defenseless. It proved to be just as easy for this flimsy and pretentious man to throw away his life as it was for him to throw out his back.

THE BIG LEBOWSKI: What makes a man, Mr. Lebowski?
THE DUDE: Dude.
THE BIG LEBOWSKI: Huh?
THE DUDE: Uhh.... I don't know sir.
THE BIG LEBOWSKI: Is it being prepared to do the right thing, whatever the cost? Isn't that what makes a man?
THE DUDE: Hmmm.... Sure, that and a pair of testicles.

Critic Roger Ager asserted that *The Big Lebowski* (1998), which is populated by weak and sexless male characters, showcases the decline of masculinity. Ager refers to them as "single guys with nothing better to do than go bowling."[17] Prominent among the bowlers is Vietnam veteran Walter Sobchak (John Goodman). Walter is, by every indication, a cranky, oversized baby. He is dim-witted, opinionated, paranoid, boisterous, and prone to tantrums.

At one point, a petty disagreement during a bowling match causes Walter to brandish a .45 caliber handgun. He starts out calmly. He informs Smokey (Jimmie Dale Gilmore), a player on the opposing team, that he stepped over the foul line before he released his ball. "[T]his is not Nam," he says. "This is bowling. There are rules." He tries his best to look officious, as if he wants to come across as reasonable and mature. But he is unable to maintain his composure when Smokey flatly denies his foot went over the line and demands that he score points for the round. Walter's voice rumbles in anger as he cautions Smokey, "You're entering a world of pain." By now, he has become frightening. This is when the gun comes out. His best friend, The Dude (Jeff Bridges), manages to restrain Walter before any harm is done. The two men later discuss the incident.

Jeff Bridges, Steve Buscemi and John Goodman consider their weekly bowling game the highpoint of their lives in *The Big Lebowski* (1998).

THE DUDE: Just take it easy, man.
WALTER SOBCHAK: I'm perfectly calm, Dude.
THE DUDE (shouting): Yeah, waving the fucking gun around?
WALTER SOBCHAK: Calmer than you are.
THE DUDE: Will you just take it easy?
WALTER SOBCHAK: Calmer than you are.

Denial is Walter's chief way of dealing with his own failures. Ager wrote, "[Walter] is almost never able to admit being wrong, even though he is wrong virtually all the time."[18] Denial is a simple defense mechanism that is often seen in children. A child breaks an object in full view of his mother and immediately exclaims, "I didn't do it!" This is motivated by a child's feelings of helplessness and vulnerability.

Walter has obviously learned to cope by combining denial with tantrums. Insecure and emotionally immature people will throw temper tantrums to get their way. Edgar Kennedy, the master of the "slow burn" comic take, was always struggling to control his temper in films. These efforts were the focus of a short comedy, *Hold Your Temper* (1943). Similarly, Ian Holm portrays Napoleon Bonaparte as a tantrum-prone man-child in *The Adventures of Baron Munchausen* (1988).

It is not surprising that The Dude, who shirks work and responsibility, would have the carefree attitude of a child. Critic Graham Daseler wrote, "The Dude ambles rather than walks, mumbles rather than talks, and slouches in any chair he can find, invariably tossing a leg over the arm rest.... [T]he role required an actor who could abandon all self-consciousness."[19]

A child, who is still developing verbal skills, will tend to regurgitate the words of others. In the same way, The Dude has a habit of borrowing other people's phrases. This idea was explored by Ager in his analysis of the film. Here are two of Ager's examples:

> He sees George Bush on the TV screen spouting: "This aggression will not stand, against Kuwait." Dude repeats this line to Lebowski: "The dude minds ... this will not stand ... this aggression will not stand, man."
>
> Maude tells him: "Little matter to me that this woman chose to pursue a career in pornography, nor that she has been 'banging' Jackie Treehorn, to use the parlance of our times." Dude repeats the line "parlance of our times" in Lebowski's limo: "Look at it, man ... young trophy wife, in the parlance of our times."[20]

Walter gets angry when his simple-minded friend Donny tries to become involved in a private conversation that he is having with The Dude. He explains to Donny that he has "no frame of reference." He likens Donny to a child who has wandered into the middle of a movie and wants to know what's happening. The truth is that every one of the film's characters is befuddled, consistently acting as if they have wandered into the middle of the movie and have no idea what is happening. That is exactly what it is like for an untrained child wandering through his formative years.

10

Problem Child

Modern comedies tend to depict men coping desperately with their failures, inadequacies and vulnerabilities. Men are in crisis in today's world. It is difficult to find motivation, direction and security amid the social chaos of our times. The tipping point could come with the Apocalypse, which could finally rally men to a simple and worthwhile cause. In *Shaun of the Dead* (2004), an unexpected crisis is certainly effective in shaking a young man out of his complacency. Shaun (Simon Pegg) is an unambitious electronics salesman. His staid businessman roommate, Pete (Peter Serafinowicz), accuses Shaun of having no direction in life. He tells him, "Sort your fucking life out, mate!" At first, Shaun is too self-absorbed to notice that hordes of zombies have invaded his town. It takes a massive assault by the zombies to finally help Shaun to find perspective and motivate him to take action.

A point could be made that society has become hopelessly corrupted and the one way to integrate into society is to become corrupted yourself. The only alternative for a person who wishes to retain their purity is to avoid the wide world altogether. The lead character of *Cedar Rapids* (2011), Tim Lippe, grew up in a small Wisconsin town, where he was sheltered from the harsh realities of the larger world. When he leaves town to attend a regional conference, he finds that his displays of naïveté and idealism put him out of place with the other people at the conference. Several people are charmed by his childlike ways, but others are either puzzled or repulsed by his peculiar behavior. In the end, Tim proves to be the most moral and mature man at the conference.

In the twenty-first century, the man-child has regularly turned up in films, assuming a variety of forms. In *Elf* (2003), Santa Claus is unaware as he delivers gifts to an orphanage that a playful baby named Buddy has climbed into his sack. Santa doesn't discover Buddy until he rejoins his elves at the North Pole. The jolly Christmas legend, who upholds himself as the patron saint of children, feels deeply responsible for the orphan boy and acts in the child's best interest by placing him in the care of a senior elf (Bob Newhart). As an adult, Buddy (Will Ferrell) finds himself a misfit among his elf peers. He comes to the conclusion that the North Pole is not where he belongs. He travels to New York City to locate his biological father, but his innocence, goodness and high spirits make it even more difficult for him to fit in among the cynical big city inhabitants. He would likely function better if he had less optimism and more insight. But how could Buddy be any different? He grew up in a winter wonderland where happy elves were dedicated year-round to making children's dreams come true. He himself

10. Problem Child

Nick Frost and Simon Pegg need to set aside their video games and drunken horseplay to defeat a zombie horde in *Shaun of the Dead* (2004).

wiled away his days assembling toys in Santa's workshop. How could a person get grumpy when their most stressful job was product-testing the latest supply of Etch A Sketch pads? Buddy is even more upbeat due to the fact that he subsists on candy, Pop Tarts and maple syrup. Unfortunately, not everyone who saw the film was charmed by this goofy, six-foot-three human elf. *People* critic Leah Rozen wrote, "Ferrell overplays his sweet, almost fey simpleton."[1] Scott Tobias of *A.V. Club* was unamused by the film's efforts to contrast New York City cynicism with Ferrell's "gleeful, near-psychotic enthusiasm."[2]

In *Failure to Launch* (2006), Matthew McConaughey plays a 35-year-old man who still lives with his parents. McConaughey is no helpless layabout. He isn't lacking in social skills, self-esteem, or business aptitude. He enjoys a substantial income from selling sailboats, which affords him numerous luxuries. He simply likes to have his mom do his laundry and cook his meals. Even more important, he knows it will discourage women from getting serious with him if they see that he's living with his parents.

The Foot Fist Way (2006) introduces viewers to taekwondo instructor Fred Simmons (Danny McBride). Aggressively arrogant and shockingly self-deluded, Simmons imparts a false and overbearing bravado in the manner of a bully on a playground. He manages with his bluster and narcissism to be obnoxious and unsettling. He extols five tenets of taekwondo: self-control, courtesy, perseverance, integrity and indomitable spirit. The film's humor largely comes from seeing how far afield Simmons is from the principles that he espouses.

In *You, Me and Dupree* (2006), Randolph Dupree (Owen Wilson) is an unemployed 36-year-old who spends his extensive free time either hitting baseballs or skateboarding with the neighborhood kids. Unable to support himself, he moves in with his best friend Carl Peterson (Matt Dillon) and Carl's new bride, Molly (Kate Hudson). Dupree's childish ways make him a nuisance to the couple. How childish is Dupree? The fact that he habitually clogs the toilet shows that the man has never gotten beyond the potty training stage.

An unplanned pregnancy can change the rules drastically. Party-loving Ben Stone (Seth Rogen) realizes that he needs to grow up in *Knocked Up* (2007). His life is devoted to hanging out with the boys and figuring out ways to have fun. A day isn't worthwhile unless these friends can come up with a silly new game. They battle each other with quarterstaffs. They box with gloves that have been soaked in lighter fluid and set on fire. In one scene, Ben gets the most out of a joint by wearing a giant fishbowl over his head and letting the smoke fill it. He has the blissful, blank expression of an idiot. But then he gets television personality Alison Scott (Katherine Heigl) pregnant during a one-stand and realizes that he has to change his life entirely.

Rogen does not exhibit Moe Howard's inability to recognize his own intellectual shortcomings, or Oliver Hardy's desperate need to be respected, or Harry Langdon's fear of sex. He is smart, self-satisfied and, when a woman climbs into bed with him, he

Will Ferrell acts like a big goofy kid in *Elf* (2003).

knows without hesitation what to do. It is his self-indulgent pursuit of pleasure and his avoidance of responsibility that makes him a big kid. Maureen Dowd of *The New York Times* wrote that the filmmaker's message "is that his lost boys must put their toys away and find the deeper fun in adult responsibilities."[3] But was that really the message? Judd Apatow, writer-director of *Knocked Up*, isn't sure. "I just find immaturity is funny. I think we all start out pretty immature and then we have to have this moment where we decide ... 'I'm not going to behave like that any more,'" he said. "And I don't even know if that's a good thing."[4] He admitted that he himself wasn't mature. "Not really," he said.

Apatow made it clear in a 2009 interview with Jezebel that his intention was to show men and women at their worst: "I don't really want to watch mature people or

Katherine Heigl and Seth Rogen are deeply troubled by an unplanned pregnancy in *Knocked Up* (2007).

smart people or people who do the right thing. I like to meet them in life, but I don't find them entertaining. And certainly not funny. So I feel like the worse people are, the more amusing [it is] and the more I root for them to figure their shit out."[5] Interviewer Anna North did not see this as a fair evaluation of Apatow's characters. She wrote that his movies "aren't really about bad people—they're about bumbling people, who are sort of trying to do the right thing even as they wonder what the right thing is and why they should care."[6] Apatow went on in the interview to defend Seth Rogen's character in *Knocked Up*: "He's gruff.... [H]e has this vicious sense of humor. But he's also very sweet. And you root for him, because as tough as he is, you kind of know his life is probably tricky. He's a really great underdog guy with a big heart who will always try to do the right thing."[7]

The two main characters of *Step Brothers* (2008), played by Will Ferrell and John C. Reilly, are described by Dan Persons of the Reelz website as "petulant, privileged layabouts."[8] The film's director and co-author, Adam McKay, described them as guys "who have no life skills, no actual power, but who walk around completely entitled as if they have *all* the power."[9] He saw these deluded characters as a product of modern America. Critic Michael Arbeiter described Ferrell and Reilly's behavior as "macho obstinacy."[10] He declared Ferrell, who had previously demonstrated his buffoonish macho jock act in *Anchorman: The Legend of Ron Burgundy* (2004) and *Talladega Nights: The Ballad of Ricky Bobby* (2006), as the "[p]atron saint of thickheaded alpha

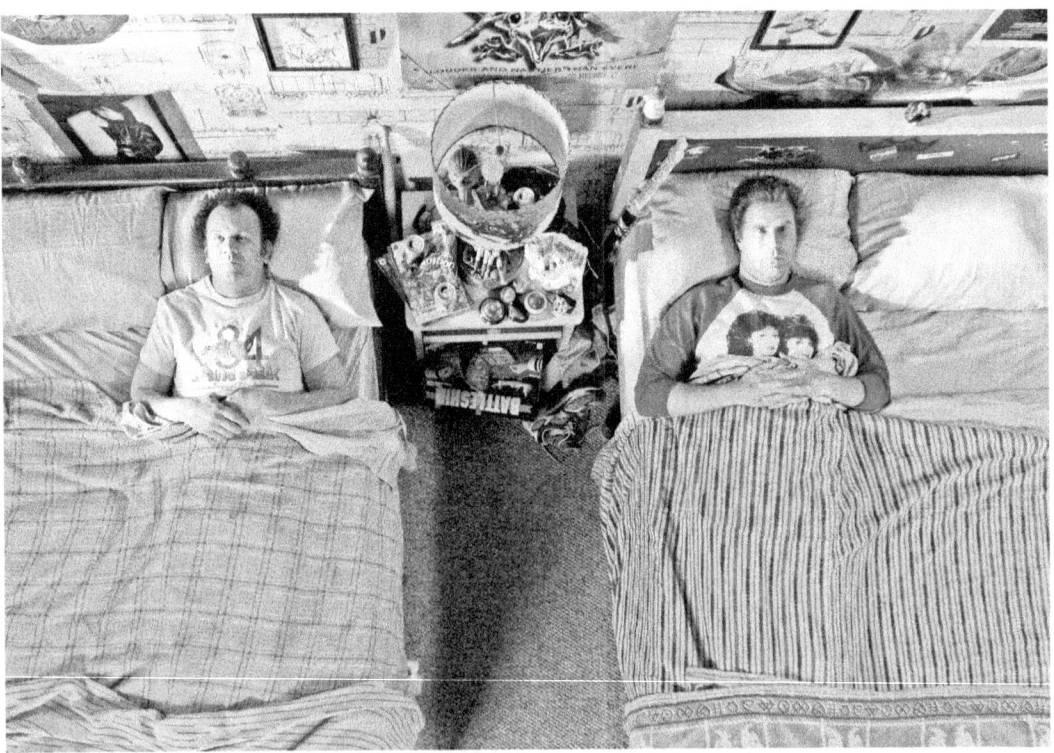

John Reilly and Will Ferrell are united by their mutual childishness in *Step Brothers* (2008).

male identity."[11] The film's message is that happiness for the man-child, and for his friends and family depends on the man-child never changing.

At the start of *Cyrus* (2010), we are introduced to hapless divorcee John Kilpatrick (John C. Reilly). Insecure and anxious, John hardly lives up to the standards of maturity. It is established in the opening scene that he still depends heavily on his ex-wife, Jamie (Catherine Keener), for emotional support. Jamie functions in his life as a mother figure, which makes it humiliating when she walks in on him while he is masturbating. Later, John is elated when he meets Molly (Marisa Tomei) at a party. This is a warm and caring woman who can transform him and make him a better man. But then he meets Molly's clingy and emotionally needy 21-year-old son Cyrus (Jonah Hill), who is more insecure and anxious than he himself has ever been. Unwilling to give up his weirdly intimate relationship with his mother, Cyrus works hard to sabotage his mother's relationship with John. Filmmakers Jay and Mark Duplass make a point to keep the rivalry from descending into unlikely slapstick antics. At times, Cyrus can be dark and devious in his tactics. Critic Ed Whitfield called him "manipulative and malicious while outwardly gracious, a nicely observed comment on a generation of young adults well versed in the rhetoric of adulthood but inwardly insecure, terrified and not yet divested of the ruthless selfishness which we normally attribute to young children."[12] In the end, Cyrus realizes that his actions have hurt his mother. He understands that, in failing to manage his fears and insecurities, he has behaved in a dysfunctional manner. He offers John a poignant apology and helps to get him back together with his mother.

Our Idiot Brother (2011) and *Jeff, Who Lives at Home* (2011), which were released less than a month apart, make it clear that slackers have better lives than their uptight siblings, who have been driven miserable by their relentless pursuit of family and career. The two films agree that it is the responsible sibling who is the real screw-up.

Roald Dahl's 1964 children's novel *Charlie and the Chocolate Factory* introduced the world to genius candymaker Willy Wonka. Author Kevin Miller described Wonka as "a mysterious, delightfully childlike man."[13] It is Wonka's wonder and whimsy that makes him the most like a child. Director Tim Burton chose to emphasize the character's childlike qualities in a 2005 film adaptation, also called *Charlie and the Chocolate Factory*. In Burton's film, Wonka is physically and socially awkward. Scriptwriter John August blames Wonka's arrested development on an unresolved conflict with his estranged father.

Overall, this varied group of films shows us many different children: the naïve child, the selfish child, the lazy child, the scrappy child, the scary child, the messy child, the possessive child, the playful child, and the genius child. These films put into question if the man-child is glorious or tragic, enchanting or repulsive, goofy or creepy.

Other less significant examples of man-child play small roles in films. In *Grandma's Boy* (2006), Jeff (Nick Swardson), a 30-year-old man, still lives with his parents. He wears footy pajamas, sleeps in a racecar bed with stuffed animals, and spends most of his time and energy playing video games. An amusing character in *Pain and Gain* (2013) is hulking, childlike ex-con Paul Doyle (Dwayne Johnson). We have seen this character in films before, for example Lennie (Lon Chaney, Jr.) of *Of Mice and Men* (1939) and Moose Malloy (Mike Mazurki) of *Murder, My Sweet* (1944).

The Guardian's Steve Rose concluded that the immature characters of modern-day films are not believable: "Hollywood's manchild heroes usually exist in an artificial reality sustained by other movie constructs. Chief among these is a mature female love interest with a blind spot about men. These heroines invariably manage to hold down a serious job, manage a family, and generally cope with the adult world while still being gorgeous, and yet they find an ungroomed layabout half their mental age irresistibly attractive."[14] He specifically referenced Seth Rogen's character in *Knocked Up*. But Rogen was not a pioneer of this trend. Let's look at Dagwood Bumstead. Dagwood's chief pastimes at home were eating colossal sandwiches and napping on the sofa. With his perpetual bedhead, he could hardly be called a well-groomed man. Yet, while Dagwood was ungroomed and dimwitted, he was married to the gorgeous Blondie, who was always around to manage family affairs and come up with quick-witted solutions to her dopey husband's problems.

In real life, a husband needs to play a responsible role in a marriage. He needs to work together with his wife for the marriage to be a success. When a mature person marries an immature person, a parent-child relationship is bound to develop. The mature spouse will have to constantly teach, motivate, correct and direct the immature spouse. This relationship cannot develop into a prosperous marriage. Marriage demands maturity because, for this close partnership to be successful, each spouse needs to confront the needs and expectations of the other.

In *Juno* (2007), Vanessa Loring (Jennifer Garner) has arranged to adopt a baby, but her husband Mark (Jason Bateman) abruptly reveals to her that he is not ready to be a father. From the script:

MARK: It all just happened so fast. We put that ad in the paper. I thought it would take months if, you know, ever and then—boom—two weeks later, she's in our living room.
VANESSA (quietly): She answered our prayers.
MARK (ignores the comment): Ever since, it's just been like a ticking clock.

This stops Vanessa. Juno [the adopted child] looks offended.

VANESSA: What are you saying?

A long hideous beat.

MARK: It just feels a little like bad timing.

Another hideous beat.

VANESSA: What would be a good time for you?
MARK: I don't know. There's just things I still want to do.
VANESSA: Like what? Be a rock star?
MARK: Don't mock me.

Vanessa sighs. It's done.

VANESSA: You're trying to do something that's never going to happen. And you know what? Your shirt is stupid. Grow up. If I have to wait for you to become Kurt Cobain, I'm never going to be a mother.

Vanessa looks defeated.

MARK: I never said I'd be a great father.

In films, a young woman might recognize value in a faithful and kind-hearted man-child and be willing to provide this less-than-ideal man with whatever support

Jennifer Garner and Jason Bateman must fully commit to adulthood to become parents in *Juno* (2007). Pictured in this scene are, from left to right, Garner, Bateman and Ellen Page.

and encouragement he needs to be successful. It is a simple premise. Behind every successful man-child is a wise, loving and mature woman. But, according to a more recent trend in films, the woman who marries a man-child is not wise, loving or mature. Yesterday's Blondie is today's harpy. In *Hall Pass* (2011), stern-faced wives habitually admonish their husbands as if these men are feeble-minded children. These films have been a way to denigrate masculinity. According to critic Michael Arbeiter, the wives in these films are required to put up with their husbands' dumb behavior and "make sure nothing catches fire."[15] That was not an exaggerated claim. In an episode of *Everybody Loves Raymond*, the dumb hubby (Ray Romano) sets his kitchen on fire while preparing dinner. Communication giant Viacom got into the habit of degrading fathers with "idiot dad" sitcoms like *Everyone Loves Raymond*, *Still Standing* and *Yes, Dear*. This can be dangerous in our times as we have become a society in which the widespread media can exert a powerful influence on political status. Camille Paglia wrote, "Men's faults, failings and foibles have been seized on and magnified into gruesome bills of indictment.... When an educated culture routinely denigrates masculinity and manhood, then women will be perpetually stuck with boys, who have no incentive to mature or to honor their commitments."[16] This modern trend is not without precedent. Laurel and Hardy were treated like children by their wives in *Sons of the Desert* (1933). The shrewish wife was a stock comic character of the era. Kathleen Howard showed the shrewish wife to full effect in *It's a Gift* (1934). Her timid husband, played by W.C. Fields, has no chance with her around to assert dominance in his home.

In medieval times, chivalrous suitors wooed their intended with sweet serenades and flowery poetry. In the Victorian era, English gentlemen made an offer of marriage by sending a pair of gloves to a woman. If the woman wore the gloves to church on Sunday, it signaled her acceptance of the proposal. These were sweet ways to propose marriage, especially in comparison to having a man engage in a bloody joust to win a maiden's hand. But these approaches would hardly be appropriate in many ancient cultures in which a man had to prove to a woman that he could be her protector and provider. Even today, a man should be required to show strength and sobriety when he asks a woman to be his wife. It doesn't seem that he would convey this if he proposed marriage by attaching a wedding ring to a kitten's collar. This is an issue that is raised in *Meet the Parents* (2000). Greg Focker (Ben Stiller) is deeply in love with elementary schoolteacher Pam Byrnes (Teri Polo), and he believes that the time is right to ask her to be his wife. Under Greg's direction, Pam's students hold up letters scrawled in finger paints to spell out "Marry me, Pam." This decidedly childlike marriage proposal foretells the series of immature blunders that Greg will make during the couple's subsequent weekend with Pam's parents.

Men no longer need to show their prowess as protectors and providers to get sex. Blogger Brett McKay wrote, "In 'the sexual marketplace,' the male demand for sex has remained the same, but its 'price' has dropped dramatically; there's no need to slay a dragon, just buy a lady dinner and invite her back to your place. The modern 'cheapness' of sex, some theorize, accounts for the way many young men are resisting commitment and floundering in other areas of their lives such as academics or career responsibilities."[17] In *About a Boy* (2002), Will Freeman (Hugh Grant) sees no consequences to sex, which makes it easy for him to lie to a woman to get her into bed. He has no problem admitting to people that he is unreliable and emotionally stunted. He speaks with pride when he acknowledges his shallow ways. He has no discernible qualities to be a husband or a father. He shuns commitment, despises children, and is crassly insensitive. His life is meaningless, revolving around sexual conquests and leisure activities. Then he meets a 12-year-old boy, Marcus (Nicholas Hoult), whose depressed mother (Toni Collette) has taken an overdose of pills. Brett reluctantly agrees to looks after Marcus and quickly develops a close relationship with the boy. Their bond brings out intimate emotions in Brett, which is something that he never before experienced. His new openness enables him to develop a loving relationship with a single mother, Rachel (Rachel Weisz). Of course, Brett's journey to intimacy is backwards as a man normally wins the heart of a woman and then takes on responsibility for a child.

It appealed to audiences to see a child's insensitive caretaker soften under the constant bombardment of the child's cuteness and eventually form a close and unbreakable bond with the child. We had seen it in films as far back as *The Kid* (1921). People may remember Chaplin as nothing but a sensitive and loving caretaker to foundling Jackie Coogan. Clips from the film always show Chaplin hugging the child, kissing the child, crying for the child. But Chaplin was not so affectionate at the start of the story. It took him time to bond with the foundling. His first instinct was to dump the bundle of joy

Hugh Grant is appalled by the prospect of marriage and babies in *About a Boy* (2002).

down into a street grating. But he did soften as so many caretakers after him would do. In more recent years, this storyline has become more popular than ever. Audiences have responded enthusiastically to these films, including *Bad News Bears* (1976), *Baby Boom* (1987), *3 Men and a Baby* (1987) and *Big Daddy* (1999). Veroff could have predicted this trend as far back as 1976. Men and women once associated their success as a parent to their status as a provider, but they now saw the extent of their closeness to their children as the ultimate measure of their worth as a parent.[18]

High Fidelity (2000) opens with Laura (Iben Hjejle) walking out on her boyfriend Rob (John Cusack). Rob is so devastated that he is compelled to reexamine his past relationships with women to figure out what he's been doing wrong. He goes as far as tracking down old girlfriends to talk with them about their breakups. It is revealed through these conversations as well as flashbacks that Rob is self-centered and lazy and he has never been willing to commit to any of his relationships. At the outcome of his self-examination, Rob realizes that he has been a dithering child and it is time for him to grow up.

The lead characters of *Sideways* (2004), Jack Cole (Thomas Haden Church) and Miles Raymond (Paul Giamatti), are not at all mature. They are not confident, secure or forthright. Though in their forties, they have yet to find what they want from life and settle down. Jack has devoted his life to getting fleeting pleasure out of short-lived affairs. After managing to avoid marriage for years, he is now engaged to the daughter of a real estate entrepreneur and he's scheduled to walk down the aisle in a matter of days. However, he has his doubts about going through with the marriage and gets the idea to have one last sexual fling before he takes his vows. Jack, who cares about no one but himself, is a scoundrel. He can't be bothered with ethical behavior or moral standards. He's undisciplined, impudent, impulsive and shifty. He repeatedly lies to his closest acquaintances to conceal his bad behavior. He's the child who hides a report card so his parents won't learn about his poor grades. At one point, Miles calls him an infant. A woman who falls for his charm and has sex with him is shocked to learn that he is getting married in a few days. She is more blunt in her assessment of Jack, who she calls "a fucking lying piece of shit!"

Miles is not much better. He is a depressed divorcee who has been unable to function well in life. He's frustrated because he's a teacher but he really wants to be a novelist. He acts like a petulant child throughout an uncomfortable visit with his mother. The visit proves, in the end, to be a ruse. When his mother is eating dinner and talking to Jack, he sneaks into her bedroom to steal cash out of her lingerie drawer. His mother keeps this stash of cash hidden inside an empty canister of kitchen cleanser. Miles cautiously twists off the top of the canister just like a child twisting the lid off a cookie jar to steal a cookie.

Mature men are men of action. They act relentlessly to attack problems and surmount obstacles. This is not the case with the manchild. We often get that moment in the manchild comedy where the manchild becomes overwhelmed by his problems and has no idea what to do next. He feels lost in the world and can do nothing more than stare off blankly into space. This is a staring off blankly into space moment enacted by Paul Giamatti and Thomas Haden Church in *Sideways* (2004).

Throughout the film, both men act furtive and jittery. They are willing to lie and manipulate to avoid exposure of their true character and to evade accountability. They are embarrassed and disappointed with themselves, but they preferred to behave badly and keep the sordidness of their actions to themselves rather than find ways to become better people. They abide by the "They'll be none the wiser" strategy that Laurel and Hardy often used without success. The film deals, in a large part, with the inevitable fall-out that results from the lies that these men tell. Take away the film's sex and nudity and you have Laurel and Hardy's *Sons of the Desert* (1933), which also deals with the fall-out from childish lies.

Late in the story, Jack shows that he has feelings. A waitress takes him to her home and, while they're having sex, her husband comes home unexpectedly. Jack has to flee without his wallet, which contains his wedding rings. He returns to Miles distraught and regressing into a blubbering baby: "Look, I know I fucked up, okay? I know I fucked up. But you've gotta help me. You've gotta help me, Miles, please! Please! I can't lose Christine, Miles. I just—I can't. I can't lose Christine. I know I fucked up. I know I did a bad thing, all right? And I know I'm a bad person. I know I am. But you gotta help me! You have to help me, Miles. Okay? Tell me you'll help me. If I lose Christine, I—I—I—I'm nothing. I just have—I'm nothing." Has Jack finally learned a lesson? It is doubtful.

Apatow established Rogen's slacker character in *Knocked Up* as, in his words, "gruff" and "vicious." But, as the story progressed, Rogen grew as a person and showed himself to have a big heart. Ferrell and Reilly's characters in *Step Brothers* start out as overgrown brats, but their love for one another transforms them. They learn through their friendship to treat others with tenderness, devotion and compassion. This was essentially the same change that Buster Keaton underwent in *The Navigator*. But, more often, it was a different sort of change that the man-child experienced in earlier eras. Let us compare Rogen, Ferrell and Sandler to silent film comedian Lupino Lane. On screen, Lane was a goofy and light-hearted character. He was unworried and irresponsible. He was able to bounce, glide and stumble through life's difficulties without serious consequence. The man-child that we see in comedy films today is also unworried and irresponsible. But, too often, he is neither goofy nor light-hearted. He is insensitive, selfish and cocky. He is dedicated to serving his own interests, he finds no shame in making the easy choices in life, and he will become petty and vindictive whenever he doesn't get what he wants. He is, to put it bluntly, a jerk. Ferrell and Reilly, who have devoted parents to support them, have no need or desire to become husbands and fathers. A man who has no ambition to be a protector or provider has no use for most of the mature qualities that we have discussed. Forget about confidence, courage, competence, commitment, discipline, determination or stability. He only needs to acquire basic social skills to engage successfully with friends. He only needs to stop being a jerk.

The contemporary definition of adulthood excludes marriage and parenthood. It now takes longer for a person to reach a position in which they are capable of supporting a family. In the past, a man could be a good provider to his family without a college degree, but job qualifications have been rewritten somewhat arbitrarily so that a college degree is required for a wide range of professions. This requires young men and women to postpone marriage and childbearing for college and graduate school. It must be stressed, too, that the cost of raising a child has skyrocketed. Economists Timothy Smeeding and Katherin Ross Phillips found in the mid–1990s that 70 percent of American men aged 24 to 28 earned enough to support themselves while fewer than half earned enough to support a family of three.

A young man is expected to abandon pleasure-seeking for the security, stability and purpose of family life. The idea is to replace a shallow existence with something more profound. But maybe that profound existence is a fraud. Maybe we are being too self-important if we see procreation as a meaningful accomplishment or, even more, a sacred duty. It is a major shift in American culture to shun marriage and refuse the burdens of parenthood. A person needs incentives to accept the increased demands of adulthood, but it is hard these days to see what those incentives are. Marriage no longer offers the security or rewards that it once did. Gender bias in divorce law reforms have made marriage a dangerous enterprise for men. It makes perfect sense for a person to reject the provider's role if it presents more risk than benefit. If adulthood is all struggle and no fun, then adulthood is worthless. A popular YouTube video features a dad and his three-year-old daughter joyfully singing a duet of "Let It Go" during a car ride. Does this encapsulate the delight and meaning of parenthood? Is this enough?

We once pursued, in order, work, marriage, parenthood and finally, if we had any energy left, self. Erikson defined these stages as industry, intimacy, generativity and ego integrity. According to Erikson, a person had to succeed in work, marriage and parenthood before they could find personal satisfaction. However, people are no longer willing to defer the self. People today have anxiety about their future and they cope with that anxiety by focusing on the here and now. In the process, it has become their primary goal to seek immediate personal pleasure.

People have come to distrust major social institutions, including government, the church, big business and the press, and this has made them feel less integrated into the social structure. They have adapted to the situation by looking inside themselves and coming up with personal adaptations to the world. We now have the flexibility to redefine old roles in personal terms.

New York Times film critic A.O. Scott wrote, "Grown people feel no compulsion to put away childish things: We can live with our parents, go to summer camp, play dodgeball, collect dolls and action figures and watch cartoons to our hearts' content. These symptoms of arrested development will also be signs that we are freer, more honest and happier than the uptight fools who let go of such pastimes."[19] But this presumes that a person with a mature perspective and mature interests can find pleasure in collecting dolls or watching cartoons. Scott continued, "[Grown people] imagine a world where no one is in charge and no one necessarily knows what's going on, where identities are in perpetual flux.... The world is [their] playground, without a dad or a mom in sight."[20] Unfortunately, this sort of unruly world could easily turn into a dangerous and uncertain place.

Men and women once defined themselves through their family roles, but they now define themselves through their work roles. A person will sacrifice family in the interest of their career. They will move away from family, leave a spouse, and terminate a pregnancy. They will seek personal fulfillment from work rather than from family relations.

Many popular sitcoms, including *Cheers, Seinfeld* and *Friends*, followed a new trend in which the comedy protagonist found free-floating relationships with friends more rewarding than committed relationships with family. These groups provided the benefits of family without the responsibilities of family. The home was replaced in these sitcoms by business establishments, including a bar (*Cheers*) and a coffee shop (*Friends*).

The home is replaced in *Dodgeball* (2004) by a gym. The out-of-shape members of a rundown gym called Average Joe's are upset to learn that their workout haven is in jeopardy. Owner Peter LaFleur (Vince Vaughn) has defaulted on the mortgage and a rival, fitness guru White Goodman (Ben Stiller), is ready to take over the facility. This motley crew of underdogs is determined to save their gym by winning a $50,000 cash prize in a dodgeball tournament. We are reminded periodically that these men are, in many ways, children. They begin their training by watching, with rapt attention, a scratchy grade school instructional film on dodgeball. They draw fangs, goofy eyeglasses and an "I Suck" word balloon on a life-size cardboard cutout of Goodman. In their first game, they go up against a group of Girl Scouts, who cow the men with their aggressive playing style. Being less powerful than little girls puts them on the same level as toddlers.

The team's odds of winning are greatly improved when they are joined by a skilled young woman, Kate Veatch (Christine Taylor). Kate seems to be a mature professional woman, but it is revealed midway through the film that Kate is obsessed with collecting unicorn figurines and paintings. She has her entire home decorated with unicorns, which makes the home look like a twelve-year-old girl's bedroom. This means that she is as childlike as the other members of the team and she actually fits in fine with the rest of the misfit group. She represents a new type of young adult who is able to successfully balance adult responsibilities and childhood obsessions. It's as if Pee-wee Herman finishes a bowl of crispy sweet Mr. T cereal and then he grabs an attaché case to head out to the office. This is the way that Harry Langdon once straddled the line between two worlds. It is what many adults do today. It's what *Time* journalist Richard Lacayo called "luxuriating in the world of childhood while also inhabiting a parallel [adult] universe."[21]

It is apparent at first that these men are woefully inadequate. At least two members of the team, Gordon (Stephen Root) and Justin (Justin Long), suffer from feelings of emasculation. Justin must redeem himself after suffering a humiliating defeat while trying out to be a cheerleader. He was deemed less than manly because he didn't have the strength to hold up a morbidly obese cheerleader, who dropped with crushing force on top of him. Because of this incident, he has come to the gym to build up his muscles. Gordon's passivity is an issue that repeatedly holds him back in practice. But, during the tournament, Gordon becomes enraged when his unfaithful wife kisses another man in the spectator stands. This give him the aggressive drive that he needs to win. He grunts. He roars. He hurls balls at the opposing players with such force that they topple like bowling pins. One terrified player covers his face to avoid a ball that Gordon has sent hurtling in his direction. David Edelstein of Slate wrote, "Nothing like getting

A misfit dodgeball team, including Christine Taylor, Justin Long, Stephen Root, Joel David Moore and Chris Williams, must learn to be confident and assertive to win a pivotal match in *Dodgeball: A True Underdog Story* (2004).

slammed with rubber balls to bring out the blubbery child in a person."²² It remains a question if Gordon, who has proven his dominance on the court, can now establish dominance in his home. But who cares about preserving the home? Preserve the gym.

At least the swinging bachelors of the 1960s were forthright about their womanizing. That is not the case with the swinging bachelors in *Wedding Crashers* (2005). John Beckwith (Owen Wilson) and Jeremy Grey (Vince Vaughn) crash weddings to meet woman and get them into bed. John has doubts about their sleazy and deceptive practices. He tells Jeremy that they are being irresponsible. Jeremy replies, "One day, you'll look back on all this and laugh. You'll say we were young and stupid. A couple of dumb kids running around." John says pointedly, "We're not that young." At their latest wedding, Jeremy is hotly pursued by Gloria (Isla Fisher), the daughter of the U.S. Secretary of the Treasury, William Cleary (Christopher Walken). Gloria brings Jeremy home to the family mansion. She can't keep her hands off Jeremy and straddles him in an open bathroom. Randolph (Ron Canada), the butler, sees the entwined couple as he walks past. He pokes his head into the room and addresses Gloria: "A little more discreet,

A wedding is nothing more than a party to playtime pals Owen Wilson and Vince Vaughn in *Wedding Crashers* (2005).

okay?" he intones. Gloria responds with a girlish *hee-hee*. The butler must discipline this immature young woman like Hobson frequently had to discipline Arthur. Later, Gloria becomes upset with her father and throws a tantrum. Jeremy remarks to John, "Looks like a little kid at Toys-R-Us."

John's doubts increase when he falls in love with Gloria's sister, Claire (Rachel McAdams). John visits Jeremy's wedding-crashing mentor, Chazz Reinhold (Will Ferrell), who lives at home with his mother. As they talk, a Betty Boop cartoon is playing on a television in the background. Betty Boop, who has a curvaceous figure and wears a scanty dress, is a caricature of a seductive woman. This is telling as the women of Chazz's juvenile fantasies are essentially cartoon characters. While at a funeral, John notices a woman deeply grieving the death of her husband. This makes him realize that marriage can be something more profound than he imagined. John comes to finally accept that wedding crashing and sexual promiscuity are juvenile.

Andy Stitzer, played endearingly by Steve Carell, is the title character of *The 40-Year-Old Virgin* (2005). An innocuous middle-aged man, he works in the stockroom at an electronics store. He is a functional adult. He does well on his job. He is, for the most part, socially adept. He will, during the course of the story, prove to be a warm and capable caretaker to children. Nothing is particularly childish about him other than his sexual anxiety and his action figure collection. In fact, it becomes clear during the film that he is more wise and well-rounded than his sexually experienced friends.

Steve Carell is a devoted caretaker to his childhood toys in *The 40-Year-Old Virgin* **(2005).**

The opening of *The 40-Year-Old Virgin*, mirroring the opening of *Pee-wee's Big Adventure*, allows us to go inside Andy's home and see the way that he starts his day. The home is stocked with an abundance of toys and other childhood paraphernalia. Most prominent is a life-sized cut-out of the Mummy that stands in the middle of the den. Berge Garabedian of the JoBlo website was allowed on the set during production and reported, "I'm standing in a geek oasis, more specifically an apartment covered from top to bottom with geek treasure. Action figures, DVDs, video games, models, posters, LPs, you name it. What's this over here? It's a leather chair, with speakers built into the headrest, and video game controllers attached to the bottom. And this? A Martin Sheen action figure from the movie *Spawn*?"[23] Lauren Jade Thompson examined this set at length in her essay "Mancaves and Cushions: Marking Masculine and Feminine Domestic Space in Postfeminist Romantic Comedy." She described the home as follows: "The interior features blue checked sheets, walls covered with pictures of spaceships, an electronic drum kit and gaming chair, and hordes of action figures arranged on surfaces of every room—even the bathroom."[24]

The action in the scene follows the action in the *Pee-wee's Big Adventure* scene in exact order: Andy is awakened by his alarm clock, he exercises, he gets cleaned up, he makes breakfast, and he rides off on his bicycle. There are, of course, differences. Unlike

10. Problem Child

Pee-wee, Andy doesn't spring up and down on his bed or wear bunny slippers. A more obvious difference is the fact that Andy awakens with a morning erection. We are aware of this fact due to a visible bulge in Andy's shorts (the bulge has been made conspicuously large to elicit the first big laugh of the film). We soon learn that Andy has a tendency to shy away from women, which makes him no different than Pee-wee, but we at least know that he has the proper working equipment to handle a sexual encounter. This was something that we were left to wonder about Pee-wee and his ilk. We only knew that Harry Langdon was capable of sex because, in *Tramp, Tramp, Tramp*, he became the father of a lookalike offspring. Andy certainly doesn't have the problem that Chance had with his "little thing" in *Being There*.

Andy's friend David (Paul Rudd) asks Andy how it could possibly be that he's still a virgin. Andy responds, "It just never happened. When I was young, I tried, and it didn't happen. And then I got older and I got more and more nervous ... because it hadn't happened yet. And I got kind of weirded out about it. Then it really didn't happen. And then, I don't know, I just kind of stopped trying."

A flashback reveals Andy's first awkward attempt at sex, which ends with him accidentally kicking his partner in the face and making her nose bleed. The young woman is unhappy, to say the least. "I'm hot," she shrieks. "But, now, you can't have any of this. You should just give up forever!"

David encourages Andy to try again: "You're 40 years old. You know, 40 is the new 20. You wanna spend the next 60 years of your life never experiencing sex? And not just sex, but love and a relationship, and laughing and cuddling and all that shit.... Look, you gotta take a risk."

It is worth noting in Andy's defense that, unlike Pee-wee, he never plays with his toys. These objects are, first and foremost, decorations. It can make people feel safe and comforted to be surrounded by items that remind them of their childhood. Second, the toys are collector's items. Andy shows himself to be a serious collector by refusing to remove his rarest action figures from their original packaging. He isn't like John Lennon, thoughtlessly playing with toys in a bathtub. Thompson found that Andy's failure to play with his toys suggests the emptiness of his life: "[Andy] has an attachment to toys but [has] a life without play."[25] But Andy's world is akin to the neat and orderly child's world that we see in Wes Anderson films, including *Rushmore* (1998), *The Royal Tenenbaums* (2001) and *Moonrise Kingdom* (2012). Anderson's characters also cling to cherished artifacts from their childhood. In *Rushmore*, Max fondly and devotedly holds onto his school awards for perfect attendance and punctuality.

Film critic Matt Zoller Seitz wrote, "[T]he now-adult children in *The Royal Tenenbaums* navigat[e] adult emotional minefields within the confines of a childhood home crammed with toys, grade-school art, and nostalgic knickknacks."[26] Anderson admitted that, as a filmmaker, he has been greatly influenced by *A Charlie Brown Christmas*. Seitz wrote, "[L]ike Schulz's preternaturally eloquent kids, [Anderson's characters seem] to be frozen in a dream space between childhood and maturity."[27]

It is interesting that, in twenty years, Pee-wee's impossible lifestyle has become the real thing for Andy and others of his kind. It is not uncommon nowadays for men to have their own playroom, which they proudly call their mancave.

Andy and his friends panic when they learn that Andy's new girlfriend, Trish (Catherine Keener), plans to visit Andy's home. Thompson wrote, "Cal (Seth Rogen) suggests that, in order to prepare, they 'take everything that's embarrassing and take it all out so that it doesn't look like you live in Neverland Ranch....' The scene cuts to reveal the living room of Andy's condo stripped completely empty, with bare walls, no furniture and no personal effects."[28] It comes across that Andy has lost his very identity and must start from scratch to develop a new one. The good news is that he does develop a better identity. He becomes confident, assertive, outgoing and sensitive. He learns in the end that sex is not about sticky emissions and body parts. It is about love and connection. It is about, as Erikson said, intimacy.

Questions were raised about the character's immaturity by the fact that he commuted to work on a bicycle. Some bicyclists were offended that the film perpetuated the notion that riding a bicycle was a juvenile quirk, not to mention a severe impediment to a man attracting a woman. Of course, Carell doesn't ride the type of bicycle that makes him look like a Tour de France champion. His bicycle is outfitted with fenders, a headlight, a milk crate bungee-corded to a rack, and two handlebar-mounted mirrors.

Does the man-child hold onto his childlike ways as an expression of nostalgia or rebellion? Or is it just straightforward, old-fashioned childishness, which needs no rea-

Steve Carell learns that sex is about intimacy and connection in *The 40-Year-Old Virgin* (2005). Pictured in this scene opposite Carell is Catherine Keener.

son to exist? Nostalgia certainly permeates *Full Grown Men* (2006). Protagonist Alby Cutrera (Matt McGrath) misses the carefree days of his childhood. When his wife insults him for being more of a playmate than a father to his young son, Alby leaves home to track down his boyhood pal Elias (Judah Friedlander).

The young adults of today reject symbols of adulthood, preferring to cling to the emblems of their childhood. Author Christopher Noxon wrote, "Take your local gas station or convenience store. Check out the snack display. You've got your adult Cape Cod Potato Chips, your teen-leaning Doritos and your kid-targeted Cheetos. What adult in their right mind would eat a snack promoted by a sneaker-clad spokescat? While snack food giant Frito-Lay doesn't release market research data, it seems clear that Cheetos have become a major flashpoint in rejuvenile's assault on age norms—adults all over are embracing the orangey goodness of Chester Cheetah's favorite snack. Many are content to casually gobble down a bag in the privacy of their workplace cubicle. Others publicly flaunt their Cheetos affiliation, proudly displaying their stained orange fingers to friends and co-workers or posting weird online video clips as proof of their playful, mischievous spirits."[29]

Michael Cera stood out as a likable man-child during this period. Ian Troub of the Texan News Service described Cera as being "typically boyish"[30] the many times that he played a "nerdy, desperately romantic daydreamer."[31] This character was seen, in one form or another, in *Superbad* (2007), *Juno* (2007), *Nick and Norah's Infinite Playlist* (2008), *Year One* (2009), *Youth in Revolt* (2009), and *Scott Pilgrim vs. the World* (2010).

Aspects of immaturity can be deeply embedded in the personality of a mentally disturbed misanthrope. This sort of character has turned up in recent films. In *Big Fan* (2009), Paul Aufiero (Patton Oswald) is a parking garage attendant who lives with his mother. A man is expected to dedicate his passion to career and family, but Paul dedicates his passion to something far less important. He cares about nothing in the world except the New York Giants. He is pathetically shallow and frighteningly crazy, which puts him into an entirely different category than baseball fan Joe Boyd of *Damn Yankees*. His mania leads him into a heated rivalry with Philadelphia Phil (Michael Rapaport), an obsessed fan of the Philadelphia Eagles. The rivalry reaches its peak when Paul assaults Phil with a paintball gun. The scene is not played for slapstick silliness. It is grim and startling. The film ends with an unrepentant Paul in prison for the assault. He is joyful that he will be released from prison at the same time that the new football season begins.

The protagonist of *Greenberg* (2010) has a myriad of problems. Roger (Ben Stiller) is high-strung, self-centered, lazy, and socially awkward. He is described by his brother Phillip (Chris Messina) as "delicate." But the first thing that we learn about Roger is that he's petty. He writes an airline a letter of complaint because the recliner button on his seat didn't work. At a restaurant, he is appalled to see a smudge on a fork that he has been given. He fixates on trivial details, which causes him to lose sight of the important parts of life, and this prevents him from arranging his priorities accordingly. Poorest of all is his social skills. Roger gets angry and abusive whenever someone tries to get close to him. He is terribly frightened to share anything of himself with others. One person who tries to get close to him is his brother's dog walker, Florence (Greta Gerwig).

The film is about Roger gradually connecting with Florence and caring about Florence's welfare. It is the plot of *Groundhog Day* without the time loop.

The Almost Man (2012), a comedy-drama from Norway, is a darker and edgier version of *Knocked Up*. Thirty-five-year-old Henrik (Henrik Rafaelsen) becomes erratic, irresponsible and outright selfish after his girlfriend Tone (Janne Heltberg) becomes pregnant. He resents having this new responsibility thrust upon him. He sulks, he cringes, he shouts. He is a little boy having an extended tantrum that, in time, comes to distress everyone around him. Tone is extremely patient with Henrik, but her patience reaches its limit when Henrik insults her friends at a party and behaves insensitively while she is laid up with morning sickness. Even Henrik's doting mother is appalled by her son's behavior. A memorable scene occurs when Henrik visits his mother for dinner. Henrik regresses further now that he is nestled back at home with Mom. He asserts his regression by discarding his formal work shoes for a pair of puppy slippers. While lounging on a couch, he becomes amused wiggling his feet to make it look as if the puppy slippers are playing together. In moments, he has one puppy slipper force itself on top of the other in what turns into a vigorously simulated puppy slipper rape scene. He is no doubt acting out the growing fury that he is feeling towards his pregnant girlfriend. Henrik's mother walks in on her son's disturbed play and she is so startled by what she sees that the poor woman is rendered speechless. Henrik's disturbed behavior creates serious problems at work, which puts his job into jeopardy. He punches a co-worker in an after-hours encounter and, after spending hours at work trifling on his computer, he abruptly flees the office without explanation.

The Almost Man (2012) is a dark version of *Knocked Up* (2007). In this scene, Henrik (Henrik Rafaelsen) has discarded his business suit so that he can sit around in primal bliss with his feet comfortably clad inside a pair of puppy slippers. He shares Huck Finn's opinion that a man can be smothered by "them blamed clothes."

Henrik's emotional turmoil reaches its peak while he is driv-

The Almost Man (2012) focuses on problems that can develop in a relationship when a couple has to deal with an unexpected pregnancy. Tone (Janne Heltberg) believes that it's time for her foolish boyfriend, Henrik (Henrik Rafaelson), to take life seriously and stop his silly antics.

ing home from work. He becomes enraged when a boy in a passing car sticks his tongue out at him. The boy suddenly represents the dreaded child that will soon be invading Henrik's life. It is as if Henrik's unborn offspring is aware of his jerky dad's distress and has miraculously materialized for the purpose of mocking him. Henrik presses his foot down on the accelerator to catch up to this car. It is a frightening moment. What is Henrik planning to do? Then Henrik loses control and runs off the road. The car comes to a sudden stop. Henrik looks shaken. Then, alone inside his car, he lets out a prolonged scream.

Henrik looks calm when he returns home. Has his screaming fit been cathartic? Has he calmed down and found perspective? He finds his girlfriend, who is preparing to take a bath, and he apologizes to her for acting "weird." The film ends at this point, but the filmmaker does not leave us with the impression that Henrik's feeble and belated apology represents a true resolution to the couple's troubles. We don't even know at this point if the expectant papa still has a job.

Almost a Man is unique in that Henrik starts out as goofy and playful as Seth Rogen, but the filmmaker manages in time to skillfully peel away Henrik's goofy and playful exterior to expose the horribly pathetic man-child that lies underneath. Maybe the other films are letting their silly fools off too easily.

11

Jack and Jill

In his films, Harold Lloyd usually left his audience to assume that the boy and the girl will live happily ever after. But it is suggested in some of Lloyd's comedies that marrying and having children might not go well for the couple. The problem with maturity is that the journey may be a lot more satisfying than the destination. In at least two films, Lloyd and his lady love have to take care of other people's kids, which allows them to perform a dry run of the duties that await them as parents. In *Now or Never* (1921), Lloyd helps a nanny (Mildred Davis) care for a little girl during a train ride. Something as simple as dressing the girl turns into an arduous task. In *I Do* (1921), Lloyd helps his wife (again Davis) babysit her brother's children. His effort to pour milk into a baby's bottle ends with him spraying milk into his face and spilling milk onto his shoes. The baby cries and kicks as Lloyd struggles futilely to rock him to sleep in his arms. The dear uncle generally looks queasy taking care of the baby. From beginning to end, the experience proves to be overwhelming for him. He receives it as dire news when, just before the final fadeout, he finds out that his wife is pregnant. In Lloyd's films, children are always something that await him in the future. Lloyd and Ann Christy daydream of having twins in 1928's *Speedy* (of course, the twins are wearing miniature versions of Harold's horn-rimmed eyeglasses). It is only in the final moments of *Why Worry?* (1923) that Lloyd learns his wife is pregnant. Perhaps showing Lloyd and his leading lady as inept parents would not have been regarded as funny at the time. We know when we watch *I Do* that Harold's brother-in-law and the brother-in-law's wife will eventually return home and restore order. The poor children are not stuck having their inept uncle as their caretaker.

Away We Go (2009) is a original take on the immaturity theme in that it shows a married man and woman struggling together to assume adult responsibility. A couple in their early thirties (John Krasinski and Maya Rudolph) approach the sudden prospect of parenthood with the wide-eyed awe and dread of children. They are a modern-day Hansel and Gretel toddling off into a dark forest. Or, just as easily, they could be seen as a slacker Jack and Jill struggling to climb a hill. Except that, rather than the couple needing to fetch a pail of water, they need to lug a diaper caddy, which is essentially a pail of pee. It is, to them, an appalling prospect.

The immature couple has become a trend. *Sex Tape* (2014) features married suburban parents, Annie (Cameron Diaz) and Jay (Jason Segel), who inadvertently leak a sex tape to family and friends on the Internet. From the beginning to the end of the

Harold Lloyd and Mildred Davis become overwhelmed babysitting for a relative's children in *I Do* (1921) (courtesy www.doctormacro.com).

film, Annie and Jay act impulsively and uncertainly. They are not an intelligent, confident or competent couple.

Immature misfits are drawn together in *Safety Not Guaranteed* (2012). Claudia Puig of *USA Today* described the two romantic leads as a "sullen young misanthrope"[1] and "a nerdy lost soul."[2] The former, Darius (Aubrey Plaza), is a twentysomething magazine intern still living at home with her parents. The latter, Kenneth (Mark Duplass), is a supermarket stock clerk trying to build a time machine.

This Is 40 (2012) stretches credibility with parents Pete and Debbie (Paul Rudd and Leslie Mann). The film provides a scary portrayal of an immature couple. It is unimaginable that a couple as petty, self-indulgent and tantrum-prone as this could have gotten as far in life as they have. Never have characters in a comedy film more fiercely resisted the process of aging. Debbie is in furious denial about her age. On her fortieth birthday, she shrieks to her husband, "I am not 40! Fuck 40! Forty can suck my dick!" This is, in fact, the way that the film opens.

During a weekend getaway at a luxury resort, Pete and Debbie agree to let loose in their hotel room by consuming marijuana cookies. Their behavior is even less disciplined than the behavior of children. Here's a comparison: In *Big*, Josh is happy to receive his first paycheck and he celebrates this achievement with his friend Billy. Josh and Billy stuff themselves with pizza, potato chips, pork rinds, soda and Oreo cookies. Afterwards, they have a Silly String battle that leaves them tangled up in the sticky stuff. These are two boys having fun. But Pete and Debbie act even more childishly than Josh and Billy when they order a tableload of creamy pastries from room service and sloppily gorge on the extravagant treats. It is almost inconceivable that this giggly, cream-smeared couple have jobs, children and a big fancy home. It is hard to believe that they have come into existence without the aid of Josh's wish machine. Sociology professor Jay Livingston shared my suspicions: "[Peter] seems like an 18-year-old who has awakened to find himself in the body of a 40-year-old man."[3]

We have seen this scene of greedy consumption played out before. André Deed gluttonously stuffed a creamy tart in his mouth in *Les Apprentissages de Boireau*. Bill Murray wolfed down creamy pastries in *Groundhog Day*. Roscoe Arbuckle, as described by Alan Bilton, managed to shove a freshly baked pie into his mouth in an unidentified comedy. This represents the powerful urge of consumption that is an obsession of a growing and self-indulgent child.

Martha Graham said, "'Age' is the acceptance of a term of years. But maturity is the glory of years." Maturity reveals itself in accomplishment, self-satisfaction and self-confidence. Maturity should never be about status and image, which is how the protagonists see it in *Neighbors* (2014). Mac and Kelly Radner (Seth Rogen and Rose Byrne) approach their responsibilities as new parents with sweaty, jittery desperation, display-

Rose Byrne and Seth Rogen have doubts as new parents in *Neighbors* (2014).

ing the uncertainty, self-doubt and anxiety of helpless children. They continuously seek reassurance from each other that they are behaving like proper, mature adults. Their biggest concern is being mature without being stodgy. It isn't as important to them to be responsible adults as it is to be "cool" adults. They want to balance work and play. They want to fulfill their commitments without giving up their freedom. But this can seem to be impossible and even ridiculous at times.

Kelly's single party-girl friend, Paula (Carla Gallo), invites them to attend a rave. This stirs up emotional turmoil in the couple. They have to stay home to take care of their baby. Mac has to go to work in the morning. But they dread admitting that they are living in captivity in the suburbs. They see their total submission to adult responsibilities as something that will weaken and diminish them. They believe that they will be incomplete if they fully relinquish their youthful ways. More than anything, Mac and Kelly fear that adulthood will force them into mediocrity. Today, young people are too self-important to accept being moderate or ordinary. Freedom and irresponsibility has become status symbols in the "We can have it all" lifestyle. Mac's ceaseless jabbering in the scene is the character's way to rationalize his fears and inadequacies, which is something that we saw with Albert Brooks' neurotic characters. Mac and Kelly finally convince themselves that they can take the baby to the rave with them, but the overworked parents fall asleep before they can make it out the door.

Will Leitch of The Concourse wrote, "*Neighbors* is your typical Seth Rogen–Apatowian coming-of-age comedy, in which an overgrown manboy learns that he has to curtail his childish pursuits of weed, video games, and general irresponsibility to become a functional member of society."[4] Critic Jake Coyle wrote, "Seven years after Seth Rogen memorably struggled with the prospect of childbirth in *Knocked Up*, he's moved on to the anxieties of young parenthood in *Neighbors*."[5] Rogen announced in interviews that he was proud of the film's premise. He said, "No one's made a movie about a couple struggling with the fact that they have a baby and they can't party anymore."[6]

Mac and Kelly reuse Lloyd's milk-spraying routine except now the milk sprays uncontrollably from Kelly's nipples rather than from a baby bottle. The filmmakers must have been confident that this scene would get a laugh as audiences had already laughed when Maya Rudolph got sprayed in the face with breast milk in *Grown Ups* (2010).

Mac and Kelly are lying in bed together, exhausted, at the end of the film. They decide that their party days are over and they need to be responsible adults.

> MAC: You made a baby. Things have changed. Everything's changed.
> KELLY: Part of our life is just totally over. It's gone. It's never coming back. We'll never not be responsible for someone until we're so, so old.
> MAC: Do you think we'll be good parents?
> KELLY: I think we'll be more good at it than bad at it.
> MAC: You know, when we had Stella, I thought we'd be missing the party, but I realized that we *are* the party. This is the only party I want to be at.

But Rogen himself has turned down his invitation to this "party." The 32-year-old comedian has adamantly shunned parenthood. He admits that, although he finds babies cute, he has no interest in becoming a father.

The modern young adult is looking to find a compromise between maturity and immaturity. Life does not need to relentlessly pump up adrenaline for the crazed fun-seeker, but it would be wrong for life in its conventional form to be agonizingly mundane and inhibited. The cautionary tale of *The World's End* (2013), in which man-child Gary King (Simon Pegg) reunites with childhood acquaintances to relive his younger days, provides a balanced outlook on the subject of maturity. A.O. Scott of *The New York Times* wrote, "Gary is not only yet another big-screen case study in male arrested development but also, it seems, a genuinely damaged soul, with decades of failure, bad debts and fruitless rehab stints etched into his face. His pals are not too happy when he shows up to drag them back to Newton Haven, but he sweet-talks, guilt-trips and otherwise manipulates them into joining him."[7] The men soon discover that their old hometown has been taken over by soulless robotic clones. The robots, who have built a society based on a philosophy of compliance and uniformity, emphasize the value of Gary's free-spirited nature. The message is that a man can be a responsible adult without suffering the misery of conformity and, even more importantly, he can reject conformity without becoming a drunken fool. A fair compromise can be found between resignation and rebellion.

Today, young people tend to reject age norms. Author Christopher Noxon coined the term "rejuveniles,"[8] which are adults who insist that they can hold onto their childlike ways while leading productive and responsible lives. Rejuveniles are prominently on display in many modern comedies. We have already met up with them in *Dodgeball* and *The 40-Year-Old Virgin*. Noxon wrote, "To rejuveniles, being grown-up means being done growing."[9] Rejuveniles strongly object to this idea. In their minds, growing means being a better person today than you were yesterday and being a better person tomorrow than you are today. If you aren't growing up, you are simply aging. But it isn't necessarily bad to stop growing up. It can be argued that maturity is stability and contentment, which aren't bad things. Frank Pittman wrote in *Grow Up!: How Taking Responsibility Can Make You a Happy Adult*, "[We are] lustily celebrating the freedom of adolescence while dreading the still, calm contentment of maturity and age."[10]

While We're Young (2014) explores some of the same territory as *Neighbors*. Middle-aged couple Josh (Ben Stiller) and Cornelia (Naomi Watts) struggle to come to terms with growing up and growing old. It is their greatest fear that, as their youth fades, they will become dull, exhausted and disengaged. Josh and Cornelia befriend a free-spirited young couple, Jamie (Adam Driver) and Darby (Amanda Seyfried), and seek to regain the openness, optimism and passion of youth by spending time with their new friends. Josh wants to be so much like Jamie that he takes to wearing a hip retro fedora just like the one that Jamie wears. He thinks that he can be young like Jamie if he becomes exactly like Jamie. *Los Angeles Times* critic Betsy Sharkey wrote, "[Josh and Cornelia] lap up the experience of being young again, no matter how exhausting or vacuous it turns out to be."[11]

Unlike *Neighbors*' Mac and Kelly, Josh and Cornelia have avoided parenthood. They have remained childless for a simple reason: they are unwilling to sacrifice their pleasures, their comforts and their social life for the sake of endless feedings and diaper-changings. Noah Baumbach, who wrote and directed the film, said that the couple is concerned that, if they take the time and energy to worry about a child, they won't have time and energy left to "worry about [their] own crap."[12] Having a child means that you have to give up being selfish, which is a terrifying prospect for the man-child. But, lately, the couple feels that the lack of a child has left an absence in their lives. Cornelia has tried to get pregnant, but she has suffered two miscarriages. Josh's friend Fletcher (Adam Horovitz), who has recently become a father, is quick to dissuade Josh from parenthood, telling him that having a child will not fulfill him or make him a better person. He says, "Having a child didn't change me as much as I hoped it would. I'm still the most important person in my life." These are the words of an arrogant, self-absorbed person. A normal person is bound to undergo profound changes after the birth of their first child, but a self-absorbed person is immune to these or any other changes. This is the sad and familiar concept we know as arrested development.

So, what is the film's message? Baumbach acknowledged that old age is not as terrible as Josh and Cornelia think it is. He said, "[If] people can get to the other side of [aging] and survive it, it can be wonderful."[13] This is the calm contentment of maturity and aging.

Immaturity is addressed in the many "battle of the sexes" comedies. Before a man and woman can come together, they must undergo a process of maturation. A romantic comedy compresses this process into ninety minutes of bickering and misunderstandings. Shakespeare understood this when, in the late 1500s, he wrote his rollicking romantic comedy *The Taming of the Shrew*. In the play, a man and woman resolve their childish ways during a tempestuous courtship. The childishness peaks with the young man, Petruchio, erupting in a tantrum which culminates with him thrashing on the floor. In romantic comedies, a pair of hard-headed and juvenile characters must develop emotionally to come together. Shakespeare's *Much Ado About Nothing* features a pair of battling lovers, Beatrice and Benedick. Benedick openly despises marriage and swears that he will never get married. An older man laughs at him and tells him that, when he has found the right person, he will get married. Critic David Denby wrote, "Why is the contact between [Beatrice and Benedick] so barbed? Because they are meant for each other, and are too proud and frightened to admit it."[14]

This idea takes on an interesting twist in *The Goodbye Girl* (1977). Bickering between Paula McFadden (Marsha Mason) and Elliot Garfield (Richard Dreyfuss) serves to determine boundaries, challenge emotions, and ultimately establish trust and intimacy. This man and woman are willing to fight furiously to find out how they fit together.

A bane of romantic comedy relationships is jealousy, a distinctly immature emotion. A large number of comedy films focus on foolishly jealous men or women, outstanding among them *Unfaithfully Yours* (1948), *Adam's Rib* (1949), *Clerks* (1994) and *High Fidelity* (2000). The Internet Movie Database lists 6,585 films that address the topic of jealousy. In the history of films, ten motion pictures share the title *Jealousy*. Jealous feelings must be overcome for a couple to establish a solid relationship.

It may seem that not all romantic comedies progress to a mature coming-together. In *Pillow Talk* (1959), Jan Morrow (Doris Day) refuses to forgive Brad Allen (Rock Hudson) for adopting a false identity in a scheme to woo her. Brad, desperate to reconcile

Doris Day and Rock Hudson have trouble getting along in the trendsetting romantic comedy *Pillow Talk* (1959).

with Jan, finds himself unbearably frustrated by Jan's resistance. Brad is, as described by film critic Rebecca Flint Marx, a "suave Neanderthal."[15] He doesn't see a need to become tender and sensitive to win the girl. It doesn't interest him to refine his social skills, or to learn to communicate and compromise with the woman that he loves. Quite the contrary, Brad seeks to win over Jan by dragging her out of her bed and carrying her into his apartment. His strategy, in fact, seems to work. But it is better to examine this scene more closely. Jan is not enamored by Brad's muscular aggression. The angry and hurt words that Brad grumbles as he carries Jan from one apartment to the other finally express his love and devotion to the woman. He reveals tenderness and vulnerability in contradiction of his Neanderthal actions. This is what actually captivates Jan.

12

Girls

Accepted wisdom says a man should want to marry a strong partner who can work with him to establish a home and raise a family. But a woman who is frivolous, daft, shallow and incapable is, at times, presented in films as the ideal mate. A childlike woman, a vision of purity and idealism, is desirable. A childlike man, simple and gullible, is off-putting.

Bringing Up Baby (1938) begins by introducing us to Dr. David Huxley (Cary Grant), a mild-mannered paleontologist. David's life is in perfect order. He is just about to complete a four-year assignment to assemble a brontosaurus skeleton for his museum, he looks forward to receiving a million-dollar donation to support his future endeavors, and he is preparing to marry his assistant, Alice Swallow (Virginia Walker). But then he meets a madcap heiress, Susan Vance (Katharine Hepburn), and his life falls into utter chaos. David is involved in a golf game with the lawyer of his potential donor when Susan comes along and plays his ball by mistake. This could be a simple problem to resolve except that David is unable to engage the screwy Susan in a reasonable discussion of the matter. If this isn't bad enough, Susan mistakes David's car for her own and dents the car's fender as she hastily pulls out of a parking space. Susan proves to be no more capable when David encounters her again at a restaurant. This time she is engaged in antics with a bartender (Billy Bevan), seeing if she can duplicate the bartender's adroit trick of tossing a cocktail olive into the air and catching it in her mouth. She misses catching the olive, which causes the olive to fall to the ground just as David is passing. David slips on the olive and falls hard on the floor.

For all of her flaws, Susan remains a breath of fresh air compared to David's fiancée. It is hard to imagine David being able to muster affection for a woman as ruthlessly businesslike and dour as Alice. In the opening scene, the couple has a brief conversation that tells the viewer everything they need to know about their relationship:

> ALICE: Why, as soon as we're married, we're coming directly back here and you're going on with your work. Now once and for all, David, nothing must interfere with your work. Our marriage must entail no domestic entanglements of any kind.
> DAVID: You mean, you mean ...
> ALICE: I mean of any kind, David.
> DAVID: Oh well, Alice, I was sort of hoping, well, you mean children and all that sort of thing?
> ALICE: Exactly. (Alice gestures with a sweep of her hand toward the dinosaur.) This will be our child.
> DAVID: Huh?

Cary Grant and Katharine Hepburn are inept parents to a baby leopard in *Bringing Up Baby* (1938) (courtesy www.doctormacro.com).

ALICE: Yes, David. I see our marriage purely as a dedication to your work.
DAVID: Well, gee whiz, Alice, everybody has to have a honeymoon and ... and ...
ALICE: We haven't time.

David is obviously distressed by Alice's refusal to be a loving wife and mother. Alice, the straitlaced scientist, represents work. Susan, the frivolous heiress, represents play. Play wins out in the end. The film's final scene takes place at David's museum. Susan climbs a ladder to talk to David, who is sitting atop a scaffold beside his brontosaurus skeleton. She becomes so excited to hear David profess his love for her that she sways wildly back and forth, which causes the ladder to become unstable. To avoid falling, she jumps onto the back of the skeleton, which causes the skeleton to collapse into a heap. This makes it clear that, as far as the filmmakers were concerned, love and companionship are more important than career and accomplishment. David's four-year project has crumbled to pieces, but it is more important to him that he is able to take Susan in his arms and tell her that he loves her. Susan has managed, in the end, to awaken a manly passion in this passive, pensive young man.

Denby found that *Bringing Up Baby* helped to create a form of romantic comedy that "transform[ed] lust into play and ritual."[1] The courtship ritual, which needed to be tamed to suit Hollywood's Production Code standards, was now reduced to a sexless child's game. Prior to David and Susan's embrace at the film's close, David does not show the slightest sexual interest in her. Denby wrote, "The man is serious about his work (and no one says he shouldn't be), but he's confused about women, and his confusion has neutered him."[2] But his boyish asexuality is not a problem to this young woman, whose own immaturity has rendered her pre-sexual. Denby continued, "In the screwball comedies, the woman doesn't ask her man to 'grow up.' She wants to pull him into some sort of ridiculous adventure. *She* has to grow up...."[3] The couple is, in every sense, Jack and Jill.

Hepburn's heiress remains lovable just the way she is and just the way she has been from the start. It is not like what we saw in *The Navigator* or *Battling Butler*. The heirs that Keaton played could not have won their beloved until they had transcended their frivolous, accident-prone ways. It was different with women.

If maturity was about toughening up boys and making them men, then what did maturity mean for girls, who were expected to be at all times gentle and demure? We, as a society, once found great appeal in a woman who maintained a feminine disposition. This was the way we wanted a woman to act. We saw the need to protect a woman from hardship because hardship could potentially coarsen the woman, spoiling her fragile femininity and preventing her from being sensitive and caring as a wife and mother. But women have always been expected in their own way to progress from girlhood to womanhood.

In *If You Could Only Cook* (1935), Jim Buchanan (Herbert Marshall) abandons the stressful responsibilities of his job as an automobile designer to rediscover the pleasures of his youth. He manages at the same time to abandon his fiancée, Evelyn Fletcher (Frieda Inescort). He has little regret about leaving his bride at the altar because he feels absolutely no love for her. Amid wedding preparations, he complains to his best man, Bob Reynolds (Alan Edwards), "Where's the romance, the glow, the silly careless rapture that's supposed to go with the whole darned thing?" Bob accuses Jim of talking like a child. But love was never meant to be the point of the marriage. Jim simply believed that, as a successful businessman, he needed to marry the aristocratic Evelyn to protect his standing in the community. He now sees the folly of that decision. During the course of the film, this runaway groom is presented as bold, independent, and virtuous. Marshall even brings an undeniable classiness to the role that makes it easy to respect Jim all the more. It could not be denied that Jim was flawed to have made his marriage plans, but it was more important that he did what was right in the end.

Filmmakers provided less favorable treatment to the fickle bride. It was presented as a sign of immaturity when a bride failed to show resolve. Betwixt and between is no place for a true adult. In the 1940s, Ginger Rogers fell into a pattern of portraying young women who were too flighty and nervous to commit to marriage. Rogers could not be more confused and indecisive when she has to consider her varied suitors in *Tom, Dick and Harry* (1941). Sean Axmaker of TCM Online wrote, "Rogers' performance verges on the overly cute, with her baby-doll voice and dreamy gazes."[4] In *Kitty Foyle* (1940), Rogers wrestles with her conscience as she tries to decide whether to marry a dentist who is honest and reliable or a charming publisher who lives in servitude to his wealthy family. In *Lady in the Dark* (1944), Rogers is again indecisive about who she should marry. In the midst of her emotional turmoil, she has a troubling dream in which she is a little girl visiting a circus. These characters, in their confusion and indecisiveness, come across at times as appalling ditherers. Indecision remains an appealing tactic for those women who wish to delay an uncertain future.

Rogers was 36 years old by the time that she starred in *It Had to Be You* (1947), yet another film that required her to play a marriage-phobic woman. Neil Doyle, an IMDb critic, was blunt but accurate when he wrote, "Ginger Rogers plays another one of her fluttery sapheads with a little girl voice and manner that becomes irritating after the first ten minutes."[5] Rogers is more than a decade older than the character that she is playing, which is especially evident in a ballpark scene in which the sunlight brings out every line in her face. It was time for this routine to come to an end. Howard Hawks exploited the absurdity of an even older (41-year-old) Rogers acting like a bratty little girl in the youth elixir comedy *Monkey Business* (1952), which we discussed earlier.

During production of *The Major and The Minor* (1942), Ginger Rogers rides a bicycle through the Paramount backlot wearing her Edith Head–designed outfit.

Brides have ditched grooms in numerous comedy films, including *Girl Shy* (1924), *It Happened One Night* (1934), *The Graduate* (1967), *Smokey and the Bandit* (1977), *Private Benjamin* (1980), *Only You* (1994), *While You Were Sleeping* (1995), *The Wedding Singer* (1998), and *Sweet Home Alabama* (2002). The tradition of the indecisive bride was ideally upheld by Julia Roberts in the appropriately titled *Runaway Bride* (1999).

In *My Best Friend's Wedding* (1997), Julia Roberts tries childish tricks to sabotage the pending nuptials of Dermot Mulroney, who she herself wants to marry. This is the worst sort of cheating. You must achieve maturity before you can become a fit spouse and parent. However, this type of cheating is found in many modern romantic comedies. In *There's Something About Mary* (1998), an awkward and shy young man resorts to deceit to win the favor of a girl he loves. You win the love of another through honesty or you really haven't won it at all. In *The Back-up Plan* (2010), Jennifer Lopez has been unable to establish a long-term relationship with a man and resorts to artificial insemination to have children. Another form of cheating can be found in a notable silent comedy film, *Three's a Crowd* (1927). Timid Harry Langdon, living alone in a tenement shack, clearly lacks the capacity to be a husband and father, but nonetheless yearns to have a family. Circumstances change when he takes a destitute pregnant woman into his home during a snowstorm. When the woman gives birth, Harry suddenly finds himself with a ready-made family.

The women in modern romantic comedies can be obnoxiously immature. According to the AV Club staff, *Bridget Jones's Diary* (2001) is "a story of a crude, foul-mouthed, dim-witted, judgmental, childishly petty girl-woman who manages to win the love of multiple men even though she pretty much lives to write horrible things about them in her titular diary."[6] Meg Ryan's character in *Sleepless in Seattle* (1993) is, by their standards, impetuous and delusional. Other women in modern romantic comedies are described as selfish, controlling, snide and abrasive. It is frightening that single young women flock to these films because they find the heroines relatable.

The central character of *Muriel's Wedding* (1994) is a naïve, socially awkward, overweight young woman named Muriel Heslop. Muriel is a shameless, obsessive dreamer. Her unrealistic view of the world proves to be a constant source of problems for her. She is fixated on getting married in an ostentatious ceremony to prove to everyone that she is someone special. She acts in dishonest and selfish ways to live out her fantasies. She tells attendants in bridal shops that she is getting married so they will let her try on gowns and take her picture. She steals a garish dress to wear at a friend's wedding.

The worst happens when she is offered a job selling cosmetics. Muriel is given money by her mother to purchase inventory, but she thoughtlessly uses it to go on a tropical vacation. This causes great tension between her parents. Later, when she moves to another city, she engages in a series of lies and denials to pretend that she's someone she isn't. She goes as far as changing her name to Mariel. She finally gets her fancy big wedding when she agrees to marry a handsome young South African swimmer, David Von Arckle (Daniel Lapaine) so that he can become an Australian citizen. Muriel is shocked to hear that her mother has committed suicide, the news making her realize that she finally needs to face the realities of life. She asks David for a divorce, telling him, "I have to stop lying now. I've told so many lies." It is at this time that she goes from being a silly and giggly girl to being a serious and responsible woman.

Boot camp provides a growth experience for the unlikely recruit featured in *Private Benjamin* (1980). Judy Benjamin (Goldie Hawn), a pampered and ditzy socialite, becomes despondent when her husband dies of a heart attack on their wedding night. Benjamin looks to find new purpose and direction in her life by joining the U.S. Army, but the grueling boot camp workout is far more difficult than she expected. It is a mismatch of person and profession, which is the main source of the film's humor. Film critic Frank Ochieng described Benjamin as "a spoiled princess in army boots."[7] This description conjures up the image of a little girl clomping around in her daddy's boots. Rescue arrives in the form of the young woman's wealthy parents, who use their clout to get her released from military service. But Benjamin, who has been sheltered for most of her life by her controlling parents, feels hurt and resentful when her father shows up at the camp to give her a dressing down. She decides that she must stick it out in boot camp to attain strength and self-respect. Her victory in military games finally achieves this goal. Critic Emanuel Levy wrote, "Private Benjamin endures the rigors of the military, and gradually she becomes transformed into a disciplined soldier—and more mature woman."[8] She has grown up, which means that she has filled out those boots.

These days, women cling to their youth just as much as men. The hugely popular *Twilight* films have an intriguing plot: Teenage Bella (Kristen Stewart) falls in love with telepathic vampire Edward Cullen (Robert Pattinson), is turned into a vampire by Edward, and joins Edward's vampire clan. The story is bound to appeal to the young girl who fantasizes about never growing up. Holly Welker observed in the article "Forever Your Girl," "When she finally does become a vampire shortly before turning 19, Bella is thrilled to realize that she will be childlike for all eternity...."[9]

Too many modern films are empty and forgettable. The end credits are rolling and viewers have already put the movie out of their head. That's why it's so special to find a film that can reach deep inside a hoary soul to scrape up a true feeling or, even better, a film that can get inside a jaded brain to stir up a deep thought or two. They don't even have to be good feelings or good thoughts, just something to remind you that you're human and other people exist who share the burden of being human. That is the sort of experience offered by *Ghost World* (2001).

The film introduces us to two teenage girls, longtime best friends Enid (Thora Birch) and Rebecca (Scarlett Johansson). The opening scene takes place at their high school graduation. The crowd is large and loud. The graduation speeches are followed by a trio of teenage girls coming on stage to perform a graduation rap. Enid and Rebecca look appalled by the trio's tasteless, amateurish performance.

At the time, many critics described Enid and Rebecca as outsiders, but an outsider can be an unappealing person who is shunned by others. Enid and Rebecca are pretty and smart young women who choose not to be part of the crowd. They, in fact, make a conscious decision to shun classmates. It would be more appropriate to call them non-conformists.

Adulthood, more than high school, demands conformity to survive. Rebecca accepts that more than Enid. Enid knows she can't remain in adolescence but she's afraid to enter adulthood, so she falls into a strange emotional limbo. A *ghost world*. The landscape of the town mirrors what she feels inside. It's being taken over by malls and fast food chains and losing every ounce of individuality and personality. Rebecca has counted on Enid to get a job and rent an apartment with her, but Enid is not ready for this and the two friends drift apart.

Enid enters into a relationship with a middle-aged sad sack named Seymour. Seymour pursues obscure hobbies and leads a loner existence. He has managed to remain outside of the mainstream, so Enid sees him as a kindred spirit and even as a hero. Seymour makes no secret he's unhappy with his life and sees himself as a loser, but Enid is convinced that his only real problem is that he doesn't have a girlfriend. She mounts a campaign to find him a mate. She's convinced that, if she can fix Seymour's life, then there's hope she can become an adult and remain happily outside the soul-devouring mainstream herself. The film, while always funny and entertaining, conveys an underlying sadness. You know nothing is going to work out well.

Birch and Johansson are the prettiest non-conformists you will ever find. Both actresses have young, innocent faces mismatched with mature, voluptuous bodies, which helps them to express their characters' conflicted transition from adolescence to adulthood.

Gary Cross, the author of *Men to Boys: The Making of Modern Immaturity*, believes that television producers have a reason to promote immaturity. The mature man who would rather preserve the household fund than waste money on the latest toys makes a terribly poor consumer. Rampant consumerism embodies immaturity and irresponsibility. This brings us to *Confessions of a Shopaholic* (2009). The protagonist, Rebecca Bloomwood (Isla Fisher), calls credit cards "magic cards" because they let her buy pretty clothing even when she has no money. She lacks the self-control that a grown woman should have. She is influenced by an overactive imagination, which causes her to envision a mannequin coming to life and talking her into buying an expensive scarf. She just has to have the scarf, which she insists is "a desperately important scarf." It is like a child who sees every toy on the store shelf as desperately important. Rebecca acts like a frightened and ashamed little girl when she hides Visa receipts under her bed. Her laid-back parents have not done a good job raising this young woman. Her father (John Goodman) offers her encouragement at the same time that he pretends to pull a coin out of her ear. It is difficult to become an adult when your parents treat you like a child. A reasonable attitude is an important element of maturity. Shoppers demonstrate it by buying only the items that they need. Compulsive shoppers, controlled by wild urges, will buy many items that they can't possibly need. As Rebecca is on the verge of bankruptcy, she

Isla Fisher must learn to control her impulsive spending habits in *Confessions of a Shopaholic* (2009).

must reassess her priorities in life. She must learn to be frugal and practical. She must, at long last, become an adult.

Immature women are everywhere in today's comedies. Nothing can be more childish than Melissa McCarthy in *Identity Theft* (2013). James Luxford of The National summarized McCarthy's performance as "running around, screaming and bumping into things."[10] In *Baby Mama* (2008), Kate Holbrook (Tina Fey) hires Angie Ostrowiski (Amy Poehler) to serve as a surrogate mother. Angie, trashy and uninhibited, creates a number of problems when she comes to live with the straight-laced Kate. Angie's lack of problem-solving skills and fundamental decorum becomes obvious in a highly memorable bathroom scene. Angie rushes into the bathroom to relieve herself, but she is unable to open a protective child lock on the toilet seat and quickly resorts to peeing in the bathroom sink. Even Oscar-winning Sandra Bullock is unable to show class or good judgment in this milieu. In *The Heat* (2013), Bullock drunkenly drops her head down onto a bar counter, burying her face in a scattering of peanut shells. When she lifts her head again, she has a peanut shell lodged in her nostril and has to blow as hard as she can to get it to shoot out.

The main characters of *Ass Backwards* (2013), Kate (June Diane Raphael) and Chloe (Casey Wilson), are clearly lacking in maturity. The young women made friends as children after they tied for last place in the Miss Neptune child beauty pageant. When the organizers of Miss Neptune invite them to compete in a special 50th anniversary pageant, the girls do not hesitate to return to their old toddler and tiara ways. As they need money to get to the pageant, Chloe sells her stuffed animal collection, one of her most prized possessions. The items that you prize say a lot about you. The stuffed animal collection is comparable to Steve Carell's collection of action figures, except for one big difference: Carell made a wise investment in his action figures, which netted him a substantial profit when he finally sold them. Wilson, however, sets out to sell her stuffed animals and receives only a few dollars for them at a thrift store.

Ass Backwards owes a great debt to *Romy and Michele's High School Reunion* (1997), a film which speculates what it would be like if the vain and superficial teenagers of *Clueless* (1995) graduated from high school and never found a way to grow up. *The Dissolve*'s Genevieve Koski describes the primary concerns of Romy (Mira Sorvino) and Michele (Lisa Kudrow) as "fashion, going to clubs, maintaining their figures, and just being around each other."[11] The filmmakers did not find fault with the pair's shallowness. Rachel Handler, also of *The Dissolve*, wrote, "*Romy and Michele* celebrates its characters for having little to no ambition; champions the importance of accepting and loving yourself, latex dresses and all; and promotes the idea that life is better if you just ignore everybody else and have a great fucking time."[12]

Like *Step Brothers*, the film stresses that it is mistake to force a man-child to become an adult. Romy convinces Michele that they should attend their high school reunion pretending to be successful businesswomen. But Michele comes to regret their deception. She tells Romy, "We always had so much fun together. I thought high school was a blast! And until you told me that our lives weren't good enough, I thought everything *since* high school was a blast." Koski wrote, "With that line, Michele taps into the slacker ethos at the heart of *Romy and Michele*: Success isn't about the job you have, the money you make, or the number of kids you have. It's about how much fun you have, and who you have it with."[13]

Yet, the film ends with the duo opening their own fashion boutique. This is much like *Step Brothers*, which ends with Ferrell and O'Reilly running a successful karaoke business. This suggests that at least one aspect of adulthood is nonnegotiable. You can avoid marriage and parenthood. You can dedicate your life to friendship and fun. But, when all is said and done, you still need to achieve success in a career and earn money to support yourself.

Legally Blonde (2001) involves an insufficiently developed young woman, ditzy sorority queen Elle Woods (Reese Witherspoon). She is hopelessly in love with cute fraternity boy Warner Huntington III (Matthew Davis), but she fails to recognize that Warner is a callous and self-centered jerk. Warner, who plans to one day go into politics, doesn't believe that blonde and fun-loving Elle will be good for his public image and he bluntly announces to her at dinner that he is dumping her. She strives desperately to win back Warner by earning a law degree at Harvard and becoming a serious, respectable lawyer. Elle, described by Film Threat's Robert Bledsoe as "an airhead Bel Air brat,"[14] fortunately discovers her brainy side while at Harvard. The film is essentially *Private Benjamin* except that it uses a hard-knocks college in place of a hard-knocks boot camp.

Anna Faris has amused audiences with a dimwitted, goofy, breathy-voiced little

A girl and her dog. Reese Witherspoon is naively enthusiastic as she arrives at Harvard Law School in *Legally Blonde* (2001).

girl persona. The actress put a fair face on the traditional stoner comedy with *Smiley Face* (2007). Not surprisingly, the blunts are thick and the plot points are thin. Faris embarks on a series of misadventures after she gorges on cupcakes that, unknown to her, are heavily laced with pot. A commanding, deep-voiced narrator defends the character in spite of her relentless foolishness. "Do not judge her too harshly," he says. "After all, how is she to know they were pot cupcakes? And ask yourselves, who amongst you would not have done the same thing?" Gorging on cupcakes, whether or not she knew the cupcakes contained pot, is somewhat childish, especially considering that her roommate had baked the cupcakes for himself and he had left a "Do Not Eat" sign in clear view. Fairy tales often featured foolish children who were punished for failing to heed obvious warnings. Faris opened her next vehicle, *The House Bunny* (2008), narrating a photo montage that combined childhood photos with storybook illustrations. Confusing fact and fantasy is a common problem that plagues this type of immature young lady. Like *Legally Blonde*, *The House Bunny* was designed to get laughs by setting down a free-spirited party girl in the middle of a formal college campus.

At the center of *Burn Before Reading* (2008) is a vain, superficial, self-obsessed and dimwitted woman, Linda Litzke (Frances McDormand). She insists that her body needs a complete overhaul. "I've gotten about as far as this body can take me," she says. She consults a plastic surgeon about restoring the volume and firmness of her breasts, removing the crow's feet from around her eyes, and eradicating the excess fat from her thighs, abdomen and underarms. She cannot see a way to interest an attractive man without making her body beautiful. Her bratty, single-minded scheme to acquire money for the surgery inadvertently causes one man to be fatally shot in the head, another man to be hacked to death with a hatchet, a third man to be put into a coma by a gunshot wound, and a final man to be locked up in prison. In the end, she is aware of the havoc that she has created and yet she remains fiercely dedicated to achieving her plastic surgery goals. Litzke is an older, darker version of Reese Witherspoon's Elle Woods from *Legally Blonde* and Anna Faris' Shelley Darlingson from *The House Bunny*. Like Witherspoon and Faris, McDormand plays her character with high energy and wide-eyed naïveté. It is not hard to imagine either Woods or Darlingson, both of whom are obsessed about their looks, panicking over the first sign of crow's feet.

Apart from the runaway bride scenarios, films tend to show an impulsive, indecisive woman in a more sympathetic light. The woman is portrayed as spirited and independent while a man who behaves in the same manner is undisciplined and irresponsible. Women are, at times, allowed to give free rein to their emotions.

This brings us to Greta Gerwig, who has come to specialize in playing the type of flighty young woman typically played by Ginger Rogers in the 1940s. This was especially evident in Gerwig's title role in *Frances Ha* (2012). According to Ty Burr of the *Boston Globe*: "Frances is yet another of the actress's adorable ditherers, turning the corner of her late 20s and shocked that her friends have decided to grow up."[15] The plot is similar to *Ghost World*. Frances' relationship with her best friend, Sophie (Mickey Sumner), is severely strained because Sophie wants to grow up and Frances doesn't. Sophie becomes engaged to Patch (Patrick Heusinger) and moves with him to Japan. Being estranged from her closest friend leaves Frances adrift.

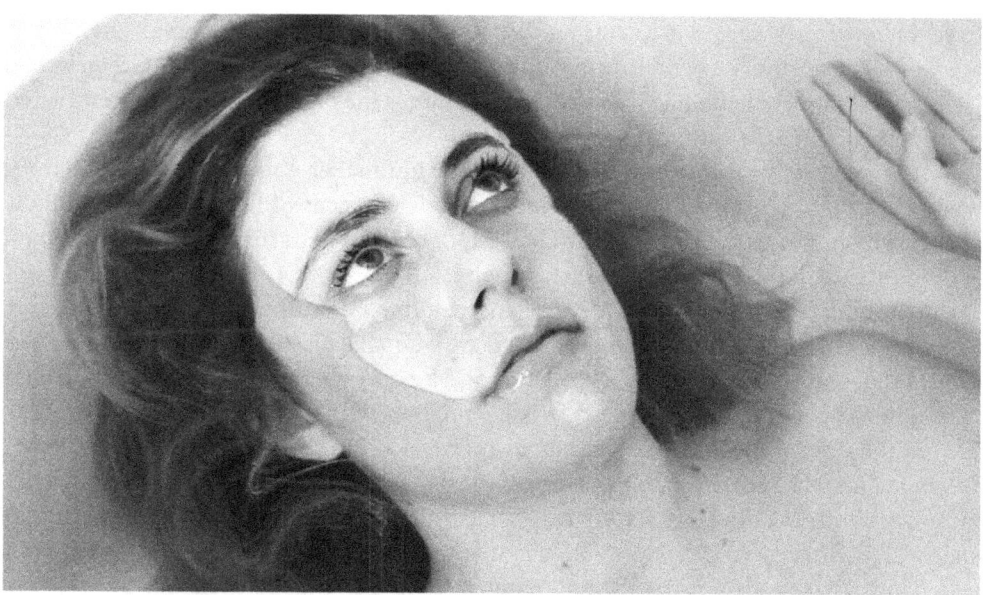

Greta Gerwig frets about her future in *Frances Ha* (2012).

Mick LaSalle of Hearst Newspapers wrote, "*Frances Ha* deals with a difficult period of life that is rarely depicted as difficult. It's the time, not right after college, but four or five years down the line, when being broke has become exhausting, when just being out of the house is no longer fun, when 30 looms in the near distance, and when the pressure is on: Do something. Do something."[16] Cath Clarke of *Time Out* was more succinct, writing, "Frances is stuck in her crazy, clueless, can't-pay-the-rent stage."[17] If most people acted like Frances when they were 27, they would quickly end up homeless. But, with the aid of her many friends, Frances is able to drag her meager belongings from one address to another. Her rootlessness is played as a joke in the film. Frances' multiple addresses are used as the film's chapter titles.

The film is largely carried along on Gerwig's charm. Moira MacDonald of the *Seattle Times* said that the director (and the actress' boyfriend) Noah Baumbach made the film "a celebration of Gerwig's coltish, goofy appeal."[18] If not for her charm, the character would barely have a chance of winning over viewers in light of her aimless, clumsy and messy ways. This was the reason that, as stated by MacDonald, "[She's] making all the wrong steps along the way, but you can't help cheering her on."[19]

It is clear in the film that Frances is not burdened by her failings. Rick Groen of *The Globe and Mail* wrote, "Frances is sublimely untormented. There's a bounce in her ungainly step…. Frances is that rare specimen who floats above her fate."[20] The key word is "floats." MacDonald similarly wrote, "Frances floats through a series of addresses, relationships and friendships."[21] She points to a scene in which Frances "runs down the sidewalks with the carefree ease of a child."[22] LaSalle described Frances as "an open spirit, floating happily through life, until she realizes that she's floating nowhere."[23] Frances is a free spirit as weightless and intangible as a fairy. She is a fairy that can cohabit the same alternate reality as Langdon's Elf. And her behavior is made to seem both enviable and exhilarating. What person wouldn't like to break out of their adult straitjacket and have fun running down sidewalks with carefree ease? Groen wrote, "Seldom has aimlessness looked so good."[24] The film is the biggest celebration of arrested development since *Pee-wee's Big Adventure*.

It is meant to be a cute and playful film. The filmmaker is an overindulgent parent who protects his irresponsible child from the consequences of her actions. Nothing is risked, which means that nothing can be lost, and this makes for boring storytelling.

Frances at least has a good heart, which is all that is really important. Yet again, the man-child is glorified for being pure and genuine in nature.

Frances is as sexless as Pee-wee Herman. She shies away from lovers using the excuse that she is "undate-able." At one point, she becomes visibly uncomfortable listening to her roommate Lev (Adam Driver) have sex with a woman in the next room.

At the start of the film, Frances has an apprenticeship at a modern dance company. When it ends, she is called into the office of the dance company director, Colleen (Charlotte d'Amboise). Colleen is happy to offer Frances an office job, but this doesn't go over well with Frances. Frances, who has thrown herself headlong into her dreams to be a dancer, is appalled at the idea of being stuck in a mundane desk job. Colleen has maternal feelings for Frances, which allows her to remain patient and caring even though Frances has reacted indignantly to her kind offer. She presents the young woman with practical advice for her future. She points out to her that she has shown more talent as a choreographer than a dancer. She expresses her willingness to let Frances have studio space to develop dance routines. In the meantime, she explains, the office job will pay Frances enough money "to keep her going." Frances is too overwhelmed by her ego and insecurities to seriously consider what this older and wiser woman has to tell her.

It is odd that the many people who surround Frances do not find her to be pathetic or reprehensible or insist that she grow up. She charms everyone she meets and, by the end of the film, everyone loves her more than ever. While rambling drunkenly at a dinner party, this woman who is jobless and has little money comes up with the foolish idea to fly to Paris for the weekend. A couple who has listened to her ramblings happily hand her the keys to their home in Paris. They look like two rational adults. Why should they do this? Shouldn't they worry that this drunken, irrational woman might burn their home to the ground? But it comes as no surprise at this point in the film. Every person in the film acts invariably polite and affectionate to Frances.

Frances finances her Paris getaway using her one overworked credit card. The trip, contrary to Frances' expectations, is neither magical nor transformative. Jet lag causes her to sleep through much of the weekend. She ends up having a gloomy and pointless stay in the City of Light.

In Chaplin's day, growing up was something that was done naturally. We might be reluctant to grow up, but it was something we still needed to do. Adulthood was as inconvertible as it was burdensome. A person either grew up or they didn't survive. The ultimate consequence was homelessness and starvation. In today's comedy films, immaturity does not cut a person off from life's niceties. Chaplin's charm and playfulness got people to give him a meal or a temporary place to stay, but his Tramp character could never fly off for a weekend in Paris. He had to contend with a fate that was more tragic than that.

Today, we do not need to have Arthur's staggering riches to have comforts and pleasures stunt our development. It is sufficient to have access to financial aid from open-handed parents or have a wallet stocked with Rebecca the Shopaholic's magic cards. Or, sometimes, all that a person needs to remain a child is enough money to buy the latest video game hardware. As it stands, the facts on this subject are simple and indisputable. The greater the wealth, the greater the chance to spoil a child. An affluent home equipped with a tempting array of distractions can easily rob a child of the opportunities to be responsible.

The last act of *Frances Ha* becomes, according to Slate critic Annie Baker, "helpless for a resolution."[25] In the same way as Frances' life, the plot becomes meandering and messy. But then, perhaps abruptly, there's a happy ending. After muddling around for awhile, Frances reconsiders Colleen's job offer. Finally seeing the wisdom and practicality of Colleen's advice, she is able to find focus and direction. It isn't long before Frances choreographs a dance number for the students to perform at a live show. After the show, Frances is praised backstage by several visitors. In the final scene, we see that Frances is living alone in her own apartment.

Young Adult (2011) sheds light on the dark side of immaturity. Protagonist Mavis Gary (Charlize Theron) is not blissful, innocent or charming. An unpleasant brat, she is selfish, doesn't care if her actions hurt others, and gets terribly bad-tempered whenever she doesn't get her way. It is understandable when a friend loses patience with her appalling behavior and tells her to grow up.

The child-woman could be dangerous. *Blackadder*'s Queen Elizabeth I (Miranda Richardson) was described by series co-creator Ben Elton as a "crazy, dictatorial, mad child-woman."[26] At any moment, the queen might have someone decapitated because he has somehow displeased her.

The poster for *Laggies* (2014) featured the tagline "A Comedy About Acting Your Age and Other Adult Decisions." Megan Burch (Keira Knightley), who dropped out of grad school, now works as a sign flipper for her dad's accounting company. She doesn't share her girlfriends' ambitions for career and family. She has remained too childish for her girlfriends, one of whom gets upset when Megan playfully tweaks the nipples of a Buddha statue at a Chinese restaurant. Megan's refusal to grow up is apparent at a glance. Ty Burr of *The Boston Globe* wrote, "Knightley's body language ingeniously suggests a teenager forcibly frog-marched into maturity."[27]

Megan flees from her boyfriend, Anthony (Mark Webber), after he proposes marriage, which makes her kin to film history's runaway bride. She's not ready for something as big as marriage and decides to lay low somewhere to figure out what to do.

Burr questioned if arrested adolescence hadn't become an overdone topic. In a general discussion of the genre, Michael Arbeiter found these films to be "getting a tad old" and "simply played out."[28] He couldn't see the man-child story having "too many folds and layers left to it."[29] With regard to *Laggies*, he wrote, "The portrait [drawn] of a young woman stalled on the edge of adulthood is so familiar by now that you may approach it with impatience. We understand, you're having trouble growing up. Get on

Keira Knightley can easily identify with a nauseated, slow-moving tortoise in *Laggies* (2014).

with it...."³⁰ Much of what happens with Megan has happened to immature characters in earlier films. Megan has a doting father, Ed (Jeff Garlin), just like Isla Fisher did in *Confessions of a Shopaholic*. Megan hangs out with a teenage girl, Annika (Chlöe Grace Moretz), which is like Kristen Bell hanging out with teenagers in *The Lifeguard*. Megan rides a skateboard with a group of children, something that Owen Wilson did in *You, Me and Dupree*. Megan finds a safe haven in Annika's bedroom, which is similar to Mikey of *Momma's Man* finding a safe haven in his parents' loft. Just like Mikey lies to his wife about flight delays, Megan lies to her fiancé about being stuck at a career seminar. The film endorses immaturity like *Jeff, Who Lives at Home* and *Our Idiot Brother*. Burr wrote, "Megan's high school friends have moved on to marriages and children, and the script by Andrea Seigel can barely hold back a sneer at their complacency."³¹

Megan cares for a sick tortoise who refuses to eat. Her kind and determined efforts cure the tortoise of its ills. She identifies with the tortoise as she believes that she, herself, is simply moving through life at a slower pace than others. Megan extends herself further when she agrees to take Annika to visit her estranged mother Bethany (Gretchen Mol), who abandoned her daughter years earlier to pursue a modeling career. Megan finds that Bethany is too immature and selfish to be a responsible and caring mother. This inspires her to stop trying to be Annika's pal and instead be the surrogate mother that the troubled girl needs. Curing the tortoise and providing Annika with support and direction makes Megan a more significant person than she was when she was twirling a sign or tweaking a Buddha's nipples at the start of the film.

The float effect came up again in *Laggies*. Megan says at one point, "I'm sure it does seem kind of stupid to make some sort of rigid plan for the future, but it's stupider not to start paying attention to who you are and what makes you happy. Otherwise, you just float." Megan finally decides that she does not want to "float around forever."

Keira Knightley continued to discuss the "float" issue in interviews. She told Refinery 29 that she didn't regard herself as a bonafide grown-up: "I think that's the thing about this character [Megan]. Particularly with people of our generation, it seems very right, and really common, that sort of float, and that feeling of 'Am I doing the right thing?' The problem of Generation Y is that feeling of 'I should be doing something to live up to my potential. Am I living up to my potential? Am I doing the right thing? Am I with the right person?'"[32] She talked to the *Guardian* about "[t]his moment where people suddenly go: 'Er, who am I?'"[33] She referred to this feeling as having "a bit of a float."[34] She added, "[E]veryone has had that at some point—and probably has it at many points."[35] The float seems by this description to involve enough heady, self-absorbed analysis to drive anyone crazy.

Filmmakers have come to recognize that a woman is not immune from immaturity. A woman, just as easily as a man, can be lazy, vain, needy, excitable, whiny, manipulative, impulsive, or superficial. She can make bad decisions and she can act inappropriately. A woman who cherishes her shoes and handbags has no right to criticize her boyfriend for caring deeply about his video games.

Epilogue

For decades, film comedians offered for our amusement poorly developed individuals who had failed to transition from childhood to adulthood. Now, though, we are seeing something else entirely. We have amassing before our eyes an epic wave of self-satisfied buffoons who refuse to make this transition whether they are able to or not.

For years, Hollywood has presented a riotous celebration of the man-child, but more recent films have acknowledged that these socially awkward misfits have a dark side. The man-child protagonists of *The Almost Man* (2012) and *Buzzard* (2014) are, to put it bluntly, scary. *A.V. Club* critic Mike D'Angelo described *Buzzard*'s slacker protagonist, Marty Jackitansky (Joshua Burge), as "a borderline sociopath … who spends his days engineering petty scams and finding other creative ways to avoid being a productive member of society."[1] Marty is far afield of his lackadaisical and free-spirited slacker forerunners. For sure, he has none of the likability of *Dobie Gillis*' guileless and happy-go-lucky Maynard G. Krebbs.

Marty, who perceives the world through comic books and horror films, has distorted attitudes about work, relationships and morality. He finds nothing worthy of his time, energy and attention other than fashioning a replica of Freddie Krueger's slasher glove. We see him repeatedly sharpening the glove's five tapered blades. We know from the Chekhov's Gun principle that something bad is going to happen with this offbeat creation. At one point, fellow slacker Derek (Joel Potrykus) playfully raises up a *Star Wars* light saber and challenges Marty to a duel. The scene becomes frightening as Marty repeatedly swipes at Derek with the glove. It seems that, at any moment, Marty's razor-sharp claws will puncture one of Derek's eyes or split open the hapless fool's carotid artery.

Marty is, in ways, a throwback to the violent and vulgar scoundrel that could be found in the Keystone comedies. We can enjoy a comic character violating rules if the rules represent a form of repression. It can, in this way, provide relief and pleasure to see these characters defy and thwart authority. Douglas Riblet made the point in an essay on the Keystone comedies that we can enjoy "an endearingly nervy scoundrel who victimizes the pretentious, the arrogant and the overly serious."[2] But scoundrel comedy has its limits. T.G.A. Nelson, the author of *Comedy: An introduction to Comedy in Literature, Drama and Cinema*, wrote, "Few of us, perhaps, can resist the lure of the demonic in comedy, but we recognize that it can reach a point where it transforms into something that is not comical at all."[3] It isn't long before Marty, with his sociopathic

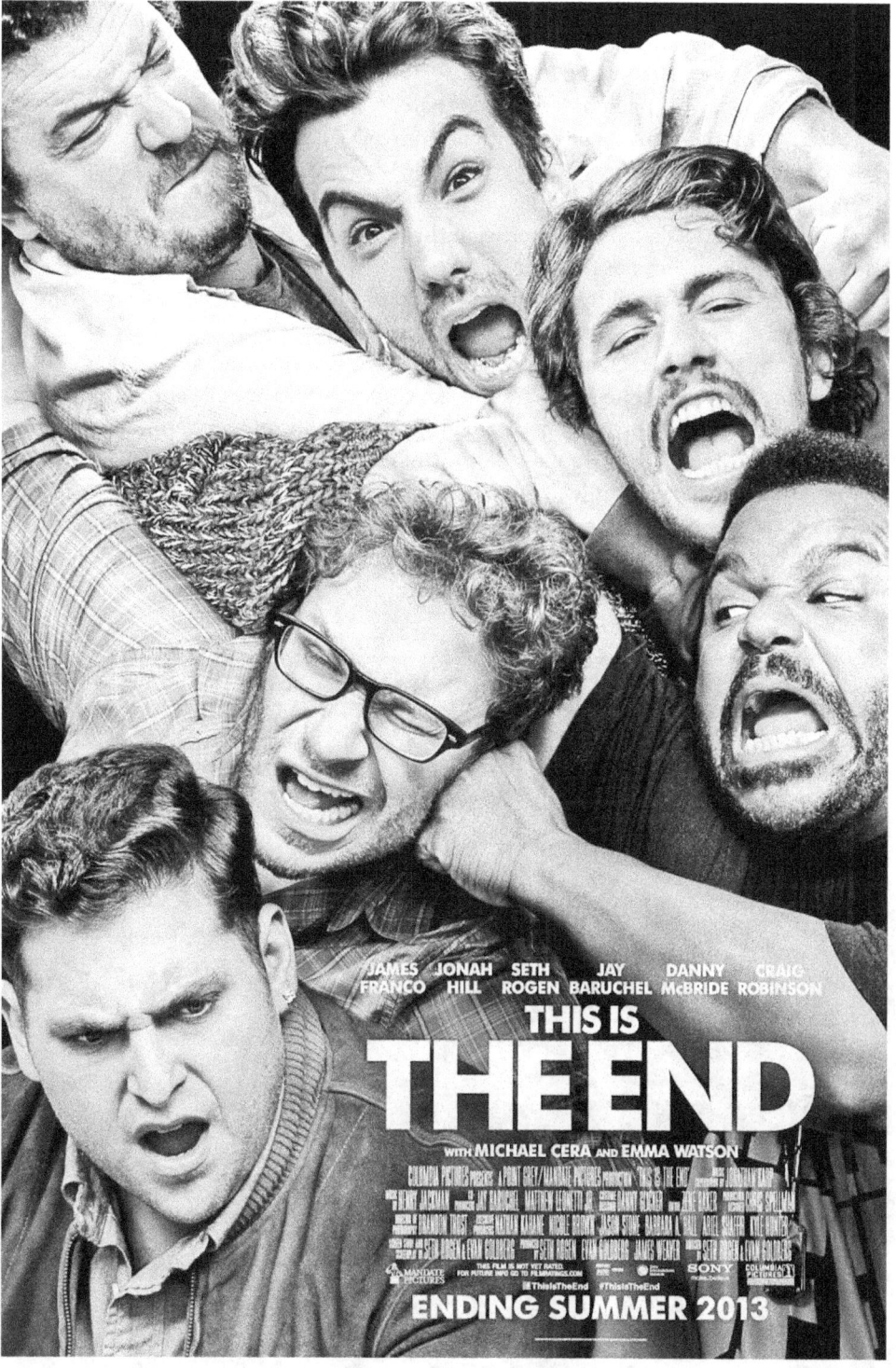

This Is the End (2013) was a $32 million, CGI-heavy meditation on maturity. A group of childish friends need to abandon their selfish and petty ways to ascend into Heaven as part of the Rapture. Pictured in this photo are Danny McBride, Jay Baruchel, James Franco, Seth Rogen, Craig Robinson and Jonah Hill.

tendencies, is no longer comical. IMDb critic Bob Lipton wrote, "All comedy starts with transgressive behavior. Bad comedy stops there."[4]

Marty is more gluttonous than either Andre Deed or Roscoe Arbuckle ever was. A key scene of the film features Marty cramming spaghetti and meatballs into his mouth, unconcerned that the food is spilling onto his chest and bathrobe. At another point in the film, he constructs a massive sandwich that consists of a layer of corn chips spread neatly between two slices of frozen pizza.

The man-child has finally regressed to bestial forms of violence and appetite. He has returned to being Kerr's monkey in the treetops.

Today, in this spectacular age of CGI, Dolby Digital sound and 3D technology, films still need to make time for character development. It is not uncommon for a film of this type to involve a protagonist struggling awkwardly and sometimes foolishly to attain maturity. Take, for instance, the plot of *Guardians of the Galaxy* (2014). The story opens in a cramped, dimly lit hospital room in the 1980s. Peter Quill (Chris Pratt), an eight-year-old boy, expresses anguish and terror as he watches his mother die. The distraught child runs out of the hospital in tears. A massive alien spacecraft astonishingly descends from the heavens and hovers directly above the boy, who is instantly

Stan Laurel and Oliver Hardy enjoy a game of checkers in *Brats* (1930) (courtesy www.doctormacro.com).

sucked up into a bright beam of light. Peter has been abducted by intergalactic bandits. He is so traumatized by his mother's death (not to mention his way-out kidnapping) that, during the years that he is held captive by the violent, grimy bandits, he remains stuck in his Earthbound past. Peter often references 1980s films and television series. He mentions the film *Footloose* (1984) when he criticizes a woman for her unwillingness to dance. He quotes a classic line from *Cobra* (1986): "You're the disease. I'm the cure." He calls someone a "ninja turtle." He has an *ALF* sticker on his spaceship. He explains that he has named the spaceship *The Milano* after his childhood crush, Alyssa Milano. He listens to 1980s pop songs assembled on a music mixtape that his mother gave him moments before she died. No matter how big and skillful he is, he is still a playful, lovable eight-year-old boy at heart. But, during the course of the film, he learns responsibility, loyalty, intimacy, selflessness, and courage. He becomes, as so many film characters before him, a true man.

After the film's big action climax, head bandit Yondu demands that Peter turn over an orb containing the powerful Infinity Stone. Peter secretly switches the orb with a ringer so that, when Yondu later opens the orb, he only finds Peter's childhood troll doll inside. Clearly, Peter no longer feels the need to hold onto his childhood by holding onto kitsch from his early years on Earth.

This type of character arc, which allows the hero to mature from child to adult, will endure despite the stubbornly childish antics of Adam Sandler and Seth Rogen. It will never go away as long as the process of maturity remains at the core of the human story.

Chapter Notes

Introduction

1. L. Molad, producer, episode 1519: "Seth Rogen Grows Up & Critics with Attitude" [audio podcast, May 9, 2014], *Studio 360*, http://www.studio360.org/story/seth-rogen-grows-up-and-critics-with-attitude/.
2. *Ibid.*
3. Bob Fischbach, "Review: Adam Sandler's 'Grown Ups 2' full of juvenile humor," *Omaha World-Herald*, July 12, 2013, http://www.omaha.com/go/review-adam-sandler-s-grown-ups-full-of-juvenile-humor/article_ba0c7794-6b44-5b2d-adba-dffbb4979614.html.
4. Justin Chang, "Review: 'That's My Boy,'" *Variety*, June 14, 2012, http://variety.com/2012/film/reviews/that-s-my-boy-1117947751/.
5. Lewis Thomas, *The Fragile Species* (New York: Simon & Schuster, 1993), 175.
6. A.O. Scott, "The Death of Adulthood in American Culture," *New York Times*, September 11, 2014, http://www.nytimes.com/2014/09/14/magazine/the-death-of-adulthood-in-american-culture.html.
7. Molad.
8. Michael Kimmel, *Guyland* (New York: Harper Perennial, 2009), 4.

Chapter 1

1. Steve Rose, "Why are there so many movies about guys who won't grow up?" *The Guardian*, May 10, 2012, http://www.theguardian.com/film/2012/may/10/movies-about-guys-who-wont-grow-up.
2. *Ibid.*
3. Andy Morris, "The most powerful man in comedy," *GQ*, May 19, 2011, http://www.gq-magazine.co.uk/entertainment/articles/2011-05/19/gq-film-judd-apatow-interview-movies-superbad/page/3.
4. Josh Rottenberg, "Talkin' 'Superbad': Modern Immaturity," *Entertainment Weekly* (August 13, 2007). http://www.ew.com/ew/article/0,,20051188,00.html.
5. David Robinson, "Rise and Fall of the Clowns," *Sight and Sound*, Vol. 56 (1987), 198–203.
6. Richard Abel, *The Ciné Goes to Town: French Cinema, 1896–1914* (Oakland, CA: University of California Press, 1998), 228.
7. *Ibid.*
8. *Ibid.*
9. Walter Kerr, *The Silent Clowns* (Cambridge, MA: Da Capo Press, 1990), 3.
10. Karl Rahner, *Everyday Faith* (Freiburg, Germany: Herder and Herder, 1968), 20.
11. Alan Bilton, *Silent Film Comedy and American Culture* (Basingstoke, UK: Palgrave Macmillan, 2013), 123.
12. David F., Bjorklund, "The Role of Immaturity in Human Development," *Psychological Bulletin*, Vol. 122, No. 2, 1997, 153–169.
13. Geoff King, *Film Comedy* (London: Wallflower Press, 2002), 87.
14. *Ibid.*
15. Tom Robbins, *Still Life with Woodpecker* (New York: Bantam Books, 1980), 19.
16. Bilton, 125.
17. *Ibid.*
18. *Ibid.*
19. *Ibid.*
20. James L. Neibaur, "Selected Short Subject: 'His Bitter Pill' (1916)," *Racine Film Examiner*, September 16, 2014, http://www.examiner.com/review/selected-short-subject-his-bitter-pill-1916.
21. Mary Desjardins, "Swanson, Moore and Bow," *Idols of Modernity: Movie Stars of the 1920s*, Patrice Petro, ed. (New Brunswick, NJ: Rutgers University Press, 2010).
22. Brian M. Raftery, "Pee-Wee Turns 20," *Entertainment Weekly*, September 1, 2006, http://www.ew.com/ew/article/0,,1515978_5,00.html.
23. Kalton C. Lahue, and Sam Gill, *Clown Princes and Court Jesters* (South Brunswick and New York: A.S. Barnes, 1970), 200.
24. Kerr, 267.

Chapter 2

1. Bordwell, David. "His majesty the American, leaping for the moon." Observations on Film Art (November 26, 2008). http://www.davidbordwell.net/blog/2008/11/26/his-majesty-the-american-leaping-for-the-moon/.
2. *Ibid.*
3. Bilton, 123.
4. Barbara Barry, "Could 'You Take It'?" *Modern Screen*, January, 1934.
5. Harold Lloyd, *An American Comedy* (Mineola, New York: Dover Publications, revised edition, 1972).
6. Mark Twain, *The Adventures of Tom Sawyer* (Hartford, CT: American Publishing Co., 1876), 255.
7. Smith, Henry Nash, *Mark Twain: The Development of a Writer* (Cambridge, MA: The Belknap Press of Harvard University Press, 1962), 122.
8. Steven D. Greydanus, "The Kid Brother (1927)," *Decent Films Guide*, http://www.decentfilms.com/reviews/kidbrother.
9. In film comedy, a man is living in high style if he can lounge in a luxurious bathtub. This is also demonstrated by Lupino Lane in *Fool's Luck* (1926), Dudley Moore in *Arthur* (1981), Eddie Murphy in *Trading Places* (1983), Mark Holton in *Pee-wee's Big Adventure* (1985) and Adam Sandler in *Billy Madison* (1995).
10. Ed Howard, "The Navigator," *Only Cinema*, April 3, 2012, http://seul-le-cinema.blogspot.com/2012/04/navigator.html.
11. Edward McPherson, *Buster Keaton: Tempest in a Flat Hat* (London: Faber & Faber, 2011), 173.
12. Geoff Nicholson, "Bustered," *Psycho Gourmet*, November 17, 2010, http://psychogourmet.blogspot.com/2010/11/apparently-theres-something-in-air.html.
13. Melissa Denes, "The double life of Harold Lloyd," *The Telegraph* (May 22, 2001). http://www.telegraph.co.uk/culture/4723674/The-double-life-of-Harold-Lloyd.html.
14. David Robinson, *Chaplin, His Life and Art* (New York: McGraw-Hill, 1985), 278.
15. Ignatiy Vishnevetsky, "A century later, why does Chaplin still matter?" AV Club (June 23, 2014).
16. Joan Mellen, *Modern Times* (London: Cromwell Press, 2006), 6–14.
17. Jürgen Martschukat, "Men in Gray Flannel Suits: Troubling Masculinities in 1950s America," *Gender Forum*, Issue 32, 2011, http://www.genderforum.org/issues/historical-masculinities-as-an-intersectional-problem/httpwwwgenderforumorgissueshistorical-masculinities-as-an-intersectional-problemmen-in-gray-flannel-suits/.

Chapter 3

1. Rob Nixon, "*The Music Box* and *Sons of the Desert*: The Essentials," *TCM Online*, http://www.tcm.com/this-month/article/190955|0/The-Essentials-The-Music-Box-Sons-of-the-Desert.html.
2. Seligman, Martin E., (1991). *Learned Optimism: How to Change Your Mind and Your Life*, New York: Knopf, 126.
3. Bjorklund.
4. Jean Jacques Rousseau, *Emile, or On Education* (New York: E. Dutton, 1762).
5. Bilton, 204.
6. *Ibid.*
7. Hal Erickson, *Military Comedy Films: A Critical Survey and Filmography of Hollywood Releases Since 1918* (Jefferson, NC: McFarland, 2012), 173.

Chapter 4

1. Wallis, John Doyle, "Pepe Le Moko," DVD Talk (January 7, 2003). http://www.dvdtalk.com/reviews/5414/pepe-le-moko/.
2. "Bon Anniversaire, Jean Renoir," program notes for Berkeley Art Museum and Pacific Film Archive (1994), http://www.bampfa.berkeley.edu/film/FN10533.
3. Ginette Vincendeau, "The Beauty's Beast: Jean Gabin, Masculinity and the French Hero," *Women and Film: A Sight and Sound Reader* (Philadelphia: Temple University Press, 1993), 115–22.
4. *Ibid.*
5. *Ibid.*
6. Tom Block, "La Grande Illusion," *Culture Vulture*, http://culturevulture.net/film/la-grande-illusion/.
7. Ivana Redwine, "Grand Illusion—DVD Review," accessed March 15, 2006, http://homevideo.about.com/library/weekly/aa080801a.htm.
8. Luc Capdevila, "The Quest for Masculinity in a Defeated France, 1940–45," *Contemporary European History*, (Cambridge, England: Cambridge University Press, 2001), 423–445.
9. *Ibid.*
10. "Reviews & Ratings for *Stormy Waters*," Internet Movie Database, http://www.imdb.com/title/tt0034093/reviews?ref_=tt_urv.
11. *Ibid.*
12. Evelyn Ehrlich, *Cinema of Paradox: French Filmmaking Under the German Occupation* (New York: Columbia University Press, 1985).
13. *Ibid.*
14. *Ibid.*
15. *Ibid.*
16. Girish Shambu, "Les Enfants du Paradis," *Senses of Cinema*, January, 2001, http://www.sensesofcinema.com/contents/cteq/01/12/enfants.html.
17. Jake Euker, "Review of *Port of Shadows* (1938)," *AMC Movie Guide*, http://movies.amctv.com/movie/1938/Port+of+Shadows.
18. *Ibid.*
19. *Ibid.*
20. Pierre-François Lacenaire, *Mémoires de La-*

cenaire avec ses poèmes et ses Lettres (Paris: Albin Michel, 1968).

21. *Movie Gazette*, "Review of The Raven," accessed March 15, 2006, http://www.movie-gazette.com/cinereviews/1217.

22. Alan Williams, "Le Corbeau," *The Criterion Collection*, Heather Shaw, ed., 2004, https://www.criterion.com/films/684-le-corbeau.

23. Ben-Ghiat, Ruth, "Unmasking the fascist man: masculinity, film and the transition from dictatorship," Journal of Modern Italian Studies, Volume 10, No. 3 (Fall 2005). 336–365.

24. Scullion, Rosemarie, "Family Fictions and Reproductive Realities in Vichy France: Claude Chabrol's *Une Affaire de femme*."

25. John Simon, "Story of Women—Movie Review," *National Review*, April 1, 1990.

Chapter 5

1. Fannie Kilbourne, "Sunny Goes Home," *The Saturday Evening Post*, Vol. 193, May 7, 1921.
2. *Ibid*.
3. *Ibid*.
4. Ibee, "Connie Goes Home," *Variety*, 22, column 2, September 13, 1923.
5. "Goodrich Picture Tops Mutual Schedule," *Motography* December 8, 1917.
6. Gene D. Phillips, *Some Like It Wilder: The Life and Controversial Films of Billy Wilder* (Lexington: University Press of Kentucky, 2010), 38.
7. Charlotte Chandler, *Nobody's Perfect: Billy Wilder, A Personal Biography* (Montclair, NJ: Applause Theatre & Cinema Books, 2004), 103.
8. Glenn Erickson, "DVD Savant Review: The Major and the Minor," DVD Talk (May 2, 2008), http://www.dvdtalk.com/dvdsavant/s2575majo.html.
9. Libby Hill, "Catfish culture: How MTV's reality show is leaching into pop culture (and reality)," *A.V. Club*, September 5, 2014, http://www.avclub.com/article/catfish-culture-how-mtvs-reality-show-leaching-pop-208104.
10. Frank Krutnik, *Inventing Jerry Lewis* (Washington, D.C.: Smithsonian, 2000).
11. James Neibaur, *The Silent Films of Harry Langdon (1923–1928)* (Lanham, MD: Scarecrow Press, 2012), 144.
12. Zach Lewis, "Review of The Ladies Man (1961)," *Letterboxd*, April 2, 2014, http://letterboxd.com/lightwisdom/film/the-ladies-man-1961/1/.
13. *Ibid*.
14. King, 81.
15. Kevin B. Lee, "The Ladies' Man (1961, Jerry Lewis)," *Shooting Down Pictures*, August 31 2009, http://alsolikelife.com/shooting/2009/08/981–113-the-ladies-man-1961-jerry-lewis/.
16. Lewis.
17. Marcia Landy, "Jerry Agonistes: An Obscure Object of Critical Desire," *Enfant Terrible!: Jerry Lewis in American Film*, Murray Pomerance, ed. (New York: NYU Press, 2002), 69.
18. Angelos Koutsourakis, "Jerry Lewis," *Bright Lights Film Journal*, Issue 63, February 2009, http://www.brightlightsfilm.com/63/63jerrylewis.php#.U9aFwmOa_G8.

Chapter 6

1. Wylie, Phili "The Abdicating Male ... and How the Gray Flannel Mind Exploits Him Through His Women," *Playboy*, November, 1956).
2. Doug Johnson, "Movie Review: Clifton Webb in *Sitting Pretty*," *Alt Film Guide*, http://www.altfg.com/blog/classics/clifton-webb-sitting-pretty-maureen-ohara/.
3. *Ibid*.
4. James J. O'Meara, "The Babysitting Bachelor as Aryan Avatar: Clifton Webb in *Sitting Pretty*, Part 2," *Counter Currents Publishing*, http://www.counter-currents.com/2013/02/the-babysitting-bachelor-as-aryan-avatarclifton-webb-in-sitting-pretty-part-2/.
5. Tasha Robinson, "The hard-bitten cynicism of Billy Wilder's *Ace in the Hole*," *The Dissolve*, June 25, 2014, http://thedissolve.com/features/movie-of-the-week/631-the-hard-bitten-cynicism-of-billy-wilders-ace-in-t/.
6. *Ibid*.
7. *Ibid*.
8. Wheeler Winston Dixon, "Dark Humor in Films of the 1960s—Part 2," *Film International*, August 27, 2012, http://filmint.nu/?p=5675.
9. J.D. Salinger, *The Catcher in the Rye* (Boston: Little, Brown, 1991), 244.
10. Gary Leva, producer, *North by Northwest: One for the Ages*, Leva Film Works, 2009.
11. Leva.
12. Justin W. Price, "'North by Northwest': The Anatomy of the Film," *HubPages*, http://pdxkaraokeguy.hubpages.com/hub/North-by-Northwest-The-Anatomy-of-the-Film.
13. Leva.
14. Brett McKay, "Where Does Manhood Come From?" *The Art of Manliness*, April 21, 2014, http://www.artofmanliness.com/2014/04/21/where-does-manhood-come-from/.
15. Jack Murnighan, *Beowulf on the Beach: What to Love and What to Skip in Literature's 50 Greatest Hits* (New York: Broadway Books, 2009).
16. Roger Ebert, "Mon Oncle," *Roger Ebert.com*, June 8, 2003, http://www.rogerebert.com/reviews/great-movie-mon-oncle-1958.
17. *Ibid*.
18. Martschukat.
19. *Ibid*.
20. *Ibid*.
21. *Ibid*.
22. *Ibid*.
23. Morris Dickstein, *Leopards in the Temple:*

The Transformation of American Fiction, 1945–1970 (Cambridge, MA: Harvard University Press, 2002.

24. Scott.

25. Ross Posnock, *Philip Roth's Rude Truth: The Art of Immaturity* (Princeton, NJ: Princeton University Press, 2006).

26. Rob Nixon, "The Apartment: The Essentials," *TCM Online*, http://www.tcm.com/this-month/article/190949|0/The-Essentials-The-Apartment.html.

27. Anonymous, "Under the Yum Yum Tree," *Crazy for Cinema*, http://www.crazy4cinema.com/Review/FilmsU/f_yum_yum.html.

28. Jake Cole, "Re-Make/Re-Model: *The Heartbreak Kid* (1972) vs *The Heartbreak Kid* (2007)," *Spectrum Culture*, October 14, 2012, http://spectrumculture.com/film/re-makere-model-the-heartbreak-kid-1972-vs-the-heartbreak-kid-2007/.

29. "TV Tropes, Man Child: Live-Action TV," http://tvtropes.org/pmwiki/pmwiki.php/ManChild/LiveActionTV. The Wikipedia page is devoted to explaining the childlike qualities of Michael Scott (Steve Carell) of *The Office*. The article reads: "He tends to overestimate his own importance in the eyes of his co-workers and cannot understand why they do not seem to have much fun at work, as he believes an office to be the 'place where dreams come true.' [His] constant desire to be the center of attention often manifests itself in selfish behavior. For example, when he burns his foot in 'The Injury,' he expects Pam and Ryan to tend to his needs, despite Dwight's much more serious concussion. In 'Michael's Birthday,' Michael spends most of this episode pouting over the way Kevin's potential diagnosis of skin cancer is upstaging his birthday."

30. *Ibid.*

31. *Ibid.*

32. *Ibid.*

33. Kenneth Keniston, "The Mood of Americans Today," *New York Times*, November 8, 1981, http://www.nytimes.com/1981/11/08/books/the-mood-of-americans-today.html?pagewanted=1.

34. Sweeney R. Emmet, "The Outsiders: *Mongo's Back in Town* (1971) and *Lifeguard* (1976)," Movie Morlocks (March 18, 2014). http://moviemorlocks.com/2014/03/18/the-outsiders-mongos-back-in-town-1971-and-lifeguard-1976/.

35. Posnock.

36. Peter Christopher Kunze, "The Tears of a Clown: Masculinity and Comedy in Contemporary American Narratives" (Florida State University DigiNole Commons, July 9, 2012).

Chapter 7

1. Canby Vincent, "Movie Review: Dudley Moore Stars as a Screwball in 'Arthur,'" *New York Times*, July 17, 1981. http://www.nytimes.com/movie/review?res=9B00E1D81038F934A25754C0A967948260.

2. Nathan Rabin, "The Longest Week," *The Dissolve*, September 4, 2014, http://thedissolve.com/reviews/1050-the-longest-week/.

3. Michael Arbeiter, "A History of Slackers in Movies," *Hollywood.com*, September 5, 2011, http://www.hollywood.com/news/movies/7836002/a-history-of-slackers-in-movies?page=all.

4. N. Murray, K. Phipps, N. Rabin, M. Singer, and S. Tobias, "Animal House Forum: Top dogs and underdogs," *The Dissolve*, November 26, 2013, http://thedissolve.com/features/movie-of-the-week/291-animal-house-forum-top-dogs-and-underdogs/.

5. Keniston.

6. George Carlin, and Tony Hendra, *Last Words* (New York: Free Press, 2010).

7. *Ibid.*

8. *Ibid.*

9. Posnock.

10. C. Bowden, C. Dieterich, Nihipali, and G. Shenk, producers, *Unseen + Untold: National Lampoon's Animal House*, Universal Studios, 2003.

11. Richard Corliss, "Review of *Lost and Found: The Harry Langdon Collection*," *Time*, http://content.time.com/time/specials/2007/article/0,28804,1665692_1665693_1705631,00.html.

12. Kerr.

13. *Ibid.*

14. David Kalat, "Harry Langdon—The Forgotten Clown [Online forum comment]," posted November 27, 2007, www.silentcomedians.com/forum/viewtopic.php?p=4765.

15. Kerr.

16. Justin DeFreitas, "Moving Pictures: Harry Langdon: Silent Comedy's Forgotten Genius," *The Berkeley Daily Planet*, December 10, 2008, http://www.berkeleydailyplanet.com/issue/2008-12-11/article/31786?headline=Moving-Pictures-Harry-Langdon-Silent-Comedy-s-Forgotten-Genius—By-Justin-DeFreitas.

17. Bjorklund.

18. F. Scott Fitzgerald, *The Crack-Up*, Edmund Wilson, ed. (New York: New Directions, 2009), 126.

19. Janet Maslin, "The In Laws (1979) Film: Arkin and Falk in Comic 'In-Laws': Comedy of Insanity," *New York Times*, June 15, 1979, http://www.nytimes.com/movie/review?res=9B03EFD61539E732A25756C1A9609C946890D6CF.

Chapter 8

1. Richard Brody, "Monkey Business," *New Yorker*, DVD of the Week Podcast, August 7, 2009.

2. Thomas C. Renzi, *Screwball Comedy and Film Noir: Unexpected Connections* (Jefferson, NC: McFarland, 2012), 62.

3. *Ibid.*

4. Anaïs Nin, *The Diary of Anaïs Nin, Vol. 4* (Boston: Mariner Books, 1971), 127.
5. Wheeler Winston Dixon, "Dark Humor in Films of the 1960s," *University of Nebraska-Lincoln: Frame by Frame*, August 27, 2012, http://blog.unl.edu/dixon/2012/08/27/dark-humor-in-films-of-the-1960s-%E2%80%93-part-2/.
6. Tasha Robinson, "The Odd Couple's odd couple has endured while the details get forgotten," *The Dissolve*, March 10, 2015, https://thedissolve.com/features/movie-of-the-week/951-the-odd-couples-odd-couple-has-endured-while-the-d/.
7. Rousseau.
8. Ty Burr, "In 'Momma's Man,' growing up is hard to do," *The Boston Globe*, September 19, 2008, http://www.boston.com/ae/movies/articles/2008/09/19/in_mommas_man_growing_up_is_hard_to_do/.
9. Ibid.
10. Bilge Ebiri, "The 16 Best Robin Williams Movie Performances," *Vulture*, August 12, 2014, http://www.vulture.com/2014/08/robin-williams-best-movie-performances.html.

Chapter 9

1. Joseph W. Smith, III, *The Psycho File: A Comprehensive Guide to Hitchcock's Classic Shocker* (Jefferson, NC: McFarland, 2009), 125.
2. Matt Singer, "Pee-wee's Big Adventure forum: Road movies, manchildren, Amazing Larry, and more," *The Dissolve*, January 14, 2014), http://thedissolve.com/features/movie-of-the-week/361-Pee-wees-big-adventure-forum-road-movies-manchild/.
3. M. D'Angelo, N. Rabin, M. Singer, and S. Tobias, "Pee-wee's Big Adventure forum: Road movies, manchildren, Amazing Larry, and more," *The Dissolve*, July 15, 2014, http://thedissolve.com/features/movie-of-the-week/361-Pee-wees-big-adventure-forum-road-movies-manchild/.
4. Nathan Rabin, "Keynote: The cartoon heart of Pee-wee's Big Adventure," *The Dissolve*, January 14, 2014, http://thedissolve.com/features/movie-of-the-week/358-the-cartoon-heart-of-Pee-wees-big-adventure/.
5. Ibid.
6. Jay Carr, "Modern Romance," *TCM.com*, http://www.tcm.com/this-month/article.html?isPreview=&id=770627|215599&name=Modern-Romance.
7. Ibid.
8. R. de Croce, M. Poole, and R. Smith, producers, "Time" [Television broadcast], *The Real History of Science Fiction*, BBC America, 2014.
9. King, 84.
10. Arbeiter.
11. Gregory Dorr, "Billy Madison: Special Edition," DVD Journal, 2004, http://www.dvdjournal.com/reviews/b/billymadison_se.shtml.
12. Ibid.

13. Matty Show, "10 Great Movies About Guys That Never Grew Up," *The Campus Socialite*, August 10, 2011, http://thecampussocialite.com/man-teen-presents-10-great-movies-about-guys-that-never-grew-up.
14. J.R. Jones, "Kings of Comedy: Chuck and Larry have got nothing on the underrated Abbott and Costello," *Chicago Reader*, July 26, 2007, http://www.chicagoreader.com/chicago/kings-of-comedy/Content?oid=925562.
15. Wikipedia, "Big Daddy (1999 film)," n.d., accessed October 25, 2014, en.wikipedia.org/wiki/Big_Daddy_(1999_film).
16. Paul Tatara, "Review: 'The Dinner Game' a one-course comedy," CNN, September 28, 1999, http://cgi.cnn.com/SHOWBIZ/Movies/9909/28/review.dinnergame/index.html.
17. Roger Ager, "Across the sands of time: Film analysis of *The Big Lebowski*," Collective Learning, 2008, http://www.collativelearning.com/big lebowskianalysis.html.
18. Ibid.
19. Graham Daseler, "The Infinite Jest," *Bright Lights Film Journal*, Issue 81, August 2013, http://brightlightsfilm.com/81/81-big-lewbowski-coen-brothers-critique.php#.U9aG1mOa_G8.
20. Ager.

Chapter 10

1. Leah Rozen, "Picks and Pans Review: Elf," *People*, Vol. 60, No. 20, November 17, 2003, http://www.people.com/people/archive/article/0,,20148606,00.html.
2. Scott Tobias, "Movie Review: Elf," *A.V. Club*, November 4, 2003, http://www.avclub.com/review/elf-5362.
3. Maureen Dowd, "Men Will Be Boys," *New York Times* (June 3, 2007).
4. Anonymous, "Judd Apatow nervous about '60 Minutes' of fame," December 27, 2012. http://www.cbsnews.com/news/judd-apatow-nervous-about-60-minutes-of-fame/.
5. Anna North, "Judd Apatow Talks About Sexism, Seth Rogen," *Jezebel*, July 23, 2009, http://jezebel.com/5321283/judd-apatow-talks-about-sexism-seth-rogen.
6. Ibid.
7. Ibid.
8. Dan Persons, "Top 10 Man-Child Movies," *Reelz*, http://www.reelz.com/article/1044/top-10-man-child-movies/.
9. Mike Sacks, *Poking a Dead Frog: Conversations with Today's Top Comedy Writers* (New York: Penguin Books, 2014).
10. Michael Arbeiter, "Steve Carell's New Movie & Why the Era of the Manchild Comedy Needs to End," *Bustle*, October 23, 2104, http://www.bustle.com/articles/45688-steve-carells-new-movie-why-the-era-of-the-manchild-comedy-needs-to-end.
11. Ibid.

12. Ed Whitfield, "Film Review: Cyrus," *The Ooh Tray*, September 14th, 2010, http://www.theoohtray.com/2010/09/14/film-review-cyrus/.
13. Kevin Miller, "Charlie and the Chocolate Factory," *Reviews by Kevin Miller*, July 19, 2005, http://www.hollywoodjesus.com/comments/kevin/2005/07/charlie-and-chocolate-factory.html.
14. Rose.
15. Arbeiter.
16. Camille Paglia, "It's a Man's World, and It Always Will Be," *Time*, December 16, 2013, http://ideas.time.com/2013/12/16/its-a-mans-world-and-it-always-will-be/.
17. Brett McKay, "The 3 P's of Manhood: Procreate," *The Art of Manliness*, http://www.artofmanliness.com/2014/03/03/the-3-ps-of-manhood-procreate/.
18. Keniston.
19. Scott.
20. *Ibid*.
21. Richard Lacayo, "Show Me the Bunny," *Time*, July 7–July 14, 2014.
22. David Edelstein, "Low Blow," *Slate*, http://www.slate.com/articles/arts/movies/2004/06/low_blow.html.
23. Berge Garabedian, "Set Visit: 40-Year Old Virgin," *JoBlo*, April 14, 2005, http://www.joblo.com/movie-news/set-visit-40-year-old-virgin.
24. Lauren Jade Thompson, "Domestic Space in Postfeminist Romantic Comedy," *Postfeminism and Contemporary Hollywood Cinema*, Joel Gwynne and Nadine Muller, eds. (Basingstoke, UK: Palgrave Macmillan, 2013).
25. *Ibid*.
26. Matt Zoller Seitz, "The Substance of Style, Part 1: Wes Anderson and his pantheon of heroes (Schulz, Welles, Truffaut)," Moving Image Source (March 30, 2009). http://www.movingimagesource.us/articles/the-substance-of-style-pt-1–20090330.
27. *Ibid*.
28. Thompson.
29. Christopher Noxon, "Age Norms and Orangey Goodness," *Rejuvenile*, November 20, 2007, http://www.rejuvenile.com/blog/2007/11.
30. Ian Troub, "Troub's Take: 'This Is the End' a comedy of apocalyptic proportions," *Texan News*, June 12, 2013, http://www.texannews.net/troubs-take-this-is-the-end-a-comedy-of-apocalyptic-proportions/.
31. *Ibid*.

Chapter 11

1. Claudia Puig, "Safety Not Guaranteed, but Satisfaction Is," *USA Today* (June 14, 2012). http://usatoday30.usatoday.com/life/movies/reviews/story/2012-06-14/safety-not-guaranteed/55604678/1.
2. *Ibid*.
3. Jay Livingston, "'This is 40'—Guilty Pleasures," *Montclair SocioBlog*, January 14, 2013, http://montclairsoci.blogspot.com/2013/01/this-is-40-guilty-pleasures.html.
4. Will Leitch, "I Guess This Is Growing Up: Neighbors, Reviewed," *The Concourse*, May 9, 2014, http://theconcourse.deadspin.com/i-guess-this-is-growing-up-neighbors-reviewed-1573931684.
5. Jack Coyle, "Seth Rogen on the Connections Between 'Neighbors' and 'Knocked Up': 'It Didn't Escape Us,'" *Associated Press*, April 26, 2014, http://www.huffingtonpost.com/2014/04/26/seth-rogen-neighbors_n_5218042.html.
6. *Ibid*.
7. A.O. Scott, "Last Call for Friends to Grow Up," *New York Times*, August 22, 2013, http://www.nytimes.com/2013/08/23/movies/worlds-end-continues-shaun-of-the-dead-and-hot-fuzz.html.
8. Christopher Noxon, *Rejuvenile: Kickball, Cartoons, Cupcakes, and the Reinvention of the American Grown-u* (New York: Crown Publishing, 2006), 2.
9. *Ibid*.
10. Frank Pittman, *Grow Up!: How Taking Responsibility Can Make You a Happy Adult* (New York: St. Martin's Griffin, 1998), 8.
11. Betsy Sharkey, "'While We're Young illuminates in delightfully grown-up ways," *Los Angeles Times*, April 1, 2015. http://www.latimes.com/entertainment/movies/la-et-mn-while-were-young-betsy-20150402-column.html.
12. Tasha Robinson, "Noah Baumbach on While We're Young's screwball spirit and universal regrets," *The Dissolve*, March 27, 2015, https://thedissolve.com/features/interview/973-noah-baumbach-on-while-were-youngs-screwball-spiri/.
13. *Ibid*.
14. David Denby, "A Fine Romance: The new comedy of the sexes," *The New Yorker*, July 23, 2007, http://www.newyorker.com/magazine/2007/07/23/a-fine-romance.
15. Rebecca Flint Marx, "Pillow Talk (1959)," *All Movie Guide*, http://www.allmovie.com/movie/pillow-talk-v38140/review.

Chapter 12

1. David Denby, "A Fine Romance: The new comedy of the sexes," *The New Yorker*, July 23, 2007, http://www.newyorker.com/magazine/2007/07/23/a-fine-romance.
2. *Ibid*.
3. *Ibid*.
4. Sean Axmaker, "Film Article: Tom, Dick and Harry," TCM Online, http://www.tcm.com/this-month/article/290016|0/Tom-Dick-and-Harry.html.
5. Neil Doyle, "Reviews & Ratings for *It Had to Be You*," Internet Movie Database, http://www.imdb.com/title/tt0039500/reviews.
6. K. Phipps, T. Robinson, N. Rabin, S. Tobias, N. Murray, S. Hyden, S. O'Neal, Z. Handlen, E. Adams, and T. VanDerWerff, "The ugliest truth: 24

romantic-comedy characters who don't deserve love," *A.V. Club*, February 8, 2010.

7. Frank Ochieng, "Review of *Private Benjamin*," *Movie Eye*, http://www.rottentomatoes.com/mobile/m/private_benjamin/.

8. Emanuel Levy, "Review of *Private Benjamin* (1980)." *Emanuel Levy Cinema*, May 1, 2011, http://emanuellevy.com/review/private-benjamin-1980/.

9. Holly Welker, "Forever Your Girl," *Bitch*, Issue 46, Spring 2010, http://bitchmagazine.org/article/forever-your-girl.

10. Luxford James, "*Identity Thief*: Thrashing around in the dark for laughs that never come," *The National*, February 28, 2013, http://www.thenational.ae/arts-culture/film/identity-thief-thrashing-around-in-the-dark-for-laughs-that-never-come.

11. Genevieve Koski, "The small dreams and big fantasies of Romy And Michele's High School Reunion," *The Dissolve*, March 31, 2015, https://thedissolve.com/features/movie-of-the-week/976-the-small-dreams-and-big-fantasies-of-romy-and-mic/.

12. Rachel Handler, and Phipps, Keith, "Forum: *Romy and Michele's High School Reunion*," *The Dissolve*, March 31, 2015, https://thedissolve.com/features/movie-of-the-week/975-forum-romy-and-micheles-high-school-reunion/.

13. Koski.

14. Robert Bledsoe, "Legally Blonde," *Film Threat*, July 12, 2001, http://www.filmthreat.com/reviews/2155/.

15. Ty Burr, "'Frances Ha' an exercise in watching Greta Gerwig," *The Boston Globe*, May 23, 2013, http://www.bostonglobe.com/arts/movies/2013/05/23/movie-review-frances-exercise-watching-greta-gerwig/NwN9BbhS1WULW4FEhzSwxL/story.html.

16. Mick LaSalle, "*Frances Ha* review: She gets the last laugh," *Hearst Newspapers*, May 23, 2013, http://www.sfgate.com/movies/article/Frances-Ha-review-She-gets-the-last-laugh-4544091.php.

17. Cath Clarke, "Frances Ha," *Time Out*, June 21, 2013, http://www.timeout.com/london/film/frances-ha.

18. Moira MacDonald, "Greta Gerwig shines in Frances Ha," *The Seattle Times*, May 23, 2013, http://seattletimes.com/html/movies/2021041982_moviefrancesxml.html.

19. *Ibid.*

20. Rick Groen, "*Frances Ha*: Seldom has aimlessness looked so good, or felt so fresh and joyful," *The Globe and Mail*, June 21, 2013, http://www.theglobeandmail.com/arts/summer-entertainment/frances-ha-seldom-has-aimlessness-looked-so-good-or-felt-so-fresh-and-lively/article12719340/.

21. MacDonald.

22. *Ibid.*

23. LaSalle.

24. Groen.

25. Annie Baker, "Life in Black and White: *Frances Ha*, America's best French New Wave film," *Slate*, November 11, 2013, http://www.slate.com/articles/arts/dvdextras/2013/11/playwright_annie_baker_s_criterion_essay_on_the_french_new_wave_influences.html.

26. R. Kelehar, A. McLean, M. O'Casey, and K. Taylor, producers, *Blackadder Rides Again*, BBC television broadcast, December 25, 2008.

27. Ty Burr, "Keira Knightley hangs with high schooler in 'Laggies.'" *The Boston Globe*, November 6, 2014, http://www.bostonglobe.com/arts/movies/2014/11/06/movie-review-laggies/tsmPrGsPZLdhRyF4V1JBJN/story.html.

28. Michael Arbeiter, "Steve Carell's New Movie & Why the Era of the Manchild Comedy Needs to End," *Bustle*, October 23, 2104, http://www.bustle.com/articles/45688-steve-carells-new-movie-why-the-era-of-the-manchild-comedy-needs-to-end.

29. *Ibid.*

30. Burr.

31. *Ibid.*

32. Daniel Barna, "Keira Knightley Still Doesn't Feel Like a Grown-Up," *Refinery 29*, October 23, 2014. http://www.refinery29.com/2014/10/76618/keira-knightley-laggies-interview.

33. Megan Conner, "Keira Knightley: 'I used to try to be sensible and good and professional.'" *The Guardian*, October 25, 2014, http://www.theguardian.com/film/2014/oct/26/kiera-knightley-interview-marriage-movies-being-a-geek.

34. *Ibid.*

35. *Ibid.*

Epilogue

1. M. D'Angelo, A.A. Dowd, J. Hassenger, A. Nayman, K. Rife, N. Schager, and I. Vishnevetsky, "The best films of 2015 (so far): A halftime report in superlatives." *A.V. Club*, July 2, 2015, http://www.avclub.com/article/best-films-2015-so-far-halftime-report-superlative-221474.

2. Riblet, Douglas. "The Keystone Film Company and the Historiography of Early Slapstick." *Classical Hollywood Comedy (AFI Film Readers)*, Kristine Brunovska Karnick, and Henry Jenkins eds. (London: Routledge, 1994), 175.

3. *Ibid.*

4. Bob Lipton, "Pro-Confederacy Films." *Nitrate Ville*, message posted June 24, 2015, http://nitrateville.com/viewtopic.php?f=3&t=20482.

Bibliography

Books

Carlin, George, and Tony Hendra. *Last Words*. New York: Free Press, 2010.

Chandler, Charlotte. *Nobody's Perfect : Billy Wilder, A Personal Biography*. Montclair, NJ: Applause Theatre & Cinema Books, 2004.

Erickson, Hal. *Military Comedy Films: A Critical Survey and Filmography of Hollywood Releases Since 1918*. Jefferson, NC: McFarland, 2012.

Fitzgerald, F. Scott. *The Crack-Up*. Edmund Wilson, ed. New York: New Directions, 2009.

Gilmore, David D. *Manhood in the Making: Cultural Concepts of Masculinity*. New Haven, CT: Yale University Press, 1991.

Gwynne, Joel, and Nadine Muller, eds. *Postfeminism and Contemporary Hollywood Cinema*. New York: Palgrave Macmillan, 2013.

Kerr, Walter. *The Silent Clowns*. Cambridge, MA: Da Capo Press, 1990.

Kimmel, Michael. *Guyland*. New York: Harper Perennial, 2009.

King, Geoff. *Film Comedy*. London: Wallflower Press, 2002.

Krutnik, Frank. *Inventing Jerry Lewis* and *In a Lonely Street: Film Noir, Genre and Masculinity*. Washington, D.C.: Smithsonian, 2000.

Lacenaire, Pierre-François. *Mémoires de Lacenaire avec ses poèmes et ses lettres*. Paris: Albin Michel, 1968.

Lahue, Kalton C., and Sam Gill. *Clown Princes and Court Jesters*. South Brunswick and New York: A.S. Barnes, 1970.

Mellen, Joan. *Modern Times*. London: Cromwell Press, 2006.

Murnighan, Jack. *Beowulf on the Beach: What to Love and What to Skip in Literature's 50 Greatest Hits*. New York: Broadway Books, 2009.

Neibaur, James. *The Silent Films of Harry Langdon (1923–1928)*. Lanham, MD: Scarecrow Press, 2012.

Nin, Anaïs. *The Diary of Anaïs Nin, vol. 4*. Boston: Mariner Books, 1971.

Pittman, Frank. *Grow Up!: How Taking Responsibility Can Make You a Happy Adult*. New York: St. Martin's Griffin, 1998.

Robinson, David. *Chaplin, His Life and Art*. New York: McGraw-Hill, 1985.

Rousseau, Jean Jacques. *Emile, or On Education*. New York City: E.P. Dutton, 1762.

Seligman, Martin E. *Learned Optimism: How to Change Your Mind and Your Life*. New York: Knopf, 1991.

Thomas, Lewis. *The Fragile Species*. Simon & Schuster, 1993.

Articles

Capdevila, Luc. "The Quest for Masculinity in a Defeated France, 1940–45." *Contemporary European History* (2001).

Movie Gazette. Review of *The Raven*, downloaded March 15, 2006, from http://www.moviegazette.com/cinereviews/1217.

Redwine, Ivana. "Grand Illusion—DVD Review, downloaded March 15, 2006, from http://homevideo.about.com/library/weekly/aa080801a.htm.

Robinson, Tasha. "The hard-bitten cynicism of Billy Wilder's *Ace in the Hole*" (June 25, 2014).

Simon, John. "Story of Women—Movie Review." *National Review*, April 1, 1990.

Scullion, Rosemarie. "Family Fictions and Reproductive Realities in Vichy France: Claude Chabrol's *Une Affaire de femme*."

Vincendeau, Ginette. "The Beauty's Beast: Jean Gabin, Masculinity and the French Hero." *Women and Film: A Sight and Sound Reader* (Philadelphia, 1993), pp.115–22.

Wikipedia. "Aftermath of Worth War I." Accessed at http://en.wikipedia.org/wiki/Aftermath_of_World_War_I.

Periodicals

The Moving Picture World (1909–1922)

Websites

All Movie Guide (http://www.allmovie.com/)
Internet Movie Database (http://www.imdb.com/)
Wikipedia (http://www.wikipedia.org/)

Index

A Plumbing We Will Go (1940) 43–44
Abbott, Bud 2, 45–46, 87
Abel, Richard 10
About a Boy (2002) 109, 154
Ace Ventura, Pet Detective (1994) 140
An Ache in Every Stake (1941) 39
The Admirable Crichton (1957) 29
Une Affaire de femme (1988) 66, 118
Allen, Woody 102
The Almost Man (2012) 166–167, 190
Anderson, Kurt 1
Anderson, Wes 163
The Apartment (1960) 98–101
Apatow, Judd 7–9, 149–150, 157
Arbeiter, Michael 141, 150, 153
Arbuckle, Roscoe 12–13, 192
Arsenic and Old Lace (1944) 47–49
Arthur (1981) 106–109, 137
Artists and Models (1955) 80–82
Ass Backwards (2013) 182
Atkinson, Rowan 16, 58, 103
Away We Go (2009) 168

Baby Mama (2008) 182
The Back-up Plan (2010) 179
Barrie, J.M. 7
Bateman, Jason 109, 152–153
Battling Butler (1926) 23, 30–33, 50, 105, 108–110
Baumbach, Noah 172–173, 185
Being There (1979) 112–113, 116–118, 163
The Bellboy (1960) 81–82
Belushi, John 111–112

Benny, Jack 7
The Best Years of Our Lives (1946) 87
Big (1988) 129, 136–139, 169
Big Daddy (1999) 109, 133, 142
The Big Lebowski (1998) 143–145
Billy Madison (1995) 141–142
Bilton, Alan 11
Boobs in the Woods (1925) 114
Bowers, Charley 134
Bracken, Eddie 49
Brats (1930) 40, 192
Bridget Jones's Diary (2001) 179
Bringing Up Baby (1938) 121, 175–177
Brooks, Albert 126, 135, 171
Buck Privates (1941) 46–47, 87
Buck Privates Come Home (1947) 87
Bullock, Sandra 182
Bumping into Broadway (1919) 19
Burn Before Reading (2008) 184
Burr, Ty 125–126, 187
Burton, Tim 151
Buzzard (2014) 190

The Caddy (1953) 68
Cantor, Eddie 76
Carell, Steve 161–162, 164
Carrey, Jim 2, 140
Cedar Rapids (2011) 146
Cera, Michael 165
Chabrol, Claude 66
Chang, Justin 1
Chaplin, Charlie 5–6, 36–38, 46, 51, 186
Charlie and the Chocolate Factory (2005) 151
Chase, Charley 14–15

City Lights (1931) 37
Clerks (1994) 141, 173
The Cocoanuts (1929) 24
Cole, Jack 102
"A Confederacy of Dunes" (novel) 119
Confessions of a Shopaholic (2009) 181–182, 188
Le Corbeau (1943) 63–65
Costello, Lou 2–3, 13, 45–46, 87
Coyle, Jake 171
Cross, Gary 181
The Cure (1917) 37
Curtis, Tony 73
Cyrus (2010) 151

Dagwood Bumstead (comic strip character) 152
Damn Yankees (1958) 125
Daniels, Bebe 19
Davies, Marion 70
Day, Doris 173–174
Dean, James 78–79
Deed, Andre 9–10, 12, 170, 192
Dickie Roberts: Former Child Star (2003) 127
The Dinner Game (1998) 142–143
The Disorderly Orderly (1964) 81
Dodgeball (2004) 159–160
A Dog's Life (1918) 36
Doughboys (1930) 51–52
Dowd, Maureen 149
Duck Soup (1933) 46, 52, 54
Dumb and Dumber (1994) 140

East of Eden (1955) 78
Ebiri, Bilge 130
Ekberg, Anita 80
Elf (2003) 16, 146, 148
Le Enfants du paradis (1945) 62–63, 65

Erickson, Glenn 73
Erickson, Hal 54
The Errand Boy (1961) 36
Everybody Loves Raymond (television series) 153
Ewell, Tom 89, 91

Failure to Launch (2006) 147
Fairbanks, Douglas 17
Farley, Chris 12, 142
Fazenda, Louise 15
Ferrell, Will 16, 146, 148, 150, 157, 161, 183
Fields, W.C. 46, 154
Fischbach, Bob 1
Fisher, Isla 160, 181
Fonda, Henry 93
The Foot Fist Way (2006) 147
Footloose (1984) 193
The 40-Year-Old Virgin (2005) 36, 161–164, 172
Frances Ha (2012) 184–187
Freeman, Kathleen 81, 83
The Freshman (1925) 25, 126
Fresnay, Pierre 63–64
Full Grown Men (2006) 165

Gabin, Jean 56–57, 59–62
Garner, Jennifer 152–153
The General (1926) 52–54
Gerwig, Greta 165, 184–185
Ghost World (2001) 180
Gill, Sam 16
Girl Shy (1924) 19, 23, 30, 178
The Gold Rush (1925) 36–38
Good Will Hunting (1997) 131
The Goodbye Girl (1977) 173
La Grande Illusion (1937) 57–60
Grandma's Boy (1922) 18, 108
Grandma's Boy (2006) 151
Grant, Cary 47–49, 120–121, 131, 175–176
Grant, Hugh 109, 154–155
Greenberg (2010) 165
Greydanus, Steven D. 25
Grodin, Charles 102
Groundhog Day (1993) 138, 140–141, 170
Grown Ups (2010) 2, 140
Guardians of the Galaxy (2014) 192

Hail the Conquering Hero (1944) 47, 50
Hall Pass (2011) 153
Hamilton, Lloyd 13–14
Handler, Rachel 182
The Hangover (2009) 98, 127–128

Hanks, Tom 136, 139
A Hard Day's Night (1964) 101
Hardy, Oliver 40–43, 70, 148, 153, 157, 192
Hawn, Goldie 179
The Heartbreak Kid (1972) 102
The Heat (2013) 182
Heigl, Katherine 148–149
Henry, Gale 15
Hepburn, Katharine 175–177
Hill, Jonah 151, 191
Hold That Ghost (1941) 45
Hollywood or Bust (1956) 80, 102
Holm, Ian 144
Hook (1991) 129–131
Hope, Bob 88–89
Hot Water (1924) 24
The House Bunny (2008) 184
How High Is Up? (1940) 44
How to Murder Your Wife (1965) 98, 136
Howard, Curly 13, 39–40, 44
Howard, Moe 39, 148
Huck Finn (Mark Twain character) 25, 142
Hudson, Rock 173–174

I Do (1921) 168
Identity Theft (2013) 182
If You Could Only Cook (1935) 177
I'm All Right, Jack (1959) 90
The In-Laws (1979) 119
It's a Gift (1934) 153

Jack (1996) 129
Jeff, Who Lives at Home (2011) 6, 151, 188
The Jerk (1979) 112, 116–118
Juno (2007) 152, 165

Kalat, David 115
Kaye, Danny 124
Keaton, Buster 17, 24–36, 46, 157
Keener, Catherine 151, 164
Keep 'Em Flying (1941) 46
Kerr, Walter 10, 12, 114, 192
The Kid (1921) 37, 154
The Kid Brother (1927) 23, 36
Kidding Sister (1917) 69
Kimmel, Michael 3
King, Geoff 11, 140
Knightley, Kiera 187–189
Knocked Up (2007) 109, 148–150, 152, 157, 166
Koski, Genevieve 182
Kunze, Peter Christopher 104

The Ladies Man (1961) 81, 83–84
The Ladykillers (1955) 95
Laggies (2014) 187–189
Lahue, Kalton 16
Langdon, Harry 13, 15, 36, 44, 80–81, 113–116, 163
Lars and the Real Girl (2007) 80
Laurel, Stan 40–43, 153, 157, 192
Lee, Kevin B. 81
Legally Blonde (2001) 183–184
Lemmon, Jack 73, 92–93, 98–101, 118, 122–123, 136
Lewis, Jerry 68, 74–84
Lewis, Zach 81, 84
Life of Brian (1979) 119
Lifeguard (1976) 103–104, 188
The Lifeguard (2013) 129
Lipton, Bob 192
Little Man (2006) 2
Lloyd, Harold 17–26, 46, 168–169
The Longest Week (2014) 109–110
Lorre, Peter 49

MacLaine, Shirley 82
The Major and the Minor (1942) 68–74, 77, 120
Martin, Dean 68, 77, 80–81
Martin, Steve 116–117
Marx, Groucho 23–24
Marx, Harpo 7–8, 23
Marx, Rebecca Flint 174
The Marx Brothers 23–24, 46, 52, 54
Massey, Raymond 47, 49, 78
Matthau, Walter 105, 122–123
Mayehoff, Eddie 77–78
McBride, Danny 147, 191
Me, Myself and Irene (2000) 2
Meet the Parents (2000) 154
Mr. Bean's Holiday (2007) 16
Mister Roberts (1955) 53, 92–93
"Moby Dick" (novel) 95
The Mollycoddle (1920) 17
Momma's Man (2008) 125–127
Mon Oncle (1958) 95
Monkey Business (1952) 120–122, 131, 178
Moore, Colleen 15
Moore, Dudley 106, 124–125
Mother (1996) 126–127
Movie Crazy (1932) 25
Movie Maniacs (1936) 44
Muriel's Wedding (1994) 179

Murray, Bill 138, 141
My Best Friend's Wedding (1997) 178
My Wife's Relations (1922) 23

National Lampoon's Animal House (1978) 110–112, 128
The Navigator (1924) 27–30, 105, 136, 157
Neibaur, James L. 13, 80
Neighbors (2014) 170–171
A New Leaf (1971) 105–107

Oakie, Jack 5
The Odd Couple (1968) 122–124
Oh, Doctor! (1917) 25
Old School (2003) 98
Our Hospitality (1923) 23, 27
Our Idiot Brother (2011) 151, 188

Pack Up Your Troubles (1932) 54, 87
Pain and Gain (2013) 151
The Paleface (1948) 88
The Patsy (1964) 84
Pee-wee's Big Adventure (1985) 16, 36, 133–136, 142, 162–163, 186
Pegg, Simon 109, 146–147, 172
Peter Pan (character) 7, 24, 114, 121
Pillow Talk (1959) 173–174
Pineapple Express (2008) 54–55
The Pink Panther (1964) 118
The Play House (1921) 25
Play It Again, Sam (1972) 102, 116
Playboy (magazine) 97
Prisoner of Second Avenue (1975) 118
Private Benjamin (1980) 179–180, 183
The Producers (1968) 101, 119
Psycho (1960) 90–92, 134
Puig, Claudia 169

Rabin, Nathan 111, 134–135
Rebel Without a Cause (1955) 78
Reilly, John C. 150–151
Rhodes, Billy 69
Robinson, David 10
Robinson, Tasha 89, 124
Rogen, Seth 1–3, 148–150, 152, 157, 170–171, 191

Rogers, Ginger 70, 72, 120, 177–178
Romy and Michele's High School Reunion (1997) 182–183
Rose, Steve 5, 151
Rousseau, Jean Jacques 44
The Royal Tenenbaums (2001) 163
Rozen, Leah 147
Rudd, Paul 163, 169
Run, Fatboy, Run (2007) 109
Runaway Bride (1999) 178

Safety Last (1923) 20–22
Safety Not Guaranteed (2012) 169
A Sailor-Made Man (1921) 17
Sandler, Adam 1, 141–142, 157
Saturday Afternoon (1926) 114
Saturday Night Live (television series) 142
Schneider, Rob 2
Scott, A.O. 2, 158
The Secret Life of Walter Mitty (1947) 86, 98, 124
Segel, Jason 6
Seitz, Matt Zoller 163
Sellers, Peter 118
The Seven Year Itch (1955) 88–92, 102
17 Again (2009) 125
Sex Tape (2014) 168
Shaun of the Dead (2004) 146–147
Sherlock Jr. (1924) 30, 116
Shoulder Arms (1918) 51
Sideways (2004) 155–157
The Sin of Harold Diddlebock (1947) 25
Sitting Pretty (1948) 85–87
Skelton, Red 85
Sleepless in Seattle (1993) 179
Smiley Face (2007) 184
Some Like It Hot (1959) 73, 76
Sons of the Desert (1933) 153, 157
Spade, David 127
Speedy (1928) 23, 168
Steamboat Bill, Jr. (1928) 24, 33–36, 84
Step Brothers (2008) 150–151, 157, 182–183
Stiller, Ben 154, 159, 165, 172
The Stooge (1952) 68
Stripes (1981) 132–133
The Strong Man (1926) 38, 75–76, 114

Superbad (2007) 165
Swain, Mack 13

Tassels in the Air (1938) 39
Tati, Jacques 81–82, 95–96
Tea and Sympathy (1956) 77
10 (1979) 102, 124
Termites of 1938 (1938) 39
That's My Boy (1951) 77–79, 84
There's a Crowd (1927) 179
This Is 40 (2012) 169
The Three Stooges 39–40, 43–44, 46–47
Tincher, Faye 15
Tobias, Scott 147
Tommy Boy (1995) 142
Top Secret! (1984) 100
Towed in a Hole (1932) 42–43
Trading Places (1983) 29
Tramp, Tramp, Tramp (1926) 36, 44, 163
Twilight Zone (television series) 124

Uncle's Finish (1914) 12, 120
Under the Yum, Yum Tree (1963) 101
Up in Smoke (1978) 116

Vaser, Ernesto 10
Vaughn, Vince 159–161

Walston, Ray 100–101, 125
The Waterboy (1998) 86
Wayans, Marlon 2
Webb, Clifton 85–87
Wedding Crashers (2005) 160–161
While We're Young (2014) 172–173
Whitfield, Ed 151
Williams, Robin 129–131
Wilson, Owen 148, 160, 188
Witherspoon, Reese 183
The World's End (2013) 172
The Yellow Cab Man (1950) 85

You, Me and Dupree (2006) 148, 188
Young, Robert 85–87
Young Adult (2011) 187
You're Never Too Young (1955) 68, 74–77, 83–84

www.ingramcontent.com/pod-product-compliance
Lightning Source LLC
Chambersburg PA
CBHW081556300426
44116CB00015B/2909